The Anglo-American Military Relationship

The Anglo-American Military Relationship

Arms Across the Ocean

WYN REES

OXFORD
UNIVERSITY PRESS

OXFORD
UNIVERSITY PRESS

Great Clarendon Street, Oxford, OX2 6DP,
United Kingdom

Oxford University Press is a department of the University of Oxford.
It furthers the University's objective of excellence in research, scholarship,
and education by publishing worldwide. Oxford is a registered trade mark of
Oxford University Press in the UK and in certain other countries

Published in the United States of America by Oxford University Press
198 Madison Avenue, New York, NY 10016, United States of America

British Library Cataloguing in Publication Data

Data available

Library of Congress Control Number: 2024931234

ISBN 9780198884620

DOI: 10.1093/oso/9780198884620.001.0001

Printed and bound by
CPI Group (UK) Ltd, Croydon, CR0 4YY

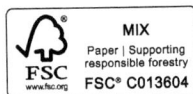

MIX
Paper | Supporting
responsible forestry
FSC
www.fsc.org   FSC® C013604

This book is dedicated to Susan, Marcus, and Sophie.

Acknowledgements

The author would like to thank numerous members of the armed services, in the UK and the United States, for agreeing to be interviewed for this book. Financial support to conduct those interviews was provided by a grant from the British Academy (SG121859). Thanks are also extended to colleagues who commented on chapters of the manuscript, including Dr Steve Marsh, and reviewers from Oxford University Press. In particular I would like to thank Dr Ruike Xu who has worked with me on the subject of Anglo-American relations.

Any shortcomings of the book are my responsibility alone.

Wyn Rees

Contents

Abbreviations and Acronyms

ACT	Allied Command Transformation
ADZ	Afghan Development Zones
ANF	Atlantic Nuclear Force
ANZAM	Australia, New Zealand and Malaya defence agreement
ANZUS	Australia, New Zealand and US pact
AQI	Al-Qaeda in Iraq
ARRC	Allied Rapid Reaction Corps
ASW	Anti-submarine warfare
AWACS	Airborne Warning and Control System
AUKUS	Australia, United Kingdom and United States
AWRE	Atomic Weapons Research Establishment at Aldermaston
BAOR	British Army of the Rhine
Brexit	Britain's exit from the European Union
BJSM	British Joint Service Mission
CAOC	Combined Air Operation Centre
CDS	British Chief of the Defence Staff
CENTCOM	US Central Command
CENTO	Central Treaty Organisation
CIA	Central Intelligence Agency
COIN	Counter-insurgency
CONMAROPS	Concept of Maritime Operations Strategy
COS	British Chiefs of Staff
CJCS	Combined Joint Chiefs of Staff
CPA	Coalition Provisional Authority
CSDP	EU Common Security and Defence Policy
CYBERCOM	US Cyber Command
DFID	British Department for International Development
EBO	Effects Based Operations
EDC	European Defence Community
EU	European Union
FCO	Foreign and Commonwealth Office
FCS	US Future Combat System
FOFA	Follow-on-Forces Attack
FRES	Future Rapid Effects System
G7	Group of Seven Leading Industrialised Countries
GCHQ	Government Communications Headquarters
GIUK	Greenland-Iceland-UK gap
GPS	Global Positioning System

ICBM	Intercontinental Ballistic Missile
IEDs	Improvised explosive devices
IFOR	NATO Implementation Force
IRBM	Intermediate Range Ballistic Missiles
ISAF	International Security Assistance Force
ISIL	Islamic State in the Levant
J7	Joint Staff insert space
JAM	Jaish al-Mahdi
JCAE	Joint Committee on Atomic Energy
JCPOA	Joint Cooperative Plan of Action
JCS	US Joint Chiefs of Staff
JDP	Joint Doctrine Publication
JOWOGs	Joint Working Groups
JRSWG	Joint Re-entry System Working Group
JSF	Joint Strike Fighter
JSOC	US Joint Special Operations Command
JSTARS	Joint Surveillance and Target Attack Radar System
JTIDS	Joint Tactical Information Distribution System
KFOR	Kosovo Force
LIC	Low Intensity Conflict
MARV	Maneuvrable Re-entry Vehicle
MC70	Military Command 70
MDA	Mutual Defence Agreement of July 1958
MNF–I	Multinational Forces Iraq
MIRV	Multiple Independently Targeted Re-entry Vehicle
MiTT	Military Transition Teams
MLF	Multilateral Force
MNC – 1	Multinational Corps Iraq
MNDCS	Multi-National Division Centre South in Iraq
MNDSE	Multinational Division South East in Iraq
MoD	UK Ministry of Defence
MRAP	Mine-resistant ambush protected vehicles
NATO	North Atlantic Treaty Organization
NCW	Network Centric Warfare
NEC	Network Enabled Capability
NFZ	No Fly Zone
NORTHCOM	US Northern Command
NSS	US National Security Strategy
OECD	Organisation for Economic Cooperation and Development
OOTW	Operations Other Than War
ORHA	Office for Reconstruction and Humanitarian Assistance
PACOM	US Pacific Command
PCRU	Post-Conflict Reconstruction Unit
PGM	Precision-guided munitions
PJHQ	British Permanent Joint Headquarters

PRT	Provincial Reconstruction Teams
PSA	Polaris Sales Agreement
PSO	Peace Support Operations
RAF	Royal Air Force
RPW	Reliable Replacement Warhead
RN	Royal Navy
SAC	US Strategic Air Command
SACEUR	Supreme Allied Commander Europe
SACLANT	Supreme Allied Commander Atlantic
SDF	Syrian Democratic Front
SDR	Strategic Defence Review
SDSR	Strategic Defence and Security Review
SEATO	South East Asia Treaty Organisation
SF	Special Forces
SFOR	NATO Stabilisation Force
SIOP	US Single Integrated Operational Plan
SIS	Britain's Secret Intelligence Service
SLBM	Submarine Launched Ballistic Missile
SOSUS	Sound Surveillance System
SSBN	Strategic Submarine Ballistic Nuclear
SSN	Strategic Submarine Nuclear
STRATCOM	US Strategic Command
TNA	The UK National Archives
TRADOC	US Training and Doctrine Command
UAV	Unmanned Aerial Vehicle
UNMIK	UN Mission in Kosovo
UNPROFOR	United Nations Protection Force
UNSC	United Nations Security Council
USAF	US Air Force
USN	US Navy
WMD	Weapons of mass destruction

1

Introduction

Since World War II, the UK has regarded the US as its closest partner and as a means of advancing its interests. The UK has sought to act as America's interlocutor with Europe, tying the US to the security of the continent. A close relationship has offered a means to offset the UK's relative decline and compensate for the loss of its Empire. Based on a common Anglo-Saxon heritage and with a shared commitment to preserving a liberal order, the UK has been content to act in a supportive role to US leadership of the West (Gamble, 2003).

In the words of David Manning, a former British Ambassador to Washington, the breadth of the so-called 'special relationship' is 'extraordinary' (Foreign Affairs Select Committee, 2010: 36): it extends across political, economic, diplomatic, and cultural domains. This study focuses exclusively upon its military dimensions. It is the quality of this military relationship that distinguishes it from other patterns of military cooperation between allies (Reynolds, 1985–1986: 4). It has continued from World War II to the present despite tensions and not a few major disagreements.

It is not difficult to understand why the US has treated the UK as a close ally. The UK has enjoyed the attributes of a global power. It is the fifth largest military power in the world and the second most influential member of NATO. It was a leading actor in the military capabilities of the European Union—until Brexit (Britain's exit from the European Union) at the end of 2019. It has been prepared to contribute to military operations not just within the NATO area but on a global basis. The UK has possessed one of the largest economies in the world and remains one of the foremost financial and trading nations. Its diplomatic influence has been considerable, reflecting its position as one of the five permanent members of the United Nations Security Council and an active participant within a range of other multilateral organizations, such as the Group of Seven leading industrial powers (G7) and the Organisation for Economic Cooperation and Development (OECD). The UK's soft power has also been formidable, derived from its language and culture, and reinforced thanks to its position within the Commonwealth and its considerable aid spending. The UK has prided itself on being a 'pivotal power' (Miliband, 2007) and that has been of value even to a country as powerful as the US.

This book focuses on the relationship between the British military and the US armed services, where there has been relatively little scholarly attention. This is what Baylis, one of the few authors to explore this dimension of UK–US relations,

The Anglo-American Military Relationship. Wyn Rees, Oxford University Press. © Wyn Rees (2024).
DOI: 10.1093/oso/9780198884620.003.0001

has described as part of the 'operational relationship' (Baylis, 1984: xviii). Wallace and Philipps describe it as part of the US–UK 'embedded substructure' (2009: 263), whilst a former Chairman of the US Joint Chiefs of Staff, William Crowe, compares it to an iceberg where much of the substance is out of sight below the waterline. With much of the post-Cold War era blighted by conflicts, cooperation between the US and UK militaries has played a vital part in responding to these international emergencies. The effort to maintain this partnership has made the British military a long-term custodian of the special relationship (Richardson, 1996).

Focusing upon the military contrasts with much of the academic literature on the Anglo-American relationship. This literature has tended to concentrate upon the elite level between governments and most particularly between presidents and prime ministers (Dickie, 1994: 258). The relationship between leaders has ebbed and flowed and has been influenced by personalities. By concentrating on the military, this book is not contending that the UK armed forces determine the relationship between the two countries. Civilian control over the military and the primacy of politics are well-established principles within the UK political system. Rather, it is arguing that the military relationship makes an under-appreciated contribution to Anglo-American relations and that this study seeks to restore that balance in understanding.

The UK military wants to be recognized as America's partner of choice, as the state to whom it turns in matters of defence cooperation. The UK has desired access to US thinking and planning so as to ensure that British interests are taken into account at the earliest possible stage. It wants to be apprised of US doctrine and be able to operate with America's armed forms in various contingencies. To this end it has sought, in the words of Xu, to 'train together, learn together and fight together' (2016: 129).

Literature on the special relationship

There is a relatively well-developed literature on the special relationship, much of it focusing on the bonds between political elites. The principal question within that literature is whether there is any substance to the claim that a uniquely close relationship exists between the two countries. Edelman (2010: 25) makes the point that the very concept of a 'special relationship' is a relatively recent invention, dating since World War II. In the nineteenth century, there was little love lost between the two countries and it would have been considered bizarre to predict that the two countries would come close together.

The functional view of the relationship has been the most prevalent, namely, that the UK and the US have always made policy decisions based upon perceptions of their own interests. Watt argues that, 'the underlying basis of the

Anglo-American relationship has always been interest' (Louis and Bull, 1986: 3) and the literature has sought to elucidate points of convergence. Writers, such as Bartlett (1992) and Robb (2013), adhere firmly to this perspective and trace the ups and downs of the alignment of their interests. Seitz (1993: 86) draws attention to 'strategic coincidence', that is, the presence of shared security interests that have kept the two countries moving in the same direction. Both sides have looked at the world through a common lens and identified common threats as well as similar opportunities. In 2010, UK Secretary of Defence Dr Liam Fox corroborated this view when he noted that there was 'a large overlap between UK interests and US interests' (quoted in Menon, 2010: 5).

The concept of overlapping interest, however, can only take us so far. Relationships between even amicable powers can be competitive in nature as each country seeks to prosper at the other's expense. The theory of Realism, for example, points to an anarchical international environment in which countries compete so as to maximize their own power. Within the Anglo-American relationship, there are numerous examples where competition rather than cooperation characterized their interaction, such as the hostile US approach to the continuation of the post-war British Empire. What is often overlooked by commentators is the extent to which the US and the UK have not only identified shared interests but have actively assisted each other in realizing them. Whilst the confluence of interests is only a precondition for cooperation, the two sides must be desirous of working together to realize them. Mutual utility has been a key feature of Anglo-American conduct, a willingness to incur costs in order to assist the other (Xu, 2016). Danchev declares 'reciprocity' to be a key feature of UK–US relations (1996). Prime Minister David Cameron described the relationship as strong 'because it delivers for both of us' (Dumbrell in Dobson and Marsh, 2013: 99).

As well as the will to work together, there must exist the capability. The British military has played a key role in making cooperation with the US possible. When the relationship has flagged during times of peace, then it has been reinvigorated during periods when the two sides fought alongside each other. Military cooperation and nuclear collaboration have been the lynchpins between the two countries. The US and the UK have sought to work in step with one another, treating the other as special in defence and security matters.

Not all authors have viewed the relationship as the pursuit of shared interests: some have viewed it as selective or even antagonistic. One perspective sees the British experience as one of subordination at the hands of the US. Beloff (1986: 256) argues that the US actively opposed Britain as a post-war imperial power but failed to fill the vacuum that it left when Britain pulled out of its Empire. Danchev (1996: 740) argues that the UK was deceived by US diplomacy and received little recompense for its slavish following of American policy. Burk (2009) contends that US behaviour was selective, in that it only treated the UK as special when it sought its help in realizing American interests.

A contending view of exploitation has regarded London as using its relationship with Washington to mask its faded leadership in the world. Thus Prime Minister Harold Macmillan talked of the British as the sophisticated and worldly-wise 'Greeks' to the all-powerful but inexperienced American 'Rome' (quoted in Ashton, 2005: 696). Dumbrell refers to a process of 'reification' by UK leaders who saw 'a permanent junior partnership with the US as the best way to manage and finesse British international decline' (Dumbrell 2004: 438; Reynolds, 1985). Seitz (1998: 325) describes the special relationship as providing Britain with an alternative to European integration, 'a bromide should Europe (and integration) ultimately prove indigestible' (Hendershot in Dobson and Marsh, 2013: 53).

The 'Terminalist' school of thought has seen the UK relationship with the US slipping away (Danchev, 1996). This approach has been built on an assumption that British power has been in gradual decline since World War II and the link with America was a means to delay that process. Analysts have identified key junctures as sounding the death knell for the special relationship. The Suez crisis was seen as a moment that captured British humiliation at the hands of the Eisenhower administration (see Chapter 3). Dickie (1994: xiv) and May and Treverton (1986) view the drawdown of the Cold War as marking the decline of Anglo-American relations. Coker posits that in the 1990s the relationship became 'an illusion of continuity for a nation that is experiencing a profound sense of purposelessness' (Coker, 1992: 409). The first Gulf War was perceived as a last gasp of the relationship before it disappeared into oblivion.

Such analysts have struggled to account for the persistence of the Anglo-American relationship in the post-Cold War era (Xu, 2017: 114). Marsh and Baylis (2006: 174) pick up this theme when they refer to the relationship's 'Lazarus quality', its capacity to revive after being considered to be moribund. Amidst the conflicts in the Balkans, the Middle East, and Central Asia, cooperation between the two powers has endured. Critics have used the argument that the UK has either conjured an 'imagined' Anglo-American community (Marsh, 2019: 311) or it has suffered from self-delusion, lured into policies in which it has falsely believed itself to be America's partner. This fantasy has been exposed when British sacrifice has not reaped the influence that it anticipated, such as after the 2003 invasion of Iraq. Nevertheless, the durability of the Anglo-American relationship and its refusal to disappear has confounded the predictions of pessimists.

Whilst a focus on interests has dominated the academic literature, another body of scholarship has seen it revolving around shared values and culture (Dumbrell, 2001). It is reasonable to expect that countries will ally with those who share their political system and values. Such alliances are likely to be long-lasting because they contain bonds within them that offer a capacity to overcome problems when they arise. This has been the 'Sentimental' school that has argued that a common language, shared history, and political and legal systems accounts for Anglo-American amity. It is also seen as the basis of a Western 'order' that has permeated through post-war organizations such as NATO and the United Nations as well as global financial and trading structures. Having these factors in common has helped to forge a shared sense of identity and has been reinforced by cultural elements such as literature, films, music, clothes, and food. President Obama reaffirmed this during a visit to the UK when he stated that, 'Our relationship is special because of the values and beliefs that have united our peoples' (Obama, 2011). These factors contribute to the soft power influence that both countries exude across the world (Dobson, 1995).

Those critical of this school of thought have argued that exponents of the special relationship have been overly reliant upon sentiment (Watt, 1986). They have either been dismissive that cultural links necessarily lead to the pursuit of common policies or have contended that the ties that once existed have been eroded. Transatlantic differences over the use of force and the values of the Trump presidency have contributed to a view that US–European paths have fundamentally diverged. Danchev notes that while the UK and US agree on values such as liberal democracy, market economics, and the rule of law, there remain cultural differences about how those are put into practice (Danchev, 2005: 432).

Baylis argues that it is the interweaving of these factors, along with shared interests, that hold the keys to understanding the Anglo-American relationship (Baylis, 1984: xviii). His view is that the sentimental linkages add a depth to the relationship and help to shape common interests. Unlike analysts such as Shapiro and Witney (2009: 16), who warn that the US will not 'sacrifice national interest on the altar of nostalgia', Baylis and Dobson (1995) contend that we should see interests and sentiments in a different way. Rather than opposing factors, interests, and sentiments should be seen as mutually complementary and helping to create a unique relationship.

Key arguments and the importance of the book

Several arguments are explored in this book. The first is that the UK's defence relationship with the US is its most important bilateral relationship. In other patterns of cooperation, the UK may be working with a peer ally like France, or with a smaller European country. Such circumstances lead to questions as to how a military task will be divided, which country will lead an operation, will they be able to bring sufficient power to bear, will they remain committed throughout the duration of the task, and what level of risk is being tolerated? Yet operating alongside the US, transforms the military calculation in a manner unlike any other ally. The US, due to its size and strength, automatically becomes the framework nation for an operation. It therefore makes sense for the UK to be aligned with the shaping power in complex operations to ensure British interests are taken into account.

The UK military perceives itself to obtain disproportionate benefit from aligning with the US armed forces.

Furthermore, US involvement transforms the prospects for operational success. As one senior military officer retorted when interviewed, 'Why would you not want to be close to the US military?' (Interview with British Army Major-General, 2012). The US has possessed the most technologically advanced and dominant armed forces in the post-Cold War era. To a military operation it can contribute critical capabilities, such as satellite reconnaissance and electronic warfare assets, that no other Western power has at its disposal. It also possesses command and control resources and precision strike and stealth capabilities that are more advanced than that of any other country. Such military strengths dramatically increase the prospects for achieving objectives as well as significantly reducing the risk of incurring casualties. The US is the country with the ability to assist the UK in realizing its objectives and to conduct a spectrum of operations, ranging from high intensity warfare to less demanding interventionary operations. In the period after 9/11, the UK abandoned the idea of engaging in large-scale operations without the US.

Anglo-American cooperation is therefore the most important security relationship for the UK. It is the cornerstone of the country's defence policy and a deeper understanding of its dimensions plays a vital part in making sense of the UK's past, present, and future. Within this policy space, the British military has a central role that sheds light on the broader special relationship.

A second argument is that employing a theoretical framework of historical institutionalism enables a better understanding of the Anglo-American defence relationship (see Chapter 2). Historical institutionalism explains how sectoral cooperation emerges between countries: the way in which patterns of collaboration are encouraged and aberrant behaviour constrained. Historical institutionalism helps to account for the durability of military cooperation and how the relationship has adapted in the face of new challenges.

A third argument is that military cooperation with a superpower is an inherently difficult thing for a UK-sized power to achieve. Contrary to the impression conveyed by armchair critics, developing military forces capable of wartime operations alongside the US is no simple matter. Both the UK and US militaries are hugely complex organizations that cannot easily be harmonized when a conflict arises. In addition, the US military is several orders of magnitude bigger than the UK and its diversity and the autonomy of its various service arms makes it a challenging actor with whom to interface. The relationship is like a multi-dimensional mosaic. To achieve cross-service collaboration in the battlespace requires detailed preparations and peacetime planning.

Interoperability with the US military—the ability to fight together—requires forces that are to a large extent similar in doctrine and tactics (Codner, 2014: 9). Achieving this demands considerable preparation. British forces have needed to look into the future, discern the direction in which the US is moving and configure their own capabilities in order to align themselves effectively. This influences the types of weapons programmes and the necessary training. The conundrum was encapsulated by former Chief of the Air Staff, Sir Jock Stirrup:

> Keeping up with the Americans presupposes that the Americans know where they are going and we just follow on a little bit behind. Actually, that is not good enough and we need to be there at the same time as they do, so we have to try to predict where they are going to wind up so that we are in a position at that moment in time to be interoperable . . .
>
> (Defence Select Committee, 2004).

The challenge for the UK military is to understand US threat perceptions and their planning for operations. In the words of Kiszely (2008: 2) it means confronting issues of, 'integration, interoperability, decision-making, and achieving unity of purpose'.

A fourth argument of this study is that UK–US military cooperation has taken place within a dynamic environment. The nature of conflict has been evolving and the US has been at the forefront of developments in warfare. During the Cold War, both sides were focused primarily on the risk of high intensity conflict with the Soviet Union that was expected to escalate to the use of nuclear weapons. With the end of the Cold War, new digital technologies impacted on warfare, and there was less clarity about threats and the type of conflict that might occur. The impact of this trend became evident in the interventions in Bosnia and Kosovo. Both the US and the UK were required to fashion new military doctrines to address peace-building and nation-building tasks. They had to prepare to encounter adversaries who pursued asymmetric strategies designed to avoid decisive engagement with Western forces.

A fifth argument is that working with the US has generated risks as well as benefits for the UK armed forces. To be America's partner of choice in military operations has involved a series of choices and trade-offs. It has required the UK to sustain a breadth of capabilities and to engage in tasks that have weighed heavily upon its resources. It has also drawn UK decision-makers into looking at global problems through a lens conditioned by US priorities. The UK has neglected other opportunities in its attempt to remain close to the US. The fact that the UK has borne these costs is testament to the importance that it has attached to working with the US.

Sources and structure of the book

This book investigates the Anglo-American defence relationship from the UK perspective. Within this agenda, it concentrates on post-Cold War operations where the armed forces of the two countries have operated together. It does not attempt to look at operations that either the British or the US have conducted separately, such as the British operation in Sierra Leone or the US mission in Haiti. As such it does not purport be a comprehensive analysis of either sides' military doctrine or the conduct of national interventions. Rather it looks at how the British military has worked bilaterally with the US military to address key defence challenges. The study investigates both the ways that they have worked together and the points of friction that have arisen between them.

This study is focused on defence rather than the broader security relationship. It does not investigate police cooperation between the UK and the US or civilian intelligence cooperation. Although intelligence has been a vital dimension of their relationship (see Aldrich 2004; Svendsen 2010), much of this collaboration has been non-military in nature. Where there is a direct military intelligence dimension then it is included in this book. By contrast, the nuclear aspect of Anglo-American relations has been incorporated because it is an integral aspect of the military relationship.

This study makes extensive use of interviews. Nearly 50 semi-structured interviews were undertaken with senior officers from all three of the British armed services. Many of the interviewees had recently retired from the military and were chosen because of their ability to talk more freely about their experiences of working with the US. Preserving their anonymity was a factor designed to encourage their candour. Insights were corroborated between officers across different branches of the armed services as well as with the secondary literature to ensure the accuracy of the data. A smaller number of interviews were undertaken with officers from the US armed forces, such as from the US Army War College in Pennsylvania, to compare with the views of British sources. In addition, the UK Director of Defence Studies was approached in order to grant access to British military personnel who were serving in the US. Interviews were permitted at the British Military Mission in Washington DC and at NATO Command Transformation in Norfolk, Virginia. In the case of Chapter 7 on nuclear relations, interviews were not sought with Royal Navy personnel due to the sensitivity of nuclear issues and that chapter relies on secondary source material.

As well as interviews, the book draws upon a range of other primary source materials. These include statements on military doctrine by the Ministry of Defence, defence reviews, historical records from the National Archives, and reports from Select Committees of the House of Commons and House of Lords. This material has been supplemented by autobiographies and books from leading military and defence officials from both sides of the Atlantic.

Secondary sources utilized in this study have included books on various aspects of defence strategy, articles in journals, think tank reports, and media publications. The wars in Afghanistan and Iraq resulted in an outpouring of military literature and post-conflict inquiries that have helped to inform this publication. Some of this literature has come from officers who fought in Anglo-American coalition operations and were able to offer first-hand accounts.

The structure of the book reflects the complex and interwoven nature of UK–US military cooperation. The two countries have prepared for different forms of conflict: this has ranged from high intensity engagement with the armed forces of an enemy state to low intensity operations against militias and irregular combatants. Post-1989, another type of operation came to the fore, one where the pursuit of victory was not the objective but force might nevertheless be necessary. The boundaries between these typologies are blurred and the strict separation between them has been made more for clarity of analysis in Chapters 4, 5, and 6, than to reflect real world practice. Each of the empirical chapters also contains a section on inter-service relationships. The pattern of cooperation between each of the British services and their US counterparts has been important dimensions in the 'special' nature of their relations.

The post-Cold War period has been characterized by a varied and unpredictable range of military campaigns involving the US and the UK. The war against Iraq in 2003 illustrates how in one campaign there may be several types of operational demands confronting Anglo-American forces. This war involved large military forces manoeuvring on battlefields with air power in support. Yet this high intensity phase lasted for a relatively short period of time. It was followed by a prolonged and complex insurgency in which fighting took place in urban centres. This phase was conducted against a range of protagonists, consisting of former members of the Iraqi Army, local militias, and foreign jihadists. The fighting was entwined with efforts to achieve a post-conflict reconstruction phase. This explains why conflicts such as Afghanistan and Iraq are discussed in both Chapters 4 and 6.

Chapter 2 sets out a conceptual framework based on Historical Institutionalism. It aids an understanding of how Anglo-American military cooperation is made possible through three key aspects. First, military doctrine between the armed forces of the two countries provides a set of 'Rules' that structures their approach to the use of force. These rules depend on the type of warfare that is envisaged. Second, 'Practices' reflect how doctrine is implemented and modified in actual conflict scenarios. Third, 'Narrative' seeks to explain how cooperation between the two countries is justified. This conceptual framework is applied to the empirical chapters of the book.

Chapter 3 provides a brief historical context of the Anglo-American military relationship in the period from World War II to the end of the Cold War. Although the book focuses on the post-Cold War era, an understanding of the themes that preceded 1989 is vital because there were continuities in issues and relationships across the periods. The Cold War witnessed close cooperation between the armed services of the two countries and the birth of their nuclear cooperation. It saw the UK emerge as a major contributor to European security and assume the role as the interlocutor between America and its European allies. Whilst Britain divested itself of its empire, it nevertheless preserved a global perspective that was to play a major part in the overseas interventions of the post-Cold War era.

Chapter 4 on High Intensity Warfighting looks at how the UK military positioned itself alongside the US as they sought to be able to conduct inter-state conflicts. This was the most demanding of requirements as the US was at the forefront of doctrinal and technological developments. It involved the British armed forces in major conflicts where they sought to make contributions that the US would find meaningful and would result in their being treated as its most important partner.

Chapter 5 focuses on 'Operations Other than All Out War'. This was one of the most complicated aspects of Anglo-American military cooperation because neither side was prepared for the types of contingencies that arose. The UK and the US found themselves engaging in interventionary operations that were not designed to secure the unconditional surrender of their adversaries. Instead they sought to bring a cessation to violence amongst conflicting parties and to police ceasefires. These types of tasks were very different from the wars that their militaries had expected to encounter in the past.

Chapter 6 on 'Insurgency and Low Intensity Conflict' charts the operations that the UK and US militaries found themselves involved in both in Afghanistan and Iraq. Although these conflicts began as inter-state wars, the very superiority of coalition forces led their enemies to resort to asymmetrical patterns of warfare in an attempt to undermine allied resolve. These conflicts imposed major strains on the Anglo-American military relationship and exposed significant differences between them.

Chapter 7 on the Nuclear Relationship investigates how nuclear cooperation evolved into a major foundation stone of UK–US relations. In spite of an initial faltering pattern of collaboration, the two sides have developed an intimate and unique way of working together. This has resulted in two generations of a US ballistic missile carried by British built submarines with British-designed warheads. A follow-on generation of British submarine is now being ordered that will preserve the UK strategic deterrent into the middle of this century.

Chapter 8, the Conclusion, reviews the insights that have been derived from this study of the Anglo-American military relationship. It also looks into the future to assess how the relationship may fare in the face of newly emerging strategic challenges.

2

Institutionalism

Introduction

In order to study the Anglo-American relationship, it is not strictly necessary to delve into a theoretical framework. Indeed, numerous studies of the broader UK–US relationship have eschewed theory. However, it is argued here that theory can offer a lens that facilitates a deeper understanding of the military relationship between the two sides in the post-Cold War era. This theoretical framework was first explained in an article by Rees and Davies (2019) that helped to build the foundation for this book-length study. The framework also draws upon the work of Xu (2015, 2016, and 2017) and I acknowledge a debt to his ideas.

The theory of institutionalism is long established within international relations and has evolved several distinct strands. This chapter posits that institutionalism aids an understanding of the Anglo-American military relationship. It illuminates how the two countries have developed a pattern of cooperation despite facing major changes in the international environment. It shifts attention away from the personal interactions of heads of state to focus on the cooperation that exists within a network of institutional linkages amongst their armed forces. It argues that this network develops a reflex to work together on a systematic and routine basis. This helps to explain the durability of Anglo-American military relations, its shared outlook, and its capacity to adapt to new circumstances.

The chapter begins by explaining institutionalist theory and the concept of 'historical institutionalism'. It explains how institutionalism can be observed in the extensive linkages between the militaries of the UK and the US. It proceeds to outline the analytical framework that will be traced in the empirical Chapters 4–7.

The development of institutionalist theory

According to Keohane (1989), an institution is a framework that political actors enter into in order to regularize their interactions. It becomes a setting, formal or otherwise, in which a specific set of issues or activities are conducted. Institutions provide opportunities for systematic dialogue between participants as well as for action. In the absence of this framework, they might struggle to cooperate or the interaction could fall into disuse. In international relations the concept of an institution is similar to that of a 'regime': a place where actors come together

The Anglo-American Military Relationship. Wyn Rees, Oxford University Press. © Wyn Rees (2024).
DOI: 10.1093/oso/9780198884620.003.0002

to deal with a particular subject (Peters, 2019: 189; For literature on regimes, see Krasner, 1983; Mayer, Rittberger, and Zurn, 1997; Young, 1980). Various types of actors may participate within an international regime, including states and non-state organizations. As a result, this study, with its focus on cooperation between the armed forces of the UK and the US, will use the concept of institutions rather than regimes.

Through the creation of a regularized setting or process for their interactions, an institution enables actors to develop routines. Institutions make cooperation easier, because they reduce uncertainty or 'transaction costs' (Keohane, 1988: 387; Hall and Taylor, 1996: 946). They demonstrate the advantages of structured cooperation and reduce the risk that the relationship will wither away. An actor can participate in an institution with a high degree of expectation that sustained patterns of mutual collaboration will occur.

The actors that come together within an institutional setting will share common values. It is this mutual outlook on the world that draws them to coalesce in the first place and makes cooperation desirable. By meeting together, it becomes possible for shared values to grow. These values enable them to evolve rules of behaviour, norms, and informal mechanisms that act as a guide to action. These become the conventions and the practices that guarantee predictability within the relationship (North, 1991: 99).

In addition to facilitating patterns of cooperation, institutions also serve as the means to constrain action that might be counter-productive. Through the development of certain behaviours, customs, and traditions, the institution prevents activity that risks jeopardizing collaboration (Sanders, 2006). Participants within the institution have the means to hold each other to account. The prevention of divergent conduct ensures that the expectations of all parties within an institution are fulfilled.

There are several strands of institutionalist theory. The first is 'rational choice institutionalism' and this strand has contributed insights relating to actors maximizing their utility and employing institutions as the means by which to realize their preferences (Peters, 2019: 24). It is within 'institutional contexts' that the preferences of actors are identified and constructed (Thelen, 1999: 375). In seeking to overcome collective action problems, actors are guided by rules and laws and they fear the imposition of sanctions if they transgress (Lowndes and Roberts, 2013: 52–53).

A second strand, 'sociological institutionalists', have provided rich descriptions of human interaction and contributed the insight that institutions are based around ideas. As such institutions are 'socially constructed in . . . that they embody shared cultural understandings' (Thelen, 1999: 386). They contribute to a 'script' from which all can draw and from which meaning can be discerned to explain various forms of interaction. An idea can lead to a pattern of behaviour that is replicated over time. Rules provide actors with 'precedents': namely, ways in which problems have been managed in the past and thus offer potential guides for the future. They signal where authoritative interpretation resides and they contribute to the smooth running of decision-making processes (March and Olsen, 2009: 7).

A third strand, 'discursive institutionalism', focuses on the ideas and narratives that are carried out within institutional settings (Schmidt, 2010). These narratives are constantly re-shaping and redefining the institution in the light of the interaction between its members. They help to give meaning to ways of doing things. As a result this form of institutionalist theory is more able to account for change and the evolution of relationships amongst actors (Peters, 2019: 135).

Historical institutionalism, the approach adopted in this book, draws upon the other strands of institutionalist theory. From rational choice institutionalism, it accepts that actors are motivated by interest and the pursuit of strategic goals. When engaging in an institution, the actor accepts a degree of constraint upon their own behaviour in the knowledge that similar constraints will be experienced by their ally. Borrowing from sociological institutionalism, historical institutionalism recognizes that ideas are powerful constitutive elements that help to bind participants together (Hall and Taylor, 1996: 938). Ideas give meaning to human behaviour (Scott, 1995: 33). From discursive institutionalism, there is an acknowledgement of the need to account for change within an institutional setting as well as to discern how language can help to structure relationships.

The insight offered by historical institutionalism is that past practice creates a context in which cooperation becomes expected and embedded. Formal rules evolve to provide guidelines for decision-making (Hall and Thelen, 2009: 9). If the participants have worked within that framework for a sustained period, and found that it serves their interests, then it will continue to be used (Lowndes, 1996: 182–183). This leads to the concept of 'path dependency' (Hall and Taylor, 1996: 942; Levi, 1997: 28) as actors follow patterns of cooperation that have worked in the past. Institutions enjoy longevity and result in actors pursuing policies along 'paths' that have become ingrained.

Historical institutionalists go a step further. They regard the institutions themselves as playing a role in shaping the identities of actors, through a process of endogenous preference formation (Hall and Taylor, 1996: 939; Keohane, 1988: 382). The likelihood of alternative preferences being chosen is reduced. Over time institutions become sources of inclination in their own right and develop a sense of their own agency (Thelen, 1999: 375). Peters (2019: 83) describes this as a process of layering or 'sedimentation'. It recognizes the importance of habit and how patterns of activity, once established, become resistant to change.

Although historical institutionalists concentrate on why institutions persist, they do not deny that change can occur. In the first place, they accept the importance of human agency in perpetuating a pattern of collaboration. Second, they identify key moments or 'critical junctures' (Peters, 2019: 90; Hall and Taylor, 1996: 94) that impact upon and provide opportunities for the reordering of the existing system. This may have resulted from a build-up of pressure or by a change in the external environment to which the actors respond. Rules and practices within the institution may be changed quickly or may prove reluctant to change and informal practices may continue in parallel.

Actors within the institutional setting may respond to changes in different ways. Historical institutionalists predict that, having established a regularized form of activity, actors are unlikely to respond to external shocks by creating new institutional arrangements. Rather, they are more likely to adapt their existing framework to meet new demands. The end of the Cold War, for example, represented a fundamental change in the threat environment faced by the US and UK that altered their calculus of interests. Nevertheless, the two countries adapted their pattern of military cooperation to new demands.

Institutionalism is important because it contributes to building trust in interstate relations. Trust is an inherently difficult attribute to engender due to the anarchical nature of the international system and the uncertainty that afflicts states when observing the behaviour of their neighbours. This uncertainty is a consequence of state sovereignty and the need for states to ensure their own survival. Wheeler (2018) has worked extensively on the concept of trust, although from the perspective of explaining how it can be built up between states that have hitherto been locked in an adversarial relationship.

Trust requires state actors to look upon their counterparts as providing the means to achieve their security objectives. Allies must possess both the capability to assist and demonstrate the political will to do so. Through Wheeler's conception of 'bonded trust' (2018: 9), actors must have amassed confidence that those with whom they have been working can be relied upon to continue replicating a pattern of cooperation. Predictability and a willingness to share sensitive information are therefore vital factors in achieving persistent cooperation. Each side has to be willing to discuss its strategic plans with its ally at the risk of exposing its own vulnerabilities. It has to have the expectation that these will not be exploited or communicated to potential adversaries (Kydd, 2005). This sort of trust is built through reciprocity and accrued over a period of time. It needs to have been tested under pressure, by resolving areas of disagreement and finding ways to engage in mutually beneficial actions. If a state proves to be inconsistent in a given circumstance then it can undermine its dependability in the eyes of its ally and trust can take a long time to be restored.

Trust is particularly hard to generate in relations between unequal states. The weaker country is likely to fear abandonment—that its security interests will be overlooked by its more powerful ally in the pursuit of wider geopolitical interests. Conversely, the powerful state will fear defection—that the costs of partnering will be deemed too great by the weaker country. Sustaining confidence in such a relationship requires constant investment. Xu argues that the Anglo-American relationship has achieved this through a track record of reliability in which, although the extent of the utility favours the UK, nevertheless both sides derive benefit from cooperation (2017: 179).

This book applies a historical institutionalist framework developed by Lowndes and Roberts (2013: 12–13), who argue that a broadly constructivist ontology is necessary to explain actor behaviour within institutions. Blending the approaches of rational, historical, and sociological institutionalism illustrates convergence on key points about the function of institutions (Lowndes and Roberts, 2013: 12; Hall and Taylor, 1996). Lowndes and Roberts (2013: 57) contend that institutions facilitate interaction through three principal mechanisms; formal rules, informal practices, and narratives. This has similarities with the approach of Scott who labels them regulative, normative, and cognitive mechanisms.

Within institutions, rules, practices, and narratives serve to both propel and constrain behaviour. They are mutually reinforcing. Rules ensure predictability within relationships and also formalize well-established practices. Practices put rules to the test and determine their appropriateness for the parties involved. Narratives typically explain and justify the existence of both rules and practices. The case for changing the rules often occurs in narrative form, and narratives can present established practices in a positive or negative light.

An institutionalized Anglo-American military relationship

This book asserts that the Anglo-American military relationship has become routinized and has acquired institutional characteristics. It is one aspect of a multi-dimensional relationship between the two countries, but it is especially important because it relates to the highly sensitive area of defence. Applying the theoretical lens of historical institutionalism helps to explain how this military-to-military relationship has contributed to post-Cold War Anglo-American cooperation.

The British and US militaries have grown together over time and have developed multiple forms of interaction: at the individual level, at a service level, and between their armed forces as a whole. Rather than calculations of short-term self-interest, the relationship has been characterized by shared ideas and experiences that have emerged from regular dialogue and consultation (Hall and Thelen, 2009). The militaries of the two countries have learned to work with each other, to build on patterns of past cooperation, and to expect future reciprocity. Institutionalism has made it possible for both sides to trust the relationship, because past experience has proven the reliability of the other party.

On the US side, institutionalism has acted as a source of constraint, entwining it into a close relationship with the UK. When the US military has looked for a partner in its overseas interventions, it has turned first to the British military. It would be difficult for the US to develop new patterns of cooperation with another country to replace the UK. For its part, the UK has developed confidence that the

US is dependable–that it will adhere to its commitments. Having more to lose and having risked dependence on the US in certain areas of military capability, the predictability of its superpower ally has been an important source of reassurance for the UK.

Because of the inequality in power between them, the British military has never taken cooperation with the US for granted. Rather they have believed that the relationship needs to be cultivated. Collaboration has been consistent largely as a result of efforts by the UK to keep investing and sustaining it in peacetime. The UK has promoted programmes for its officers to work in the US, and it has engaged in large-scale joint exercises. This pattern of working together has become systematized to the extent that both countries reserve personnel positions for the other side in their armed forces. It has accorded the UK a privileged awareness of US thinking: its threat perceptions, strategic planning, and military doctrine.

This has been given additional impetus in times of war. Rules, practices, and narratives have provided the two countries with the means to transition to a warfighting capability when required. Although this has been challenging for the UK, it has nevertheless been treated as a priority. The UK's defence establishment has engaged in a close dialogue with the US military. This helps to explain how the relationship has been able to adapt to new security challenges and thereby remain relevant over many decades.

Rules

Institutions represent routine patterns of cooperative behaviour. Actors can move beyond routines to formalize their actions into rules that provide guides to action. These can take the form of laws or treaties and can create obligations to which decision-makers are expected to abide and are held to account (North, 1991: 99). 'Rules (and) laws . . . provide parameters for action rather than dictate a specific action' (March and Olsen, 2009: 10). The actor interprets what is relevant through the lens of their experience and within the culture in which they operate.

In the case of armed services, rules and laws are represented by military doctrine. These are the parameters on which armed forces are configured, they are written in peace time to provide principles for action in war time. Doctrine gives military commanders the guidelines within which they must design actual operations. Such doctrine provides an insight into the thinking of how military forces may be utilized in a given set of circumstances, the means at their disposal, and the priorities that will be pursued (Long, 2016: 20).

According to Posen (1984: 13), military doctrine should be understood as a 'set of prescriptions . . . specifying how military forces should be structured and employed'. Posen postulates that doctrine emerges through a competitive process that results in resources and status being allocated to particular groups within an organization. Military organizations are broadly similar in nature: they incline towards preparing for missions with which they are familiar, namely those that have resulted in past successes. Yet planning for operations alongside other states has the effect of complicating doctrinal thinking. Coalition or alliance activities require bringing doctrine into alignment with another state or group of countries in order to ensure that armed forces can function effectively together (Interview by telephone with Director of the Defence Concepts and Doctrine Centre, 2020). The extent of the doctrinal alignment will depend upon the degree to which allied military forces are integrated in the battlespace or whether they are assigned separate sectors of responsibility.

Since the end of the Cold War, the UK has found itself in a multifaceted position in relation to military doctrine. This is because, in addition to acting alongside the US, it is also a permanent member of NATO. The UK has been committed to preserving a leading position in NATO: it holds the role of Deputy Supreme Allied Commander Europe (D-SACEUR); it serves as framework nation for the Alliance's Allied Rapid Reaction Corps (ARRC); and it has provided the Commander and Deputy Commander role in the International Security Assistance Force in Afghanistan as well as leadership of the Very High Readiness Joint Task Force. NATO is itself highly institutionalized, its decisions are made by consensus, and it promotes common military standards and equipment (Walt, 1997: 168–169). NATO doctrine is formulated within Allied Command Transformation in Norfolk, Virginia, with inputs from national representatives and then signed off by all member states. As a result the UK has needed to work with both NATO and US national doctrine.

NATO is a complex alliance composed of democratic states from Europe and North America. It has evolved into Deutsch's concept of a 'pluralistic security community', where there exists a sense of trust and predictability amongst the members (Deutsch 1957: 129). As Wheeler (2018: 120) observes, it is exhibited by institutional linkages and predictability of behaviour. It has evolved into a group of like-minded states for whom force is no longer an instrument for resolving differences. The existence of shared values has enabled NATO to transcend the shared threat that led to its formation and to remain together for post-Cold War missions. US and UK representatives sit in the NATO forum together and at the highest level in the North Atlantic Council. British and American officers have been stationed together at various military commands within the Alliance.

The US and UK have not formed a bilateral organizational relationship because their cooperation has been nestled within the existing structure of NATO. Yet the Anglo-American relationship has also acted separately from the Alliance. Collaboration in nuclear and intelligence matters has been conducted through bilateral channels. Even in the case of conventional military actions, wars such as those against Iraq in 1990–91 and 2003 were conducted as coalition operations led by the US. Whilst they drew extensively upon NATO operating procedures, these conflicts were conducted outside the scope of the Alliance. On such occasions, the US acted as the framework nation for the coalition: it would determine the nature of the operation and designate the land and sea areas in which coalition forces would operate (Interview with Royal Navy Admiral, 2012a). The US would also contribute 'enablers', such as satellite intelligence or electronic warfare assets, that would be critical to the military outcome. Because of its size and strength, US involvement in an operation has tended to result in it playing the dominant role.

A British military publication affirms that, 'Except where there is a specific need for national doctrine, the UK will adopt and deploy NATO doctrine' (Joint Doctrine Publication 0-01, 2014). Utilizing NATO doctrine is regarded as maximizing interoperability: the UK only produces national doctrine where Alliance doctrine is inappropriate (DCDC, 2020). On occasions when the UK differs from aspects of NATO doctrine, it inserts 'green paragraphs' into papers that explain and account for its divergent position (Interview by telephone with Director of the Defence Concepts and Doctrine Centre, 2020). The US shapes much of NATO doctrine because of its leadership role within the Alliance. However, whilst the US is a vital player in the formulation of NATO doctrine, it does not necessarily adhere to it and composes its own national doctrine (Interview by telephone with Director of the Defence Concepts and Doctrine Centre, 2020).

A further complication for the UK is that the construction of US military doctrine derives from two sources. The first is from within each of the powerful single services, the US Army, Navy, Air Force, and Marines (Hallion, 2011: 115). Each of the US armed services has its own doctrine formulation centre. For example, the US Army has its Training and Doctrine Command (TRADOC) at Fort Eustis, Virginia. The UK has posted liaison officers to these doctrine formulation centres because it is from here that technological and warfighting ideas originate. While the UK does not always possess the resources, or the need, to emulate all US doctrinal developments, the desire to be apprised of them is paramount (Interview by telephone with former British Army Liaison Officer to the US Training and Doctrine Centre, 2019).

The other source of US doctrinal development is from within the Joint Staff (J7) that operates under the auspices of the Joint Chiefs of Staff (JCS). In a military operation, the US Joint Staff liaise with the British Permanent Joint Headquarters (PJHQ). British officers have been placed on the J7 staff in both the Pentagon and NATO's Allied Command Transformation in Norfolk, Virginia to better understand US concepts. The mission of the Joint Staff is to weld the doctrines of the Army, Air Force, Navy, and Marines into a shared doctrine that can guide the activities of all of the services (Interview by telephone with Director of the Defence Concepts and Doctrine Centre, 2020). The US has sought to ensure doctrinal compatibly with its NATO allies through the creation of Combined Joint Operational Services. The US military has been propelled towards 'jointery' (the ability of all of its armed services to operate together) since it was recognized as a concept in Field Manual 100-5 in 1962 (Kretchik, 2011: 182) and then prioritized in the Goldwater Nichols Act of 1986. The size and rivalries within each arm of the US armed services has constrained the extent to which jointery has been successful (Rumsfeld, 2002: 31).

As a result of these conflicting pressures, the UK has found it necessary to build its military doctrine around NATO whilst simultaneously monitoring the advancement of doctrine within the US military. Where UK forces have undertaken operations in US-led coalitions, they have sought to place a senior British officer beneath an American commander in order to minimize the potential for frictions over force utilization. In addition, liaison officers have been deployed to ensure inter-operability in the battlespace. These efforts have made it possible for UK armed forces to be 'closer to the US . . . [in] doctrine, than any other military power' (Freedman, 2004: 112).

Practices

Military doctrine can only serve as a guideline: it remains abstract until it is tested in practice. Doctrine needs to be adapted for use in wartime, taking account of the particular circumstances in which force is to be applied. The resulting experience can have the effect of reinforcing doctrine or it can demonstrate its inappropriateness to operational requirements (Helmke and Levitsky, 2004). An institution can play a significant role in shaping practice: it can determine the doctrinal ideas that are put to the test, how they are judged in light of experience, and how they are revised. Based upon the knowledge derived from testing, new practices may be developed and these may later be turned into rules (Lowndes and Roberts, 2013: 57).

The process by which ideas and doctrine emerge as military practice is moulded by organizational culture. The concept of culture is intangible: it is a reflection of several interacting factors such as identity, history, material resources, and contemporary circumstances. It serves as a filter through which the world is interpreted and helps to determine what analogies are regarded as relevant and how actors should behave (Long, 2016: 8–9). There is a well-developed literature on 'strategic culture' and it is not the intention of this book to explore this subject and add to that body of work (see for instance, Johnston, 1995; Snyder, 1977; Giegerich, 2006). The point here is that there are different cultures between the militaries of the UK and the US (Foley, Griffin, and McCartney, 2011: 254). This has the effect of influencing their interactions and their capacities to cooperate together.

General Martin Dempsey (2014), former Chairman of the US JCS acknowledged that the US and the UK militaries 'share a remarkably close relationship'.

Common values, beliefs, and objectives have brought the armed forces of the two countries together. Their professionalism has made it possible for the two sides to collaborate. In rare instances, the armies, navies, or air forces of the two countries shared common interests that led them to support each other even when this caused tensions within their own national armed services. This occurred when a role or a weapons system brought competition with their own forces. For example, the navies of the two countries have competed with their respective air forces over how to provide airpower to expeditionary operations: by aircraft carriers or by land-based air power.

Yet as well as shared interests, there have been differences between the armed forces of the UK and the US that has reflected the societies from which they are drawn, as well as their size and resources. The US military has more of a German culture, with an emphasis on hierarchy and the carrying out of orders (Interview with British Defence Attache, 2014). In its approach to waging war, the US has shown a predilection for heavy firepower (Wiegley, 1960; Clark, 2001: 315), the use of overwhelming strength, and for seeking absolute victory (Mahnken, 2008: 4). After serving as the Deputy Commander alongside the US military in Baghdad in 2006, UK General Sir Nicholas Parker commented that 'the US Army is probably more different from us than the French' (Parker, 2013: 134).

The British military tends to be less hierarchical and less wedded to the use of firepower than its American counterpart. Whilst the US has tended to be concerned about force protection in the aftermath of conflict, the British have been more willing to take risks (Interview with US Army Colonel, 2014). The British military has been more reluctant than the US to write extensive doctrine. This has reflected an innate predisposition towards 'muddling through', on the grounds that military operations will always need to adapt to circumstances. Based on their historical experience, the British military have tended to see conflict as taking place along a spectrum and that it may be necessary to move flexibly up and down that spectrum. Egnell (2009: 115) describes British military culture as 'an intuitive approach from past operations, an empirical, pragmatic military tradition'.

Practices in peacetime

The US and the UK have turned to each other repeatedly for military cooperation since the end of the Cold War. This has been due to the fact that they have created, within their bilateral relationship, a 'deep infrastructure for consultation and cooperation' (Niblett, 2007: 627). This institutional framework has been assembled during peacetime to enable their militaries to interface with one another at all levels. It has made it possible to discuss how military doctrine should be translated into operational planning and how each country should respond to threats. This has guaranteed them knowledge of their ally's threat perceptions and its range of responses. Whilst it has not precluded disagreements, it has resulted in them being discussed behind closed doors. In the words of former US National Security Advisor, Henry Kissinger, the UK was treated as a government whom 'we exchanged ideas with so freely, or in effect permitted to participate in our deliberations' (quoted in Self, 2010: 106).

At the top of the structure, interaction has taken place between the US JCS and the British Chiefs of Staff (COS). This draws upon a distinguished heritage: in December 1941, after the Japanese attack on Pearl Harbour, the US and the UK established the Combined Joint Chiefs of Staff (CJCS) (Danchev, 1986). The shared threat from the Axis Powers pushed the two countries into a closer embrace than they might ever have envisaged possible (Reynolds, 1985: 5). The military-to-military relationship was kindled at the Arcadia conference where they sat together planning the strategy for the war and orchestrating their logistical efforts. Field Marshal Sir John Dill was the Head of the British Military Mission in Washington and he played a key role in putting the collaborative infrastructure in place. In the words of Watt (1986: 5), the militaries developed 'habits of easy intercourse'. It was the way in which World War II was fought that fostered, 'the depth of a relationship that has since come to seem inevitable' (Clarke, 2014: 237)

The discontinuation of the CJCS after World War II was widely lamented on the British side. In his 1946 Iron Curtain speech in the US, Winston Churchill called for the re-institution of the CJCS for the post-war era. This did not take place but in March 2013 twice yearly meetings of the UK COS and US JCS Committee were resurrected. The first meeting was hosted by the US at Fort McNair in Washington DC, and provided a chance to compare perspectives about worldwide issues. It also encouraged personal relationships to be cultivated between heads of the armed forces so, if a problem emerged, they could be resolved based on personal trust. The UK proceeded to host a follow up meeting in June 2014.

The British Chief of the Defence Staff (CDS) has a direct relationship with his American opposite number, the Chairman of the JCS, through a British officer based in the Pentagon (Interview with Liaison Officer for the British Chief of the Defence Staff, 2014). This officer has access to the Chairman on a weekly basis. The link was particularly important during operations that involved the armed forces of both countries, such as in Iraq and Afghanistan. The CDS can also interact with the Pentagon through the UK Defence Attache in Washington and the US Defence Attache in London (Interview with former UK Defence Attache, 2012). As an illustration of the close personal relationships that can develop, General David Richards, flew across the Atlantic to attend the retirement parade of Admiral Mike Mullen, former Chairman of the JCS in Washington (Richards, 2014: 305).

The British Joint Service Mission (BJSM), co-located with the Embassy in Washington, has the job of coordinating the UK's entire military presence in the US.

This presence comprises nearly 800 people, led by a two-star Defence Attache. Under the Attache are one-star representatives from each of the British armed services that interact with their equivalent ranks in the US armed forces. The BJSM interfaces with the central US government, oversees the procurement of military equipment, and orchestrates the through-flow of British military and defence personnel on visits to and from the US. As well as British officers and personnel embedded within US structures, the BJSM also oversees the myriad British defence companies who operate in America, such as British Aerospace. The strength of contacts between the two sides is illustrated by the fact that a British team of defence officials were accorded unprecedented access to the US 2005 Quadrennial Defence Review (Foreign Affairs Select Committee, 2010: 23).

The UK has secured the placement of its officers in each of the US major commands. These include Northern Command (NORTHCOM), Cyber Command (CYBERCOM), Pacific Command (PACOM), and Special Operations Command (SOCOM). In Strategic Command (STRATCOM), UK officers represent the UK as well as the European dimension of NATO's nuclear planning representatives in Mons (Miller, 2008: 177). It is supplemented by a bi-annual conference on nuclear matters between the two countries. In the case of PACOM, UK representation has been increased to take account of greater US attention being paid to the Indo-Pacific region. The largest contingent of 30 British military personnel has been under a two-star general at US Central Command (CENTCOM) in Tampa, Florida that handles planning for the Middle East and Central Asia. According to McCausland (2009: 176), 'No other state has the daily involvement in the planning and preparation of operations that the UK has with the United States'.

The heads of each of the British armed services have representatives on the staff of their American counterparts (Interview with Royal Navy Captain, 2014). This provides a direct line of communication between each of the services and is supplemented by regular staff talks. For example, the British Army and the US Army meet at three-star level for staff talks each year (Interview by telephone with former British Army Liaison Officer to the US Training and Doctrine Centre, 2019), while their training and doctrine centres regularly interact and share best practice (Interview with British Army Lieutenant General, 2015). Similarly, the Royal Navy conducts staff talks with the US Navy once per year and wargaming exercises are hosted annually at the US Naval College at Rhode Island. The submariner communities meet twice per year (Interview with former First Sea Lord, 2015). The First Sea Lord meets with the US Chief of Naval Operations at least twice per year and there is a US naval officer on the staff of the First Sea Lord (Interview with former First Sea Lord, 2012), plus a US officer on the operational staff at the Permanent Joint Headquarters (PJHQ) at Northwood (Interview with Royal Navy Captain, 2014). The only other relationship that comes close to the intimacy between the two navies is that between the Special Forces of the two countries.

Practices in wartime

While talking together in peacetime is important, acting together in war time has required an even higher order of cooperation. Such circumstances raise the stakes, compress the timeframe, and impose all manner of strains. To prepare for this to the greatest possible extent, the US and the UK have engaged in a range of exercises and joint training that attempt to replicate the operational environment. Exercises have provided an opportunity to bring the armed forces of the two nations together and to test aspects, such as logistical support and medical evacuation. The UK has been involved in regular bilateral exercises with the US. For example, the Royal Air Force (RAF) has engaged in 'Red Flag' exercises at Nellis Air Force base in the Nevada desert, since 1977, where various packages of UK and US aircraft conduct simulated sorties. NATO exercises have afforded opportunities for British Army and US Army units to operate in tandem whilst naval units operate frequently together. There are also one-off exercises that are arranged between each of their armed services. For example, in 2021, the UK Royal Marines practiced with the US Marine Corps in 'Operation Green Dragon' in the Californian Mojave Desert.

Due to its area of responsibility, CENTCOM has been at the heart of recent wars. In the case of the 2003 Iraq conflict, an enlarged British team was sent out to Tampa to participate in the planning prior to the invasion (Interview with British Army Lieutenant General, 2015). British personnel were afforded the opportunity to understand US strategy prior to the commencement of military operations and to determine protocols on issues such as rules of engagement. A larger British presence at CENTCOM was also important from the point of view of the unique nature of America's wartime command structure: namely, that the CENTCOM commander reported directly to the secretary of defense and the president, not through the JCS (Joint Doctrine Publication 01, 2014: 64). Thus it was important for the British military to have an input into CENTCOM thinking if it wanted to impact US policy in Iraq.

During conflicts, US coalitions are conducted under an American commanding officer and supported by a British deputy. The British subordinate commander provides the link between the US military and the Permanent Joint Headquarters in the UK. Subordinate US officers control each of the major land, air, and sea combatant commands, with British officers as their deputies. By providing the second largest troop or aircraft contingents, the UK has secured these deputy billets beneath US officers. UK one star officers have worked closely with their US counterparts in such positions as the Combined Air Operation Centre (CAOC) at al-Udeid or the US Fifth Fleet base at Bahrain. Fighting alongside each other represents the hardest test for the two countries' armed forces. Although in ground operations the US and the UK have been assigned separate zones of responsibility, their ground forces inevitably come into contact with one another and have to coordinate their actions. In the case of air and naval forces, their conflict zones have overlapped and it has been important to establish clear lines of demarcation to prevent fratricide and military accidents.

Narratives

Narratives have long been recognized as important in politics and institutions are seen to influence actors through constructing and perpetuating them. March and Olsen (2009: 5) argue that it is necessary to find, 'structures of meaning that explain and justify behaviour—roles, identities and belongings, common purposes, and causal and normative beliefs'. Narratives provide an explanation for a course of action and its relative priority. They are often articulated through stories and are aggregated over time: they come to represent the 'symbolic architecture of institutions', to use the words of Lowndes and Roberts (2013: 63; Feldman et al, 2004).

Narratives and discourses embody values and ideas: they can empower certain types of behaviour whilst constraining others (Lowndes and Roberts, 2013: 63; Miskimmom et al, 2013). By explaining why things are done in a particular way, they legitimize and justify practices, while rendering others illegitimate. Sociological institutionalism contends that actors follow a 'logic of appropriateness' that results from them perceiving what is in their interests as well as internalizing the values of the institution (March and Olsen, 2009: 2).

The choice of narrative grows from the strategic culture of the state concerned. When the UK works with the US, it has sought to develop a narrative about the motivations behind the relationship and its sources of legitimacy. When collaboration with the US was initiated in World War II, the UK regarded itself as a global power and expected to remain so in the post-war period. It set about reasserting its empire and fulfilling its obligations as one of the five permanent members of the United Nations Security Council. Although this mindset was eroded by the experience of relative decline during the Cold War, the UK still regarded itself as the natural partner of the US. In the words of Gamble (2003: 87), Anglo-America became an 'imagined community' of action.

Critics meanwhile have contended that the narrative has been distorted and manipulated in order to construct a myth of Anglo-American amity (Baylis, 1998: 118). According to this perspective, the wartime cooperation between the US and the UK was romanticized so as to hide the decline of the UK's power. The UK attempted to harness US power for its own ends. Danchev (1996: 738) argued that it was a reflection of an 'Evangelistic' group of commentators who tried to divert attention from the absence of UK–US common interests in the post-war years. According to this view, the UK has engaged in a deliberate process of manipulation to convince the US that their two countries share interests in common. Danchev (1996: 743) listed one of the qualities of the 'special relationship' as 'mythicality', the capacity to generate a myth in order to justify a relationship. An analysis of US–UK relations needs to be alive to this possibility and cast a sceptical eye over UK government statements. Marsh (2019: 317) agrees that there is a 'mythologised relationship between Britain and America, which is designed to conjure the impression of unique, intimate relations between equals'.

Set against this is the observation that the US military remains a difficult actor to hoodwink. The US armed forces have a reputation for hard-headedness and pragmatism (Interview with former Commander of British Land Forces, 2015). If the UK military was intent upon convincing its American counterpart of a pattern of cooperation that was hollow, it is difficult to see how such a pretence could be made credible and durable. It is likely that a sceptical US military establishment would have rejected any attempt to be deceived in this way.

Whether myth or not, perpetuating a narrative has evidently been made easier by the shared language, culture, values, and norms within the UK–US relationship (Renwick, 2016: 41). A sense of shared identity and history has made it possible to construct a narrative that is both powerful and coherent. This has led to criticism from some allies of the US and UK who have regarded it as exclusionary: France, for example, has decried the 'Anglo-Saxon' identity. The narrative has been communicated through symbols and rituals, as well as by conventional forms of dialogue (Schmidt, 2008; 2010). Schmidt (2008) pushes the point further by arguing that the narrative helps to shape the institution: by developing a narrative of a uniquely close and cooperative relationship, the UK has helped to realize its ambition.

This shared identity, language, and value system has created bonds of friendship between the militaries of both countries. It has helped to smooth over inequalities and promote a sense of 'specialness' (Hendershot, 2013: 53). The ability to draw upon shared historical and cultural reference points has deepened the sense of common purpose. The Anglo-American relationship has stimulated professional contacts between officers at various military levels that have been sustained over time, in some cases throughout whole careers. Comradeship can act as a crucible in which deep personal bonds can been forged. Such networks serve as 'important lubricants of the defence relationship' (Marsh, 2013: 179), making it possible to overcome frictions that might otherwise undermine the capacity to work together. For example, Sir Mark Stanhope served on a US Virginia class submarine as a Royal Navy exchange officer but progressed in his career to become First Sea Lord (Interview with former First Sea Lord, 2014). Norman Schwarzkopf, the US Commander of Coalition Forces in the First Gulf War described his British subordinate, General Peter de la Billière as a 'good friend' and one whose advice he sought, 'on even the most sensitive military issues' (Schwarzkopf, 1992: 478). It was de la Billière who convinced the US commander to deploy British Special Forces in hunting for Scud missiles that were being used against Israel (Interview with British Army Lieutenant General, 2012). General Wesley Clark, NATO's Supreme

Allied Commander, described his Deputy, Jeremy MacKenzie as 'a close colleague and friend . . . (we) were both armour officers, we socialized and played sports together' (Clark, 2001: 115). This has been a dimension of the 'sentimental relationship' that is rarely discussed. The personal friendships between officers and officials from both countries have facilitated smooth interchange between the two countries in times of both peace and conflict (Interview with former Commander of British Land Forces, 2015).

Last but not least, both countries send their military personnel to attend courses at the other's military establishments. This occurs at initial officer training for the various strands of the British and American armed services and also at senior levels. In this way officers on both sides have the opportunity to learn about the thinking of their counterparts. The UK sends officers to the US War Colleges and academies. In return, the US places some of its military representatives in the Defence Academy at Shrivenham and the Higher Command and Staff Course in London.

Conclusion

Institutionalization has helped to create a web of day-to-day contacts that provide the life blood of the Anglo-American military relationship. It has built habits of cooperation that have ensured that the two sides see the world through similar lenses and prioritize the same threats. Through working with the US on security issues, military relationships have become interwoven and resulted in well-practiced patterns of cooperation. This has contributed to path dependency and has acted as a restraint on alternative courses of action.

Through institutionalizing patterns of cooperation, a reflex towards acting together has been embedded. This helps to account for the longevity of Anglo-American military relations. It also helps to explain how it has proven to be capable of adapting in the face of new security challenges.

3
A History of Anglo-American Military Relations 1945–1989

Introduction

Whilst the focus of this book is the post-Cold War period, it is nevertheless important to appreciate that Anglo-American defence cooperation did not start in 1989. It can be traced back to World War II and the onset of the Cold War. This chapter seeks to provide the historical context in which key themes that resonate in the post-Cold War era will be explored. In doing so, this chapter provides more of an overview of the strategic contours of the US–UK relationship during the Cold War, rather than detailed aspects of the cooperation between their armed services.

The chapter begins by assessing how the British envisaged the defence of Europe in the aftermath of World War II and the central role that nuclear weapons were expected to play, in concert with the US. These military plans drew the British armed forces into a tight embrace with the American military and sparked a sustained debate about the relative importance of conventional forces versus nuclear weapons. Although the British military would have welcomed an interdependent relationship with their superpower ally, US hostility to the British Empire meant that it remained necessary to preserve independent capabilities. As British power diminished, the US become more sympathetic to their concerns and was desirous of preserving a British presence around the world, as well as within Europe.

Roles

Of the types of conflict that the British armed services were preparing for, during the Cold War, high intensity conflict conducted on a global scale was accorded overwhelming priority. It amounted to war against the Soviet Union and its allies and, whilst the least likely, it threatened the very existence of the West. The main theatre in which it would occur would have been Europe but the severity of the conflict meant that there would be implications for non-NATO regions as well. It was envisaged that NATO conventional forces could only hold an attack for a limited period of time, and that escalation to the use of tactical, theatre, and finally strategic nuclear weapons would take place. As soon as a national nuclear capability was achieved, the UK saw her own nuclear forces as a 'lever' upon the

The Anglo-American Military Relationship. Wyn Rees, Oxford University Press. © Wyn Rees (2024).
DOI: 10.1093/oso/9780198884620.003.0003

US in matters where the very survival of the country might be at stake (TNA FO 371-ZP5/02/G, 1955).

The UK military was supportive of a nuclear-focused defence strategy to offset the conventional force preponderance of the Warsaw Pact. Early US Cold War strategy was orientated around the concept of 'Massive Retaliation', namely that aggression would be met by massive nuclear destruction of Soviet population and industrial centres (Croft, 2001: 73). As early as the Global Strategy Paper of 1952, it was acknowledged by the British Chiefs of Staff that nuclear weapons were essential for the defence of the West (Baylis and Macmillan, 1993). This strategy was subsequently endorsed in the 1957 Defence Review by Duncan Sandys based on both a strategic and an economic rationale (TNA, DEFE 5/80, COS, 1957).

There were important policy debates within NATO, and parts of the UK and the US militaries took contrasting positions on some issues. One debate was over the role assigned to conventional forces during high intensity warfare. A widely held view was that conventional forces were required only to hold Soviet aggression until the nuclear bombardment could be brought to bear. The contrasting view was that a war against the Soviet Union could be protracted in nature with an initial nuclear phase followed by a period of indeterminate duration in which there would be conventional operations. Supreme Allied Commander Europe, General Alfred Gruenther, and subsequently General Lauris Norstad, believed that NATO might force a 'pause' upon the Warsaw Pact before or after the release of nuclear weapons (Wampler, 1990: 34). In light of this, the US wanted NATO to stockpile equipment and ammunition for a sustained period of fighting. The official British position was that a conventional phase of operations was unlikely and should not be part of planning. Whereas Norstad called for 30 divisions and 90 days of stocks, the British were only willing to prepare for 30 days (TNA, DEFE 5/84 COS, 1958). The 'Minimum Essential NATO Force Requirements' that were enshrined in Military Command 70 (MC70) in 1958 reflected US views of the need for large conventional capabilities and defied British pressure for total reliance upon nuclear weapons.

The British Chiefs of Staff resisted the idea that a limited war, short of the use of nuclear weapons, could be fought in Europe. They pointed to formal NATO planning documents: 'The NATO Strategic Concept does not envisage a limited war with Russia. The United Kingdom Chiefs of Staff accept this view and believe most firmly that NATO could only hope to defeat Russia by using nuclear weapons from the outset of a war' (TNA, DEFE 4/96 Annex to JP, 1957). It was from within the RAF that the most vociferous voices for the dominance of the nuclear offensive could be heard. The RAF was the service responsible for the deterrent and was most focused on its role in high intensity warfare. By contrast, the British Army and Royal Navy were more preoccupied with conflicts outside Europe.

The British military was vulnerable to the criticism that their strategic stance was inflexible and risked a probing military action by the Soviets that would result in a massive nuclear response. There were views within the British armed forces that the balance between East and West was in the process of changing. As Soviet nuclear stockpiles reached parity with the West, it was credible that the Kremlin would become less risk averse and more willing to test allied resolve. At the same time, the readiness of the US to respond with nuclear weapons to anything less than all-out aggression by the Soviets was diminishing. America was contending that its allies required sufficient conventional capabilities to deal with low-level aggression by the Warsaw Pact without recourse to strategic nuclear war.

The Royal Navy, under Lord Louis Mountbatten, and the British Army, under Sir Gerald Templer, expressed their opposition to the views of the Chief of the Air Staff, Dermot Boyle, and argued that the UK had to be ready to fight with conventional forces in the absence of a release of American nuclear weapons (Jones, 2019, 1: 105). Mountbatten and Templer were sympathetic to their US military counterparts who envisaged either a long war or a limited conflict in which nuclear weapons were not used (TNA, DEFE 4/129, COS, 1960). The Royal Navy, in particular, envisaged a 'broken-backed' conflict in which there could be nuclear exchanges between the Soviet Union and the West that were interspersed with conventional military operations (TNA, DEFE 4/129, COS, 1960). They put forward the view that there was also an important role for naval forces in wars that were limited, either in their geographical coverage or the weapons employed. Such 'limited wars' might necessitate controlling the seas, conducting strikes against land targets, and keeping maritime communications open (TNA, DEFE 4/95 COS, 1957; Kennedy, 2012: 69). There was also widespread support amongst the Army and Navy for deployments in the Middle East and Asia. Secretary of Defence Denis Healey noted the preference of the armed forces to fight in the 'glamorous Orient' rather than 'patrolling the North German plain' against a Warsaw Pact enemy that never materialized (1989: 293).

The US Navy, the US Army, and the Supreme Allied Commander Atlantic (SACLANT) were all of the view that conventional forces needed to be maintained at much higher levels to deal with low level conflict and to be able to contribute to conventional operations within a nuclear conflagration (TNA DEFE 4/101 JP, 1957). The US Army wanted to focus on large-scale conflict yet was having to engage in limited conflicts around the world that detracted from its perceived core mission (Kretchik, 2011). They were mindful lest a solely nuclear-focused strategy weaken the rationale for maintaining high force levels. They also appreciated that wars could occur outside Europe where the crossing of the nuclear threshold was unlikely (TNA DEFE 4/103 COS, 1958).

The British military was under pressure from political masters that were concerned about the weight of defence spending on the civilian economy as well as the need to retain forces for operations outside Europe. Conventional forces were seen as exerting the greatest strain because of their costs and the manpower that they consumed. In 1952 extending the length of National Service increased the armed forces to 872,000. But the 1957 Defence Review changed this direction of travel and reduced overall numbers to 375,000. The British Chiefs of Staff stuck to the official position that the nuclear phase of a war with the Soviet Union would likely be decisive, even if periods of conventional conflict were not ruled out. The UK had anticipated American dissatisfaction with the tenor of the 1957 Defence Review and the Minister went to the US to explain his strategy (TNA, FCO 371, 1957).

The Kennedy administration was the first to seek options, other than automatic recourse to the use of nuclear weapons, in the event of a conflict in Europe (TNA DEFE 6/32 JP, 1955). The strategy of 'Flexible Response' was hammered out in the 1960s and placed a premium upon robust conventional forces defending the inner German border. A possible ladder of escalation was envisaged from conventional to tactical nuclear and then theatre nuclear systems, each level seeking to force a cessation in hostilities and restore deterrence. This strategy had arisen in response to the fundamental dilemma whether a US president would be willing to sacrifice cities such as New York and Chicago in defence of allied cities, such as Berlin, Paris, or London. The introduction of the strategy of Flexible Response in 1967 (Strom-seth, 1988) seemed to confirm America's reluctance to fulfil its extended nuclear guarantee to NATO. From the late 1960s NATO practised large-scale Return of Forces to Germany (Reforger) exercises annually to test the ability of the US to reinforce Europe with land and air forces.

Although British defence planning was dominated by considerations of high intensity war, the likelihood of it breaking out was thought to be low. Instead, the UK government saw the threat from Soviet inspired subversion and its sponsor-ship of national liberation movements as the foremost challenge. A British Chiefs of Staff paper from 1956 noted that 'subversion or covert aggression . . . are now recognised as the main danger' (TNA, DEFE 5/72, 1956). UK armed forces were deployed throughout the Empire in bases that were designed to support each other in the event of conflict. Although the political authorities cut the size of the mili-tary, they were reluctant to reduce colonial possessions commensurately: all were considered to be vital interests (Healey, 1989: 299). Even the granting of indepen-dence to overseas territories did not always result in the termination of defence guarantees. The result was that the armed forces found themselves fighting in numerous wars across the world that were limited in terms of their geography, their opponents, and the means that were employed. The British government's view was that the military were not only protecting imperial interests but also resisting the encroachment of Moscow's influence around the world. In the words of a Joint Planning Staff document, 'The United Kingdom . . . has special responsi-bilities in regard to the need to counter Communism on a world-wide basis' (TNA, DEFE 4/96, 1957).

Many of the wars in which the British military was engaged, such as in Malaya, Kenya, and Borneo, were classified as counter-insurgency campaigns.

This involved fighting against a part of the population that was resisting British control. Such wars were complex and required the careful balancing of military means and political strategy. They were also frequently protracted: the conflict in Malaya, for example, went on for 12 years between 1948 and 1960. The UK armed forces earned a reputation for navigating these conflicts successfully, although it took time to develop a strategy appropriate to each situation. British Army officers, such as Gerald Templer, Robert Thompson, and Frank Kitson, became synonymous with developing effective counter-insurgency campaigns. These tended to involve separating the insurgents from the civilian population, frequently by re-settling villagers to dedicated compounds.

Inter-service relationships

Within this Cold War framework of high intensity war, limited war, and counter-insurgency, links developed between British and US armed forces. This grew out of relationships that had been established during World War II and were perpetuated in the post-war period. It was made more complicated by the fact that the UK and the US had different political relationships with countries around the world.

The Royal Navy enjoyed the closest and most consistent cooperation with the US Navy during the Cold War (Wells, 2017: 17). Although imperial duties led to minimum overlap between the navies, the task of anti-submarine warfare (ASW) in the Atlantic, under the auspices of NATO, kept surface and sub-surface forces working closely together. ASW involved a complex tapestry of effort between frigates equipped with towed array sonars, maritime patrol aircraft, and hunter-killer submarines. The Royal Navy was highly proficient at ASW and this resulted in the UK and the US dominating the eastern Atlantic (Interview with former First Sea Lord, 2012; Interview with former Royal Navy Vice Admiral, 2012). The Navy helped to protect US lines of communication to Europe (McGwire, Booth, and Connell, 1975) through their role in policing the Greenland–Iceland–UK (GIUK) gap (Wells, 2017: Chapter 4). There were also around 45 high quality British naval analysts based at Norfolk, Virginia, who participated in the Sound Surveillance System (SOSUS) underwater listening capability that detected submarine signatures in the GIUK gap (Interview at Naval Ocean Processing Facility, 2014).

In the ASW role, the UK was content to play a subordinate part in US naval operations against a shared adversary. In the latter stages of the Cold War, the Royal Navy's status in US naval thinking was enhanced. John Lehman, President Reagan's Secretary of the Navy, presided over a more aggressive naval doctrine known as the Concept of Maritime Operations Strategy (CONMAROPS) of 1981 (Grove, 1991: 18). As part of an expansion to a 600-ship navy, it was envisaged that the US Navy would assume offensive aircraft carrier operations against the Soviet

Northern Fleet in the Norwegian Sea. Rather than trying to stop the adversary from breaking into the North Atlantic, it was envisaged that offensive operations would be conducted against the Northern Fleet with the aim of bottling them up (Interview with Royal Navy Rear Admiral, 2012). The Royal Navy would provide ASW to four US carrier battle groups that would be the core of offensive operations (Grove, 1991: 15). The US Defense Secretary Caspar Weinberger pressed for and was successful in establishing a US–UK Defence Cooperation Working Group to inject American views into UK thinking (Doyle, 2017: 873). A particular American ambition was to preserve the British naval presence in the north Atlantic, but that was subsequently reduced in the 1981 Nott defence review.

The extent of the cooperation between the RAF and the US Air Force (USAF) varied during the Cold War. In 1946, US General Carl Spaatz and Air Chief Marshal Arthur Tedder agreed that US aircraft could conduct deployments to UK bases (Duke, 1987: 17). Along with the Berlin Airlift, this helped to renew the bonds between the two air forces. The nuclear deterrent became the backbone for much of the early cooperation between the two air forces: as the V-bombers came on stream from the middle 1950s it led to coordination with the nuclear offensive of the US Strategic Air Command. The growing role of the US Navy in submarine ballistic missile technology resulted in common cause between Strategic Air Command and RAF Bomber Command in the provision of airborne nuclear forces. When Royal Navy Polaris submarines took over responsibility for the strategic nuclear deterrent in 1968, Bomber Command reverted to the tactical nuclear role and its relationship with its US counterpart diminished.

The British Army had the least intimate Cold War relationship with its American counterpart. In NATO, there was relatively limited overlap between US and British forces on the continent: they occupied different stretches of the front line. In northern Germany, 1 British Corps was accompanied by the Dutch, Belgian, and German Corps, whilst US and German forces occupied the Central Army Group region. The British adopted a mobile linear defence posture. They were deployed up to the frontline in peacetime but in the event of war envisaged falling back and conducting their main defence from prepared positions (McInnes, 1996). This was consistent with the strategy of 'Forward Defence' in which the allies were committed to defending as much of the Federal Republic of Germany's soil as possible. It was thought unlikely that allied forces could hold a concerted attack by the Warsaw Pact for more than a few days and that they would have to seek recourse to battlefield nuclear weapons.

The British Army and the US Army were brought closer together in the 1980s by a change in US strategy that was facilitated by technology. Rather than adhere to a defensive approach, US Army thinking began to explore a more agile ground force strategy that involved taking the offensive to the enemy. This would be achieved by attacks upon rear echelons of Soviet tank and infantry formations (Lewis, 2018: 308). This concept was informed by the experience of Arab–Israeli conflicts and became known as 'AirLand' battle (US Army Field Manual 100-5, 1982 and 1986). Deep strike technologies underpinned this approach, such as radars that could track advancing formations, long-range artillery, battlefield missiles, and fighter bombers and attack helicopters (Kretchik, 2011: 204). Under SACEUR General Bernard Rogers the idea of 'Follow-on-Forces Attack' (FOFA) envisaged degrading and disrupting waves of Warsaw Pact forces in order to limit the damage that could be inflicted on NATO front lines, blunt the numerical superiority of the adversary, and raise the nuclear threshold. This strategy required better intelligence, target acquisition, rapid movement, precision strike, and sophisticated management of the battlefield.

This evolution in US Army thinking complemented a change in thinking that was taking place in the British Army of the Rhine (BAOR). In 1981 Lieutenant General Sir Nigel Bagnall became the Commander of 1 British Corps and sought to move Army thinking from a succession of fighting retreats, to a strategy that envisaged a defensive phase followed by a counter-attack (British Army, 1989). According to this approach, forward-deployed forces would absorb the first wave of a Warsaw Pact attack, buy time, and enable the main axes of the enemy's aggression to be identified (McInnes, 1996). Then large reserve forces would seek to regain the initiative and start conducting offensive operations. The attraction of the strategy was that it was less reactive and made it possible to consider manoeuvre and defence in depth. Like the Americans, the British were equipping their forces with a new generation of weapons systems: Challenger tanks, Warrior infantry fighting vehicles, Apache attack helicopters, and multi-launch rocket systems. British and American thinking dovetailed and, in so doing, brought the two armies closer together.

Practices

The objective of UK forces was to tie the US into the defence of Western Europe because it believed only American involvement was sufficient to deter Warsaw Pact aggression. In British eyes, the US alone possessed the strength to counterbalance the Soviet Union (TNA, DEFE 6/60, 1959). America served two other vital functions: it contained the risk of a resurgent Germany and it provided the cohesion that could overcome rivalries amongst European states.

America was perceived as a benign hegemon whose power did not threaten the security of its European allies (Ikenberry, 2001). Whilst the UK regarded the American commitment to Europe as vital, it did not assume it was inevitable. The abrupt termination of 'Lend-Lease' after the end of the war highlighted the risk that US calculations could change and its focus of attention shift away from Europe. Thus it was necessary for the UK to share the burdens of security alongside the US. This was the case both in Europe and in conflicts elsewhere in the world such as Korea. The British military sought to convince Washington that Europe was worth defending and that a meaningful contribution was being made by allies.

In turn, the US encouraged the UK to lead in Western Europe. It was the reluctance of the UK to commit to the European Defence Community, proposed by France in the early 1950s, that led to its collapse (Fursdon, 1980; Eden, 1960: 36). The US Secretary of State, John Foster Dulles, expressed his disappointment at British policy and threatened an 'agonizing reappraisal' of the US commitment to Europe. The failure of the European Defence Community and the implicit threat of US withdrawal led the UK to pledge to maintain forces on the continent of four divisions plus the 2nd Tactical Air Force for the next 50 years. In response the US undertook to station a large military presence in Europe. From this point onwards, a transatlantic defence framework, NATO, rather than a defensive community composed of European states, became the mechanism for guaranteeing continental defence.

The UK positioned itself as the special ally of America by becoming 'primus inter pares' amongst NATO states (McKercher, 2017: 76). It held the second most powerful military position within the Alliance, guarding the north German plain and taking responsibility for the Channel and the eastern Atlantic. American tactical nuclear weapons were held by the British under dual-key control. As the consistent supporter of NATO's right of first refusal for interventions, the UK was able to block French attempts to challenge American leadership. The UK acted as a bulwark against greater European autonomy in defence.

Occupying the role of America's deputy within NATO made reductions in force levels difficult to justify. The 1957 Sandys Defence Review made swingeing cuts to the size of BAOR and the Second Tactical Air Force with the rationale that missiles, rather than conventional forces, were more appropriate contributions in the modern era. In the second half of the 1960s, further cuts of up to a one third in the size of BAOR were mooted (Dockrill, 2002: 124). The UK was wary of reducing the size of its forces in Germany for two reasons. First, it feared that cuts could have stimulated corresponding reductions in US forces, leading to wholesale disengagement. The US subsequently pressured its European allies by initiating troop reductions as part of the 'Mansfield Amendments'. Second, there was a risk that the returns for the US of treating the UK as special would not justify the costs and the US would downgrade its importance. The UK was perpetually seeking to convince the US of its worth as an ally.

UK military capabilities independent of the US?

The financial constraints on British military power were a constant theme in the post-war period. Suffering from relative decline, the UK was painfully aware that its position on the world stage owed much to how it was treated by the US. A

Cabinet paper noted that, 'We shall become increasingly dependent on their [the US] support and our status . . . will depend upon their readiness to treat us as their closest ally' (TNA, CAB 139/1929, 1960: 24). US cooperation and consultation would only be forthcoming if it could be convinced of the UK's value. In the Korean War, for example, the UK provided over 60,000 personnel and its Far Eastern Fleet, a contribution second only to the US. On the one hand, it was evident that America prized Britain's global perspective and its commitment to international organizations like the United Nations (UN) and NATO (Wallace and Philips, 2009). There was 'a congruence . . . of interests' between Washington and London on a host of international issues (Self, 2010: 104; Holmes, 2013: 106). On the other hand, maintaining Britain's military contribution was harder to achieve. Washington could see that British forces were stretched thinly around the world and that this factor was accelerating the decline of British power (Dumbrell, 2004: 438). Britain spent much of the post-war period trying to trim its defence spending to fit its reduced circumstances (Darby, 1973).

A potential solution for the UK was to align itself even more closely with the US. In 1956, for example, the Chancellor of the Exchequer questioned whether, 'we (should) not cease altogether to think in terms of local wars . . . (without) the United States?' (TNA, Air 8/2046, 1956). Operating in conjunction with the US military offered access to additional resources and reduced the capabilities that the UK would need to preserve independently.

Yet this seductive idea was not a realistic option for the British military. The US was deeply suspicious of post-war British attempts to revitalize their colonial interests in a manner inconsistent with the 1941 Atlantic Charter. (The Atlantic Charter was an attempt to lay out values that the two sides shared and could guide their relationship). During World War II, the US had suspected that Churchill's motives were driven more by the needs of empire than the defeat of the Axis powers. US Chief of Staff George Marshall commented of the British that, 'Their military objectives were conditioned upon political aspects of guaranteeing their post-war position' (quoted in Renwick, 2016: 58).

Washington was determined that American power should not be harnessed to the preservation of British colonies and its closed sphere of economic interest (Baylis, 1998). Three other factors weighed on American thinking. First, there was the potential for the US and UK to compete for influence and commercial advantage in various theatres. Second, supporting the UK could detract from America's other foreign relationships. As the self-declared champion of free peoples, the US was aware that its relationship with the UK was inconsistent with its ideals. Third, there was concern that British strategic thinking was being distracted from the primary focus on the Soviet threat.

The Middle East was a particular area of friction, as the US was reluctant to acknowledge UK experience in the region and appeared eager to compete for influence. American hostility towards Britain was evident in its refusal to join the Central Treaty Organization (CENTO) or 'Baghdad Pact'. This alliance had been instigated by the UK as a sort of NATO for the Middle East, but was seen in Washington as serving selfish UK interests (Devereux, 1990: 105). Despite encouragement from the UK to join, the US remained outside the organization, preferring to conduct bilateral relationships with key members, such as Iran, Iraq, and Pakistan. The British military pressed the Americans to agree that a conventional defence of the Middle East in a global war would be impossible and that a concept of defence had to be 'based on the effects of the strategic air offensive and nuclear attack' (TNA, DEFE 4/82, 1956; Louis, 1986: 277). The US championed an anti-colonial agenda (TNA, DEFE 6/61, 1960). The US did discreetly coordinate some of its activities with the UK: the two countries worked together in the overthrow of the Mossadegh regime in Tehran and laid plans to defend Iranian territory in 1955 (TNA, DEFE 4/82, 1956a). They also coordinated their respective interventions in Lebanon and Jordan in 1957 (McKercher, 2017: 67).

The 1956 Suez Crisis was illustrative of the damage that could be inflicted on the UK by a breakdown in relations with the US. The British were focused on the threat they perceived from Arab nationalism, whereas the US viewed the issue through the lens of growing Soviet influence. The Anglo-French military operation to seize the Suez Canal, following its nationalization by Egypt's President Nasser, had been agreed clandestinely with Israel (Watt, 1986: 71). President Eisenhower's administration was incensed at British duplicity in occupying the Canal on the pretext of keeping Israeli and Egyptian forces apart (Renwick, 2016: 203). Yet London had indicated on numerous occasions the likelihood of it resorting to force. They thought that they had signalled the seriousness of their intent to Washington and that the US would most likely stand passively on the side lines of the conflict. What was so hard for the UK was that America did not merely criticize 'Operation Musketeer' but actively sought to disrupt the amphibious landings. The US then threatened sanctions and blocked financial support from the International Monetary Fund, causing such pressure that the British government was forced to order a humiliating withdrawal. Suez extinguished any lingering doubts that Britain could act as an equal partner of the US and exposed the over-stretch of British deployments (Richardson, 1996).

Nevertheless, the damage to Anglo-American military cooperation appears to have been limited. Baylis (1984: xxi) notes that the pre-existing cooperation between the militaries of the two countries continued despite the political fall-out from the Suez campaign. Hendershot quotes President Eisenhower as describing the British as, 'still my right arm' (2013: 62) whilst Eberle observed that 'Harmony abounded—and at the military level was little affected by the events of Suez' (1986: 155).

A similar lack of Anglo-American military trust was evident in the Far East. The South East Asia Treaty Organization (SEATO) was signed in Manila in September 1954 between Australia, France, New Zealand, Pakistan, the Philippines, Thailand,

Britain, and the US. Yet Washington refused to bring London into their confidence regarding defence planning for the region. This was especially hard for the British to take as they had previously been excluded from the Australia, New Zealand, and US (ANZUS) pact of September 1951, despite expressing an interest in joining. The British Chiefs of Staff complained of US hostility towards UK interests in Asia and that the exchange of information was exclusively from the UK to the US (TNA, DEFE 5/60, 1955). The US military appeared to want to preserve the maximum latitude for action and refused to commit itself in advance (TNA, DEFE 4/101, COS, 1957). Even efforts to harmonize policy through the British Defence Coordination Committee in the Far East were unfulfilled (TNA, DEFE 6/49, 1958). It led the British Planning Staff to wonder whether the US had thought in depth about military action within the region and whether they actually had any plans to share (TNA, DEFE 6/33, 1955).

The lesson that the UK derived from America's reluctance to share its planning was that they needed to preserve the capacity to act alone. This meant that the British military had to retain their own balanced military capabilities (TNA, DEFE 4/101, 1957). In addition, the UK chose to maintain bilateral defence obligations with some countries after independence had been granted, in order to support newly formed governments. For example, post-independence guarantees were made to Malaya under the Australia, New Zealand, and Malaya (ANZAM) defence agreement, in the face of the threat posed by President Sukarno's Indonesia. The UK portrayed its bilateral defence contributions as part of its wider commitment to the SEATO area and the upholding of international order (TNA, DEFE 4/96, 1957).

Changing US attitudes towards the UK's global role

The gradual dissolution of the British Empire and the rise of the Commonwealth removed an important source of tension in Anglo-American policy and created a stronger sense of shared interests. Ironically it stimulated a contrary concern in the US: namely a fear that Britain's narrowing European focus would lead it to lose its globalist perspective. By the 1960s, US Secretary of Defense Robert McNamara was opining that Britain's defence contributions in Asia were of greater value than its role in Europe (TNA, CAB 148/30, 1967). Washington began to actively campaign to maintain a British contribution to the defence of Asia, where about a third of its armed forces were based. Prime Minister Harold Wilson reassured US Secretary of State Dean Rusk that, 'he would rather pull half our troops out of Germany, than move any from the Far East' (TNA, PREM 13/124, 1965; Dockrill, 2002: 168).

A major factor behind this change in American attitudes was its deteriorating position in Vietnam. At a time when Britain was drawing down its forces in

Asia, America was being sucked inexorably into a quagmire. As the Vietnam conflict dragged on, it became evident that US military doctrine was inappropriate for this form of unconventional warfare (Kretchik, 2011: 282). The situation was made worse by the unpopular nature of the war domestically and the perception that the US lacked the will, both militarily and politically, to prevail. There was a palpable desire by the US to obtain allied support (Gill, 2014: 134). President Johnson invited the Wilson government to make at least a symbolic contribution of British military forces, but this was refused (Hendershot, 2013: 67). The British were already fighting a jungle conflict in Borneo and resisted US attempts to lure it into Vietnam. President Johnson's response was that British force reductions were leaving the US to 'man the ramparts all alone' (quoted in Marsh, 2018: 282). The US understood that the vacuum left by the withdrawal of British power would not be replaced by another country.

Despite this change in American attitudes towards Britain's global role, overwhelming economic pressures forced London to reduce their defence obligations. Crises over the value of sterling led to the imposition of a defence budget ceiling of £2000 million and military commitments were determined within that overall envelope. The British military were clear that if the Far East Command at Singapore and the Middle East Command at Aden were ended, then the whole structure of a British presence beyond Europe would be fatally undermined (Dockrill, 1988: 89). In 1967, the withdrawal of over 50,000 British troops from East of the Suez Canal was announced, following the ending of the 'Confrontation' between Malaysia and Indonesia. Air transport capability was also cut back with the result that Britain would be unable to reinforce overseas territories at short notice. The emergence of states hostile to Britain flying reinforcements over their territory rendered it increasingly problematic to defend far-flung bases. British forces had been overstretched for too long. It was a critical juncture in policy as the military was signalling the end of its global presence and reducing its focus to Europe.

The next generation of large aircraft carriers was cancelled (Wells, 2017) despite an offer by the US to provide such vessels at reduced cost (Dockrill, 2002: 141). The Royal Navy was strongly opposed to the decision as they saw it as undermining their power projection and diminishing their status in the eyes of the US Navy. In place of the large aircraft carriers, in the early 1970s, the Royal Navy was authorized to order the Invincible class of smaller aircraft carriers. These vessels were dedicated to ASW duties in the Eastern Atlantic. In 1968, the decision was taken to accelerate the timetable for withdrawal from the Far East from the mid-1970s to 1971. US pain was compounded by the cancellation of the F-111 order of 50 long range strike aircraft.

The transition from Empire to Commonwealth and the withdrawal of British forces from the Far East effectively put an end to the extra-European dimension of the Anglo-American relationship. A former US Secretary of State Dean Acheson had accused the UK of losing an Empire but not yet finding a role and the withdrawal from East of Suez appeared to realign the UK's focus to Europe. Dickie (1994: 169) argues that the special relationship effectively ended at this time with the conclusion of Britain's global presence, while McKercher (2017: 87) describes it as entering a period of 'suspended animation'. This was illustrated at the time of the Yom Kippur War in October 1973 when the Heath government refused to allow the US to use British airbases to resupply Israel. Others contend that it was more of a cyclical trough in relations and that it was resuscitated in the 1980s. Nevertheless, 'functional connections' persisted even in the 1970s in the realms of military and intelligence matters (Watt, 1986: 4).

In 1982, the US chose to intervene in support of a British colonial operation in the Falkland Islands. This was an interesting case because British interests were heavily engaged whilst US interests were not. The initial response of the Reagan administration was to attempt to appear even handed in the crisis and to try to secure a diplomatic resolution. First Sea Lord Admiral Sir Henry Leach convinced Prime Minister Margaret Thatcher that it was possible to retake the islands by force following the Argentine invasion. Thatcher was incensed by the shuttle diplomacy of US Secretary of State Alexander Haig because she interpreted it as condoning aggression and failing to recognize the difference between an authoritarian and a democratic government.

Behind the scenes, US Defense Secretary Caspar Weinberger and Chairman of the Joint Chiefs of Staff, General David Jones, offered material support to the UK at an early stage. The personal linkages between Admiral Terence Lewin and General Jones illustrated the benefits of a relationship between the two militaries that had been cultivated for many years (Richardson, 1996: 165). The US provided over a hundred AIM-9L Sidewinder missiles for British Sea Harrier aircraft, Stinger hand-held missiles were sent for ground forces, Shrike anti-radar missiles for aircraft, and huge stocks of fuel were made available from emergency stores (Dickie, 1994: 4). US satellite information and signals intelligence was substantial and gave the UK an edge over their adversary (Williams, 2016: 111; Wallace and Phillips, 2009: 273). There was even consideration that the USS Guam, a ship capable of carrying aircraft, could be offered to the UK in the event that a Royal Navy aircraft carrier was damaged (Dickie, 1994, 8). Admiral Sir Henry Leach, later commented that, 'Support from the United States was wholehearted' (Badsey et al, 2005: 74). The US had decided that a British military operation such as this could not be allowed to fail (Freedman, 2005).

The Falklands conflict restored some of the pride and self-confidence within the British military that had been draining away in past decades of steady withdrawal from overseas territories. It made the US military look at the British in a new light, impressed by the determination that had been demonstrated in the South Atlantic. Nevertheless, the fragility of power lay just beneath the surface. The 1981 Nott Defence Review had preceded the Falklands and had targeted the Royal Navy for substantial reductions. Two of the aircraft carriers and the amphibious assault ships that had proved vital to the expedition had been destined either to be sold or scrapped as part of the Review. Britain sought to be America's closest partner but there was no hiding the huge disparity in capabilities between the two countries.

The nuclear dimension

The history of the Anglo-American nuclear relationship is an unusual one: whereas the post-Cold War era has witnessed stable cooperation (see Chapter 7), the early period was characterized by turbulence and uncertainty. The US closed the door on a wartime collaboration that had seen Britain share its nuclear secrets with America and involved British scientists working on the 'Manhattan Project' in the New Mexico desert. This collaboration on nuclear fission had emerged from the Quebec Agreement of 1943 (Baylis and Stoddart, 2012: 333). However, the nature of the Quebec Agreement had been kept secret and as a result, in August 1946, the US Congress's Joint Committee on Atomic Energy (JCAE) proposed the McMahon Act which effectively obliterated cooperation on nuclear research between the two countries. The Congress was largely oblivious to the secret Anglo-American effort during the war. In the post-war world, 'the US pressured even its closest allies to eschew independent nuclear forces' (Gavin, 2015: 15) as it feared the loss of its monopoly and the diffusion of this dangerous knowledge.

A small inner circle of the British Cabinet, with the support of the Chiefs of Staff, took the decision to proceed with the development of a British atomic weapon in 1947. They saw it as essential to the UK's status in the world and a mark of a leading technological power (Gowing, 1974: 21). The British military were wary of relying on the US: they foresaw potential circumstances in which UK interests could diverge. If future Soviet nuclear strength overtook that of the US then it might cause a president to hesitate about responding to an attack on Europe. Simpson (1983: 220) argues that this period was characterized by British determination aimed 'at demonstrating an ability to make nuclear weapons ... in order that they would have a say in superpower councils where the fate of the world could be at stake'. In 1956, Ronald Ivelaw-Chapman, the Vice Chief of the Air Staff, declared that a nuclear capability 'was the measure of military power in the modern world' and vital if Britain was to avoid a foreign policy that 'slavishly follow[ed] American ideas' (TNA, Air 8/2046, 1956a). The UK felt that it was vital to have a say in American policy (Kandiah and Staerck, 2005).

From July 1948, 60 US B-29 nuclear-capable bombers were permanently based at ten British airfields including Mildenhall, Upper Heyford, Alconbury, Fairford, and Greenham Common (Murray, 1995: 16; see also Baylis, 1995). Not only did this footprint in the UK bring the Soviet homeland into range but it also gave the US a staging base for potential global operations. It made the UK a target for

Soviet attack despite the fact that the UK had no say over the use of the aircraft. Two agreements subsequently solidified the basing rights: the Johnson–Chilver Arrangement of January 1949 and the Ambassadors Agreement of April 1950 (Miller, 1995: 19).

Once the V-force was operational this created a linkage between RAF Bomber Command and US Strategic Air Command (SAC). Some of SAC's weapons were made available to the RAF, under 'Project E', because the UK's limited bomb production capabilities meant that there were more aircraft than bombs available to be delivered to targets (Mackby and Cornish, 2008: 9). The two air forces shared their strike plans and UK personnel were seconded to the US for consultation over targeting (Wynn, 1994: 254–255). Preventing duplication of effort was at the heart of their efforts (Menaul, 1980: 91). The long-term interests of the two armed services became entwined as the debate about the future of manned aircraft versus missiles impacted upon them both. Neither side wanted to lose responsibility for the deterrent and neither wanted the future of their service to lie in the manning of underground missile silos.

Two developments served to draw the RAF and the US Air Force closer together. The first was the US desire to base Thor Intermediate Range Ballistic Missiles (IRBMs) in the UK. The Soviet launch of its Sputnik satellite in October 1957 had caused near panic in the US as they interpreted this as evidence that their enemy was more advanced in ballistic missile technology (TNA, DEFE 4/100 Annex to COS, 1957). The 1500-mile range of the Thor missiles necessitated their placing on British soil and the USAF requested that 60 be installed at 20 RAF bases in the UK. The RAF was pulled into a tight embrace with its US counterpart because they were deployed under a dual-key arrangement (Clark, 1994: 422) in which Britain was accorded a status unlike any other of America's allies (TNA, DEFE 4/101 COS, 1957; see also Dickie, 1994: 101). The US even discussed transferring the ownership of the Thor missiles to the UK, minus their warheads (Boyes, 2019: 106). The siting of Thor in the UK helped to heal some of the political tensions in Anglo-American relations following the Suez imbroglio. Not for the first time the military-to-military relationship proved to be a source of reconciliation between the two countries.

The other development between the air forces of the two countries arose when the US offered 100 WS-318A Skybolt air launched missiles to the British. The cancelling of the land-based British Blue Streak missile in April 1960 and the decision to purchase Skybolt was a major watershed for the UK as it signalled the end of a nationally produced strategic nuclear weapons system (Jones, 2019, 1: 209). The RAF lobbied strenuously for the project (Clark, 1994: 283) as both they and SAC regarded the 1000-mile range missile as a means to prevent the obsolescence of manned bombers. It was also only an interim solution as Soviet air defences would eventually put the bombers at risk of interception. An RAF–USAF working party was created to determine the specifications for the missile and the British participated in the choice of the Douglas company to develop Skybolt (Clark, 1994, 251). According to Eberle, 'the RAF made certain that they were in the closest cahoots with the US Air Force' (1986: 156). In the event, technical difficulties resulted in the cancellation of Skybolt. The US did offer to continue the development programme if the UK chose to take over its funding or provide the Hound Dog missile as an alternative.

Yet even as the US was cooperating closely with the British over nuclear weapons, there was a spectrum of opinion within the American politico-military establishment over whether the UK should remain a nuclear power. Dean Acheson, US Secretary of State, told the National Security Council in April 1961 that, 'Over the long run, it would be desirable if the British decided to phase out of the nuclear deterrent business' (Jones, 2019, II: 247). Defense Secretary Robert McNamara's notorious speech at Ann Arbor described independent deterrents, such as the UK's, as 'dangerous, expensive (and) prone to obsolescence' (quoted in Boyes, 2019: 167). There were others, such as George Ball and Walt Rostow, who were known to be hostile to the UK's independent nuclear capability. The decision to cancel Skybolt, based on US strategic calculations, offered an opportunity to squeeze the UK out as a nuclear actor.

It took the intervention of Prime Minister Harold Macmillan to secure a replacement for Skybolt in the form of Polaris, the submarine-launched ballistic missile system. By exploiting emotional arguments and manipulating US fears that the UK would have to reduce conventional defence spending to fund independent nuclear capabilities, Macmillan was able to secure a front-line American nuclear system (Stoddart and Baylis, 2014: 75). It marked the demise of the RAF responsibility for the deterrent and the switch to the Royal Navy.

In the 1960s, the US was looking for ways to assuage German and French demands for a greater voice in decisions over nuclear strategy as well as to increase Europe's sense of responsibility for its own security. The US proposed a Multilateral Force (MLF) of 25 mix-manned NATO ships each armed with eight Polaris ballistic missiles that would be under SACEUR's command. This was strenuously pressed on the UK by the Johnson administration (Baylis, 1984: 145; Clark, 1994: 265). The UK was openly sceptical of the MLF concept. It did not think that the concept was viable and it opposed the idea of having to contribute financially to such a scheme. The MLF concept exposed the long standing tension in UK–US nuclear relations between a superpower that wanted the nuclear deterrent to be a source of solidarity amongst its NATO allies and a government in London that sought a unique bilateral relationship. The UK feared that its own deterrent would be merged into the MLF and wanted to preserve its special nuclear status in NATO (TNA, DEFE 4/103, COS, 1958a). However, it did not wish to be seen to be opposing an American initiative. The UK proposal for an Atlantic Nuclear Force, to which the UK would contribute its V-bombers and Polaris submarines, was designed as an alternative to the MLF. Procrastination over MLF and the development of the Atlantic Nuclear Force concept were two strategies the UK pursued in derailing US nuclear policies within NATO.

Narrative

The risk of conflict with a mutual adversary provided the soil in which the Anglo-American security relationship was able to grow. It is therefore unsurprising that the UK has developed the narrative of the 'special relationship' within the crucible of the largest and most successful conflict fought by the two countries. World War II provided a backcloth against which the relationship has been extolled and justified. It was part of the great struggle against fascism, a war that had stretched the capabilities of both countries and involved huge sacrifices. Out of that searing experience, the two countries established a foundation for their collaboration that was to prove extremely durable. It was to be a form of mythology to which the British would return constantly during the Cold War and afterwards.

The wartime experience was an important part of the narrative of US–UK cooperation. There was a sense of solidarity between the two militaries that had fought and shed blood together. In the early years of World War II, the two powers had made a broadly equitable contribution and this had lauded the role of the UK as a partner of the US. Only later in the war did America's larger population and mobilization of its latent industrial potential result in it becoming the dominant partner. In a visit by the British Prime Minister in 2012, the White House said it would be 'an opportunity to recall the valour and sacrifice of the US and British armed forces and their long tradition of standing shoulder to shoulder' (quoted in Marsh, 2019: 317).

The narrative of fighting together was important for each of the UK armed services. Each branch of the services developed a relationship with its US counterpart and led to respect for the others' professionalism (Eberle, 1986: 158). In the case of the British Army, it was the fighting in North Africa, Italy, the Normandy landings, and the experiences of pushing the Wehrmacht back across Europe. For the Royal Navy, it was the cooperation with the US Navy in the Battle of the Atlantic against the U-boat menace and in conducting major amphibious operations. For the RAF, it was the cooperation with the US Eighth Air Force based in the UK: the US conducted daylight raids whereas the RAF operated night-time attacks. Each military service was able to look back to a golden age in which a strong bond was created with its US equivalent.

This narrative of brotherhood tended to gloss over wartime tensions between the two sides. The UK lobbied for, and eventually won, the strategic argument that defeating the European Axis powers should be the primary objective of Anglo-American policy. The result was that the allies struck first in North Africa (Operation Torch) and then Sicily and Italy before undertaking the grand amphibious invasion of Northern France (Operation Overlord) in June 1944. It was testament to the strength of their relationship that this was agreed; after all, the US had been attacked in the Pacific theatre and it fought a largely separate campaign against Japan until victory in August 1945. Tensions persisted throughout the war. Churchill pushed for an indirect approach that sought to restore Britain's pre-war status as well as limit the gains that the Soviet Union could make in the eastern half of the continent. The US argued for a decisive attack upon northern Europe, with the encouragement of Stalin. The US was fearful that alienating the Soviet Union could sow the seed of post-war mistrust and confrontation. Even while the two allies fought side-by-side in many theatres, there was 'co-ordination' between them rather than 'combined' operations (Eberle, 1986: 152).

Nevertheless, Haglund (2013) has noted that the two powers emerged after the war without the rivalry and antagonism that is usually associated with a power transition between countries. Britain was exhausted and its foreign exchange reserves depleted. The abrupt termination of US Lend-Lease, the lending of military equipment to Britain, and the McMahon Act boded ill for the future of the relationship. It was to be the common cause against the Soviet Union that gave the Anglo-American relationship a new cause around which to coalesce. The 1949 US Military Defense Assistance Act and the 1951 Mutual Security Act led the American government to provide the UK with hundreds of millions of dollars of defence assistance with which to purchase US weaponry to confront potential Soviet aggression in the Cold War (Marsh, 2013: 181).

Conclusion

This chapter has sought to draw out some themes from the history of Anglo-American relations that will figure in the rest of the book. Foremost amongst them has been recognition that the UK–US military relationship has been required to address the risk of conflict occurring at various levels; ranging from high intensity to counter-insurgency warfare. In order to exert influence the UK has felt it necessary to make a substantial contribution to US-led operations (Hood, 2008: 186). It has needed to possess balanced forces for this purpose and reject the option of indulging in role specialization.

A second theme has been the constant financial pressure on the British military. The end of National Service reduced the Army to only 165,000 personnel and over 55,000 of these were permanently deployed for the defence of Europe. The Chiefs of Staff were forced to treat the BAOR as an extra-European 'manpower reserve' (Darby, 1973: 275). Britain could not keep up with the US. Throughout the Cold War there was the perpetual question of what size of contribution was sufficient to convince the US it was worth cooperating with Britain. Richardson (1996: 215) describes Britain as 'pragmatically and persistently purs[uing its relationship with the US] . . . as a means of exercising more influence internationally than would be warranted by an objective assessment of its power'.

A third theme has been the self-interested policies of the US towards the UK. Despite British overtures to the US for cooperation in South East Asia and the Middle East, America remained opposed. This reflected American fears of being tarnished with the brush of British imperialism. There were numerous areas of tensions between the two sides during the Cold War and Dumbrell (2013: 84) refers to 'rows' that were often fiery in nature. For its part, the UK prioritized its relationship with the US over all other allies. It believed that American was vital not only to Britain's global role, but also to the security of Europe. By deferring to the US, the UK may have paid 'an unreasonably high price' in its cooperation with other European countries (Wells, 1986: 149).

A fourth aspect has been the relationship that each branch of the British armed forces developed with the US armed services. The British Army, Royal Navy, and Royal Air Force have all cooperated with their American counterparts. The extent of the cooperation has ebbed and flowed over time but it has created a whole that is greater than the sum of its parts. Personal friendships between British and American officers have contributed to a narrative that has extolled trust and collaboration.

A final aspect has been the Anglo-American nuclear relationship. It added a further dimension to the military linkages between the two countries. It emphasized the specialness of the relationship because no other European country was treated in this way. The inequality between the two countries was stark, and this made the British dependent upon US generosity. If America had chosen to do so, it could have forced the British out of the strategic nuclear business.

4

High Intensity Conflict

Introduction

This chapter investigates the way in which the UK military has planned to conduct high intensity conflict in conjunction with the US. High intensity conflict is
conceived of as conflict between states that involves great levels of violence and is
organized across land, sea, and air domains. The militaries of both the US and the
UK were tasked to prepare for this possibility, but the post-Cold War environment
reduced its likelihood. Planning for such an eventuality influenced decisions about
the weapon systems that were procured and the doctrine and practices for their use
(Posen, 1984). The UK was the only European power, other than France, with the
capability and the desire to intervene rapidly beside the US around the world with
sufficient forces able to undertake high intensity war-fighting (Rynning, 2010).

With the end of the Cold War, the principal adversary against which Western
policy had been planned for 45 years had collapsed. Although Russia remained a
major power, its military was reduced in size and it retreated from Eastern Europe.
One of the challenges for the US and UK during the 1990s was how to configure
their military forces for what Kagan (2006: 200) called a 'strategic vacuum'. Both
sought to realize 'peace dividends'. In 1993, the Pentagon's 'Bottom Up Review'
adopted a 'Base Force' concept in which the US Army was downsized from 18 to 10
divisions, the surface fleet was reduced to 400 ships, including 11 aircraft carriers,
and the Air Force was cut from 15 to 11 Air Wings (Aspin, 1993). The US went
on to publish a National Security Strategy (NSS) in July 1994 that envisaged being
able to fight two 'Major Theatre Wars' simultaneously: one to be a major effort
whilst the other was to be a holding operation. This planning assumption was not
formally abandoned until the Obama presidency in 2012 (Kagan, 2006: 182).

A similar mindset pervaded British military policy. There was a 30% cut in the
size of the British Army after the Cold War with a reduction from four divisions to
two (Dannatt, 2011). There were comparable cuts to the Royal Air Force (RAF)
and Royal Navy in the 'Options for Change' defence review (Ministry of Defence,
1990). This led to a change in military posture in which forces based in Germany
were cut until there was no longer a forward presence. Like other NATO powers,
the British benchmarked themselves against the US in the expectation that they
would fight in concert with them in the future.

Whilst the risk of major inter-state conflict decreased in the Euro-Atlantic area,
the potential for conflict elsewhere increased. The first Gulf War of 1990–1991,

The Anglo-American Military Relationship. Wyn Rees, Oxford University Press. © Wyn Rees (2024).
DOI: 10.1093/oso/9780198884620.003.0004

the war in Afghanistan 2001 and the war against Iraq 2003 all required military mobilization against state-level actors in which the occupation of the adversaries' territories was either contemplated or carried out. Furthermore, the experience of the first Gulf War showed that even a regional war could require a high proportion of the US armed forces to be involved. Russia's rearmament from 2007 (Michta, 2019: 61–62), its invasion of Crimea in 2014 and then the whole of Ukraine in 2022, as well as the rise of China, all served to increase the risk of conflict with a major military power. In 2015, the UK Strategic Defence and Security Review acknowledged the need to attach a higher priority to such a possibility.

Rules

Rules have existed in the Anglo-American military relationship in the form of legal frameworks that have shaped their patterns of interaction. Both countries have been members of the North Atlantic Treaty (1949) that has bound states together. The UK and the US have also constructed a range of bilateral agreements that have structured their military cooperation.

Network centric war

High technology has been central to US ideas about waging large-scale conflict. The Cold War taught the US military that it could not afford parity in numbers against the Warsaw Pact. However, it could offset its own numerical inferiority by developing technologies that would have a force multiplier effect. In this way, the US exploited its inherent superiority in technology and simultaneously reduced the demands for personnel. It came to emphasize 'short, intense and decisive' engagements (Lewis, 2018: 311).

America pioneered the concept of 'Network Centric Warfare' (NCW), which was the marrying of digital information technology to land, sea, and air forces. Sensors of all kinds were developed to gather information that was then processed and prioritized. That intelligence and targeting data was linked to a sophisticated command and control system to export it to frontline units to track and destroy enemy assets (Mahnken, 2008: 177). US forces benefitted from information dominance enabling them to identify, target, and destroy their adversary whilst minimizing their own vulnerability. US military forces were able to 'see first, understand first, act first, and finish decisively' (Mitchell, 2009: 101). This represented a shift from a 'platform-centric' to a network-centric approach (Hammes, 2005: 21). The advantage conferred would enable smaller and more agile forces to exert the same strategic effect as much larger force structures. They would achieve their objectives within a timeframe that would incapacitate the adversary.

NCW, or 'military transformation', was the driving concept behind developments within the US military in the 1990s. Admiral William Owens, Vice Chairman of the Joint Chiefs of Staff in 1994, was one of its leading advocates (Mahnken, 2008: 177). Owens conceptualized NCW as a 'system of systems' (Shimko, 2010: 109) that would afford US forces an all-encompassing awareness in military operations (Boot, 2003). The concept of transformation reached its zenith in the George W. Bush administration under its first Secretary of Defense, Donald Rumsfeld. In the 2001 Quadrennial Defense Review, led by Andrew Marshall, the emphasis was on small and nimble forces that were capable of precision strikes. An Office of Force Transformation was established in the Pentagon, consisting of 20 personnel, under the direction of Admiral Cebrowski (Cebrowski and Gartska, 1998). This was complemented at the NATO level by the creation of Allied Command Transformation in Norfolk, Virginia. The US pursued a deliberate policy of trying to prevent its European allies from falling so far behind its developments that they would become incapable of interoperability (Terriff and Osinga, 2010: 189).

In order to be able to fight alongside US forces, the British military recognized that they would need to invest in elements of network centric warfare (Ministry of Defence, 2015). However, the British were more circumspect about the potential of transformation. First, they were more sceptical than the US military about the potential benefits (Farrell and Bird, 2010). According to Weisner 'the British military have a natural tendency to be critical of US military operational concepts, which are often regarded as too technology-focused' (2013: 75). They were wary of the dependency and the vulnerabilities that technology created and placed a greater premium on the quality of personnel and human decision-making (Weisner, 2013: 82). Second, the British military were more constrained in the resources that they could devote to new technology (Mitchell, 2009: 111). Theirs was a less ambitious and less costly version of transformation, because they did not seek to be as capable as US forces (Clarke, 2014: 5).

The British armed forces used and adapted the American model to their own needs as well as to what they could afford. They developed 'Network Enabled Capability' (NEC) (Ministry of Defence, 2015: 1), adjusting US ideas 'to suit British circumstances and sensibilities' (Farrell, 2008: 805). NEC was flagged up in the New Chapter of the UK Strategic Defence Review (Ministry of Defence, 2002) as a form of enabling, rather than a determining, factor in operations. It was embodied in the Joint High Level Operating Concept. The 2003 Defence White Paper noted that British armed forces, in order to be able to operate alongside US forces, had to be able to 'match (their) operational tempo and provide those capabilities that deliver the greatest impact' (Ministry of Defence, 2003: 8).

In a similar fashion to NCW, the UK adapted the US concept of 'Effects Based Operations' (EBO) (Boyce, 2003) The concept of EBO involved marrying up military power with other instruments of national power to achieve the rapid defeat of an adversary. It focused on achieving an objective with the most effective means available. It was derived from US Air Force thinking regarding an enemy's centre of gravity, seeking to target those elements until an enemy collapsed (Elliott 2015: 70).

Interservice relationships

Each of the US armed services has championed a core mission. US Defense Secretary Robert Gates, described the US Army as planning for, 'conventional force-on-force conflicts against nation states … for the Navy, conventional maritime operations on the high seas (and) for the Air Force, high-tech air to air combat' (2014: 118). The British armed forces have sought to be able to fight alongside their American counterparts, so they have preserved a full spectrum of capabilities. According to Victoria Nuland, a former US Ambassador to NATO, 'You (the UK) and the French are the only full-spectrum allies left in the alliance' (Defence Select Committee, 2018b). Like their ally, the British military has focused on high-end warfighting tasks (Dunne, 2004: 902) based on the assumption that such capabilities afford the ability to perform a range of less demanding tasks, should the need arise.

Each US service has represented a large and powerful bureaucratic actor with its own specific vision about the configuration of its forces. In turn, the UK military considered the extent to which they wanted to embrace US approaches. The RAF has been particularly close to the USAF: Boyes describes their relationship as the 'strongest partnership in the world' (2019: 132). It was underpinned by operating together almost constantly between the first Gulf War and the 2014 drawdown of combat operations in Afghanistan. The USAF was at the forefront of technological developments and the RAF followed closely in its wake (RAF, 1991). Based on David Deptula's authorship of 'Air Force and US National Security' (Department of the US Air Force, 1989), the USAF argued that the inherent flexibility of airpower enabled it to conduct precision strikes anywhere in the world, using platforms such as the B-52, B-1, and B-2. This decreased the importance of allies by fostering the impression that the US alone could defeat an adversary (Pape, 1997: 94), although the provision of bases like Diego Garcia, by the UK, give the USAF the ability to strike targets in the Middle East and Asia. These 'deep strike' platforms were part of a complex envisaged within the NCW concept (Weiner, 2009) that linked to advanced target acquisition systems, such as the Joint Surveillance and Target Attack Radar System (JSTARS) and Global Hawk Unmanned Aerial Vehicle (UAV). It also included space-based satellite intelligence systems with optical, infrared, and radar sensors.

The RAF did not share the ambition of its American counterpart to exercise global power (RAF, 1999; Clarke, 2014). There was the obvious difference in scale between the two air forces and in the 2010 Strategic Defence and Security Review the RAF lost its entire Harrier force. The RAF acquired Reaper UAVs for both persistent surveillance and strike, based on its operational needs in Afghanistan and Iraq. A close relationship grew up between 39 Squadron at Creech Air Force Base, Nevada, and 13 Squadron at RAF Waddington. The RAF has joined the RC-135W Rivet Joint intelligence gathering programme in which British crews have trained in the US (Interview with Royal Air Force Air Chief Marshal, 2012). F-35 Joint Strike Fighters have been purchased and the UK has invested £3bn in the programme as the only Level 1 partner. (Note that Anglo-American defence industrial cooperation is a major subject within the special relationship but it lies outside the confines of this study.) The RAF and the Royal Navy have purchased different variants of the Joint Strike Fighters and the RAF has built up a close relationship with the US Marine Corps over the F-35B (Interview with Royal Air Force Air Marshal, 2020).

The Royal Navy's relationship with the US Navy, in relation to preparations for high intensity conflict, has been especially close. After 1989, both services struggled with the lack of a peer competitor to justify their spending: the former Soviet northern fleet rotted in Murmansk. In the face of a lower threat environment, the US Navy rethought its doctrine and published 'From the Sea' (Department of the Navy, 1992) and 'Forward from the Sea' (Department of the Navy, 1992), that emphasized the role of naval power in amphibious assault and attacks against the shore (Friedman, 2009: 80). The US Navy adopted the concept of jointery as well as sharing data amongst its air, sea, and sub-surface platforms, through the Link 16 system. This 'ForceNET' approach gave the US Navy its 'Cooperative Engagement Capability' (Friedman, 2009), namely the ability to share radar and data between weapons platforms so as to optimize offensive and defensive capabilities. In 2013, the UK First Sea Lord George Zambellas and US Chief of Naval Operations Jonathan Greenert commissioned a study, 'Combined Seapower: A shared Vision for Royal Navy-US Navy Cooperation', to investigate future areas of cooperation (Rosamond, 2015). That vision planned for close interoperability from the outset and research into maritime autonomous systems. The two navies shared the objective of a maritime renaissance, reasserting the role of sea power in national security policy and emphasizing its forward presence (Swartz et al, 2017; Defence Select Committee, 2021).

Two categories of naval vessel have symbolized the Royal Navy's determination to remain the partner of the US Navy: hunter–killer submarines (SSNs) and large aircraft carriers (Till, 2010: 38). Despite the decline of the Russian Navy after 1991, the UK continued to invest in highly capable submarines, such as the Astute class. SSNs from the Royal Navy continued to perform vital intelligence gathering roles (Ring, 2001). The US Navy has demonstrated its high regard for its British counterpart by putting some of its submarine commanders through the Royal Navy 'perisher' training course (Jones, 2016) and by adding advanced communications equipment to British submarines (Interview with former First Sea Lord, 2012).

With the re-emergence of Russian maritime capability after 2007 (Interview with Royal Navy submarine Captain, 2012) and the rise of the Chinese Navy, this form of naval power has regained its earlier importance (Interview with former First Sea Lord, 2015). Whilst the breadth of Anglo-American submarine operations have diminished, the depth of cooperation between the two communities has been preserved (Interview with former First Sea Lord, 2014).

The other category of naval power, aircraft carriers, experienced a turning point in the 1998 UK Strategic Defence Review (Elliot, 2015: 63). The desire to be able to undertake expeditionary warfare led the Royal Navy to procure two new Queen Elizabeth class aircraft carriers, each of 65,000 tons (Rosamond, 2015). There was a hiatus after 2010 when the existing aircraft carriers were scrapped and before the Queen Elizabeth came into service. Armed with US F-35 aircraft, the new carriers offer a range of capabilities including loitering off-shore, air defence, shore-based operations, and carrier strike (Joint Doctrine Publication 0-10, 2017). The US–UK 'Statement of Intent' led to US Navy assistance to return the Royal Navy to complex carrier aviation operations (Ministry of Defence and the US Department of Defense, 2012). A team of British officers were resident at the US naval base in Norfolk, Virginia (Interview with Royal Navy Aircraft Carrier Liaison Officer, 2014), Royal Navy pilots trained with the US Navy and a 'Long Lead Specialist Skills' exchange programme was created with the US (Navynews, 2013).

Resurrecting a large carrier capability was not without controversy in the UK, even within the armed services. A former head of the British Army, for example, expressed doubts about the rationale, arguing that aircraft carriers present large and vulnerable targets in an age of long-range ballistic and cruise missiles (Interview with former Chief of the General Staff, 2014). Retaining the aircraft carrier programme led to the cutting of the Nimrod maritime patrol aircraft in 2010; the UK's maritime patrol capability was only renewed in the 2015 Strategic Security and Defence Review when nine P-8 Poseidon aircraft were ordered. Unlike the US Navy, the Royal Navy possesses only a limited number of surface vessels and submarines to protect its carriers. This means that its carriers would only act alone against less capable enemies and would need to operate with the US or major allies against a peer adversary (Interview with Marshal of the Royal Air Force, 2020).

The British Army was shrunk after the Cold War to two heavy brigades, three medium weight brigades, and one light brigade (Farrell, Rynning, and Terriff, 2013: 130). Its US counterpart emerged from the Cold War with a desire to adapt to the information age and demoted the former priorities of firepower and massed armour (Interview with former Commander of British Land Forces, 2015). The US Army Chief of Staff, General Gordon Sullivan, sought to develop enhanced situational awareness, improve the speed of decision-making, and increase the synchronization between military units. In 1994, there was a project to create a battlefield internet that would give commanders a detailed overview of the entire battlespace that became part of the so-called 'Force XXI' programme (Serena, 2011: 44). Subsequent Chiefs of Staff, such as General Dennis Reimer and General Eric Shinseki, proceeded with these ideas in the 'Joint Vision 2010' programme (Mahnken, 2008: 177). It was envisaged that digitized units of brigade size would become self-sufficient, with embedded artillery and aviation assets, and not need to be part of divisional or corps formations (Mitchell, 2009: 21). But there were also fears within the US Army that transformation was a screen for imposing cuts on the size of ground forces (Rayburn and Sobchak, 2019: 38).

The British Army shared many of the objectives of its US counterpart in being smaller but more lethal, with better communication and more precise weaponry (Wither, 2006: 53). Cuts were inflicted in the 2010 Strategic Defence and Security Review and although the 2015 Review went some way to rebalance capabilities, the reductions were not reversed. Like the US, the British have aimed to digitize the battlespace and develop the capability to share information between different platforms. The British Army used the same information distribution system as the US, CENTRIX, and opted for the Bowman communications systems in land vehicles and the Falcon communication systems, with a Skynet 5 satellite providing much greater bandwidth (Interview, with US Army Colonel, 2014b). The British Army has bought some US equipment, such as the Multi-Launch Rocket System and AH-64 Apache helicopters, that has allowed them to mirror US operational concepts (Deni, 2012).

All three of the British services have experienced patterns of cooperation with their US counterpart. These US services understand British operational roles and the pressures that they face. Thus, the British and American armed services have been able to share with each other in ways that they cannot with their own national services. This has resulted in intimate relationships developing between them and it has helped to foster trust and confidence between the two armed forces. Theorists of institutionalism have pointed to the way in which the institutions themselves become an active part of the relationship between state actors (Thelen, 1999).

It has also created a temptation to lobby their opposite allied service for support and influence when inter-service tussles over resources and roles have arisen domestically. The militaries on both sides of the Atlantic represent interest groups within their nations, advancing the visions of their respective tribes. The British military have been drawn into inter-service competition within the US military and vice versa (Seitz, 1998: 329). One example of this has been when British governments of various political hues have cut defence expenditure and this has been followed by criticism from across the Atlantic from senior military officers warning that the special relationship is being put at risk. It takes little imagination to appreciate that such interventions have been invited by British military colleagues eager to put pressure on their own government.

Practice

Whilst the US and British armed forces configured themselves for high intensity operations, they have not confronted a peer competitor on the battlefield. Instead they have faced state level actors of considerably less sophistication than the Soviet military. This is not to deny that Saddam Hussein's Iraq was a formidable adversary in 1990, with the fifth largest army in the world, and possessing military equipment from the former Soviet Union and France. But it was a second tier adversary with an outdated conceptual approach to warfare. What made it more challenging was that the war against Iraq materialized just as the Cold War ended and amidst expectations of a new and more peaceful international order. At the very moment in which the demise of the Soviet Union appeared to consign the special relationship to history, a new threat in the Middle East rekindled cooperation (Self, 2010: 93).

In the first Gulf War of 1990–1991, the British Chiefs of Staff considered making only a modest contribution of RAF, Royal Navy, and Special Forces contingents. However, it was decided in the prelude to the conflict that a large land force would be offered. To this end, an additional team of military planners was despatched to reinforce the British officers already present at Central Command (CENTCOM) in Florida (Interview with British Army Lieutenant General, 2015). A British armoured division, approximately 15% of the size of the US force was decided upon (Foreign Affairs Select Committee, 2010: para 60), comprising two armoured brigades plus artillery, engineers, logistics, and aviation elements. To field such a force meant cannibalizing British military stocks held in Germany. Here was the first post-Cold War opportunity for the UK military to prove itself as the partner of choice for the US. Several factors influenced this decision. First, the size of contribution was deemed sufficient to demonstrate Britain's determination 'to stand shoulder to shoulder with the Americans' (Farrell, Rynning, and Terriff, 2013: 124). Second, it was the minimum size of force that could manoeuvre on the battlefield and be sustained independently. Third, it secured the UK military leadership positions within the US-led coalition. General Peter de la Billière was appointed as the deputy to US General Norman Schwarzkopf, a British brigadier was placed in the US planning cell (Kiszely, 2013: 126), and an RAF wing commander sat on the USAF planning team.

The British division was originally designated to operate alongside a US Marine Division and enter Kuwait from the south. This reflected a US presumption that the British Army's equipment was unreliable (McInnes, 1996: 87). But the US relented when political pressure was exerted from London because the British military wanted a key role alongside US forces (Billière, 2008: 152). The division was put under 7 US Corps, thereby causing consternation amongst the US Marine Corps who had welcomed the potential British help in fighting to reach Kuwait City. Instead, the British division was able to participate in the flanking movement by American forces through the desert to attack the Iraqi forces from the rear. Robin Renwick, the British Ambassador to the US, commented on, 'the ability of the American and British armed forces to operate together in a more cohesive manner than any other allies' (2016: 375). Since the time of General Bagnall's reforms of land warfare strategy (see Chapter 3), the British had adopted a 'Manoeuvrist Approach' that combined rapid mobility with the application of firepower (McInnes, 2006: 168; Dannatt, 2011). Its cognitive element entailed the capacity to think and take decisions more quickly than the adversary, so as to maintain tempo and preserve the initiative on the battlefield (Joint Doctrine Publication 0-01, 2014). The British achieved their objective of 'plugging' into US structures and played a significant role in the defeat of Iraqi forces.

The maritime dimension of the first Gulf War was a less satisfying experience for the Royal Navy. They had extensive experience of working alongside the US Navy in the Persian Gulf as part of the Armilla patrol during the Iran–Iraq War (Interview with Royal Navy Admiral, 2015). During the so-called 'tanker war' of the 1980s, the British deployed a destroyer and two frigates, as well as six mine counter measure vessels, to patrol between Bahrain and the mouth of the Persian Gulf (Sander, 1990: 185). In the Gulf War, a major US–UK naval formation was held off the Kuwaiti coast and it was rumoured that an amphibious invasion was intended (Wells, 2017: Chapter 9). The First Sea Lord, Sir Julian Oswald, wanted a Royal Navy role and used his American counterparts to exert pressure on political decision-makers but it was resisted (Interview with Royal Navy Admiral, 2012). The naval force served as a feint to tie down Iraqi forces and distract attention from the centre of gravity of the coalition attack. The US Navy conducted attacks with cruise missiles and with carrier-borne aviation. The Royal Navy came away from the conflict disappointed that there had not been an opportunity to play a bigger role (Interview with Royal Navy Rear Admiral, 2012).

By contrast the RAF, alongside the USAF, played a decisive part in the campaign. The US Joint Force Air Component Commander, General Chuck Horner, along with Brigadier General Buster Glosson and Colonel John Warden planned the air war and operationalized many of the concepts that had been latent in transformational thinking (Weiner, 2009). The conflict was an ideal environment for the decisive application of airpower as there was a profusion of ground targets, little opportunity for the enemy to practice concealment, and a low risk of collateral damage (Shimko, 2010: 102). Britain contributed 6100 sorties to the air campaign (Dannatt, 2016: 207) whilst the US provided 76% of the coalition airpower overall (Lewis, 2018: 340). The coalition targeted the Iraqi leadership and its command and control, as well as the ground forces that were occupying Kuwait (Warden, 2000: 131). The USAF was able to put to the test technologies that had been developed to fight the Soviets: stealth, precision-guided munitions (PGMs), the Global Positioning System (GPS), and ground tracking radar. The difference was that the Iraqi forces were dug into defensive positions in Kuwait, rather than engaged in offensive operations as foreseen in AirLand Battle (Kretchik, 2011: 216). The war refined thinking about the application of airpower and how it could maximize its advantages of speed, range, precision, and lethality (Hallion, 2011: 108). The lessons drawn from the first Gulf War proved to be both influential and seductive in the ensuing era.

It was perhaps inevitable that the RAF was drawn into the afterglow of the success of USAF operations against Iraq. US technology had proven its worth and the part played by precision airpower had enabled the ground war to be completed in just a hundred hours. However, the early stages of the air war were costly for the RAF. Their tactics of Tornado aircraft flying at low level with runway cratering munitions had resulted in the loss of aircrews and resulted in the decision to switch to medium-level attacks (Cox and Ritchie, 2002). Furthermore, the absence of laser designators for precision munitions highlighted their relative lag in technology compared to the USAF. After the war, the RAF set about emulating many of the US practices that had proved so effective in the campaign.

Afghanistan

The 2001 War in Afghanistan was a different sort of conflict from the Gulf War for two main reasons. First, it was a conflict against a poorly armed adversary. Despite the natural advantages that Afghanistan enjoyed in terms of its mountainous terrain and inaccessibility, it was unequal to the might of the US. Second, the US was determined to exploit its concept of transformation. Secretary of Defense Donald Rumsfeld saw this as an opportunity to test the ideas that he had championed (2002), emphasizing smaller ground forces with enhanced deployability and lethality. Boot (2003) argued that it represented a 'new way of war' that made sense against an enemy for whom traditional concepts of 'fire and manoeuvre' were of little relevance (Russell, 2013: 61).

It was ironic that transformation had been designed to facilitate a US victory against a peer competitor: yet the first time it was put into practice was against a country many orders of magnitude militarily inferior. The US adopted an approach that drew upon assets from both its military and intelligence agencies. A force of just over 300 US Special Forces and 100 Central Intelligence Agency (CIA) personnel were deployed into the country (Mahnken, 2008: 197), thereby sidelining the US Army. They linked up with anti-Taliban forces of the largely Pashtun Northern Alliance who provided the majority of ground forces. These were supported by US Navy aircraft operating from aircraft carriers and USAF aircraft, such as B-2 and B-52 bombers, armed with precision-guided weapons and flying from the British owned airfield at Diego Garcia in the Indian Ocean. The speed of the Taliban collapse was dramatic and it confirmed the assessment of those that had argued against a protracted build-up of forces (Shimko, 2010: 135).

The US declined offers of assistance from NATO nations who had operational-ized the Alliance's Article V commitment for the first time following the 9/11 attack. US experience working with the United Nations in Bosnia and with NATO allies in Kosovo, had made the US military wary of being constrained by the con-flicting objectives of allies and conducting a war by committee. In addition, with such an unorthodox strategy, Rumsfeld feared that allies would be an encum-brance and insisted that in the case of 'Operation Enduring Freedom', 'the mission should determine the coalition' (Washington Post Online, 2001). The US did accept offers of assistance from the UK that served to confer a sense of legitimacy on an otherwise national operation. The UK provided diplomatic linkages with the government of President Musharraf of Pakistan that facilitated access to airbases. In the initial phase of the operation a British submarine fired Tomahawk cruise missiles at targets in Afghanistan, aerial refuelling assets were provided (Finlan, 2014: 100), and British special forces collaborated with American forces.

The role of naval forces in Afghanistan was significant in the earliest stages of the operation but diminished over time. As a land-locked country, carrier-based air-craft were essential before there was access to airfields within the theatre. Around 30% of the initial airpower was from aircraft carriers (Weiner, 2009: 108) but the US possessed sufficient long-range strike aircraft that they did not need to turn to the Royal Navy. *HMS Illustrious* was already in the Persian Gulf in 2001 as part of exercise 'Saif Sareea II' and it was converted from an aircraft carrier role to a commando carrier role (Childs, 2009). In November, Royal Marine Commandos were helicopatered from Illustrious to Bagram to seize the airbase (Joint Doctrine Publication 0-10, 2017; Interview with Royal Navy Admiral, 2015a). But the role of naval power was quickly eclipsed as neighbouring countries provided airbases and soon even the US Navy was no longer needed.

The part played by allied air forces in Afghanistan was limited by the dearth of high-value targets. The USAF was able to have aircraft circling, waiting to be called into action by ground controllers (Weiner, 2009: 108). Kagan describes the US strategy as 'very high-tech close air support' (Kagan, 2006: 309) and it was clear that the USAF were especially adept at this type of operation (Farrell, 2017: 183). The RAF contributed intelligence assets, transport aircraft, air to air refuelling, and helicopters (Peach, 2014: 93). After the Taliban were defeated, there was a larger role for allied airpower in supporting the ground operations of the NATO Interna-tional Security Assistance Force (ISAF). At this point the RAF was able to operate much more closely with its US counterpart (Interview with Royal Air Force Air Commodore, 2014). The USAF gave the RAF aircraft access to the Joint Tactical Information Distribution System (JTIDS) which provided them with secure com-munications and with access to data from a variety of platforms. JTIDS enabled the RAF to receive data from US Airborne Warning and Control System (AWACS), the JSTARS ground surveillance system, and Rivet Joint. The RAF found itself oper-ating in concert with the US with a much more capable system than the rest of the UK armed forces which continued to rely on the Bowman communications system (Interview with Royal Air Force Air Marshal, 2020).

The Iraq War of 2003

The political context surrounding the 2003 War against Iraq was an important factor in shaping how the conflict unfolded. From the time that Prime Minister Tony Blair visited President George W. Bush at his ranch in Crawford, Texas, the British were convinced of the likelihood that the US was going to use force against Iraq. Blair concurred with the US assessment that Iraq was a long-term threat, that Saddam Hussein was determined to acquire Weapons of Mass Destruction (WMD) and that the sanctions regime, imposed upon the country after 1991, was crumbling (Kampfner, 2003: 22; Riddell, 2003). Aligning with the US was consistent with Britain's vision and values. From the Prime Minister's perspective it was necessary to share in America's operations if you wanted that country to provide leadership, as well as be able to exercise restraint over its ambitions (Self, 2010: 97). The leader of the House of Commons, Robin Cook, expressed the widely held view that Britain was being forced into military action by a timetable determined in Washington (House of Commons, 2016: 39). These contrasting positions created a political framework in which the British military operated.

Blair believed that, 'We are stronger with the US because we are in Europe, and a bridge between the two' (Blair and Brown, 1999). He thought that he could act as spokesperson for Europe, closing any policy differences in the transatlantic relationship, and helping to obtain a UN mandate for operations against Iraq (Blair, 2010: 401; Naughtie, 2004: 213). The traditional British approach was to try to agree on a policy with the US before presenting the issue to Europe (Niblett, 2007: 627). Ultimately this did not succeed because both the French and German governments were unconvinced of the imminent need to use force. In the face of Franco-German opposition, the UK chose to follow the US lead into a war with Iraq.

What added to the complexity was the dysfunctional relationships that existed within the higher reaches of the US government and military. Donald Rumsfeld and Vice-President Richard Cheney differed in their approach from Secretary of State Colin Powell (Jackson, 2007: 319). Cross (2013: 71) records the 'deep animosities' that existed between agencies in Washington DC in the run up to the Iraq War. Both the US and the UK agreed on the broad strategic objectives: namely, the removal of Saddam's government and the dismantling of WMD. But there was a lack of clarity about how the war was to be prosecuted as well as the planning for the post-war situation. Neo-conservatives in the administration and Iraqi emigres, such as Ahmed Chalabi, advised that the US would be welcomed as liberators and that after the removal of the despotic regime, it would be possible for American

forces to quickly withdraw. The State Department had conducted post-war planning for Iraq but it was overridden and responsibility for post-conflict stabilization
was invested in Rumsfeld's Pentagon (Interview with Royal Air Force Air Chief
Marshal, 2012).

Compounding this tension were differences within the US military chain of
command over planning for the various phases of the conflict. CENTCOM
was focused on the military plan for the defeat of Iraqi forces. The Office for
Reconstruction and Humanitarian Assistance (ORHA), under General Jay Gar-
ner, which had only been established at the beginning of 2003, was left critically
short of personnel (Cross, 2013: 69–75). When ORHA did enter Iraq after the
war, there were insufficient forces to assure its protection and it was hampered
in its task of getting the ministries of the Iraqi state back into operation. General
Tommy Franks at CENTCOM was deeply resistant to allowing the US Joint Chiefs
of Staff to interfere in his military planning, insisting that he reported only to Secretary Rumsfeld and the President (Rayburn and Sobchak, 2019: 38). Lieutenant
General Ricardo Sanchez proceeded to have a stormy relationship with the head
of the Coalition Provisional Authority (CPA) in Iraq, Paul Bremer.

For their part, the British military had looked to the Iraq Planning Unit within
the Foreign and Commonwealth Office (FCO) to conduct post-war preparations.
This Unit was only set up in February 2003. It experienced hostility and non-
cooperation from the Department for International Development (DfID) whose
Secretary of State, Clare Short, was opposed to the war. The UK government was
wary of the costs that might follow with the reconstruction of Iraq (Maciejewski,
2013: 159; Synnott, 2008: 137) and was frustrated at their inability to influence US
policy (House of Commons, 2016: 80). The British military were badly let down
by other agencies.

General Anthony Zinni, Franks' predecessor at CENTCOM, had an operational
plan for war with Iraq that envisaged a force of around 400,000 troops (Finlan,
2014: 111). Rumsfeld rejected these planning estimates and, based on the experience of Afghanistan, called for a much leaner force that exploited the conceptual
thinking that had been embodied in transformation strategy. Rumsfeld turned
down representations from the Joint Chiefs of Staff that lobbied for larger force
goals for 'Operation Iraqi Freedom'. When Lieutenant General David McKiernan
assumed the position of Land Component Commander he insisted on the addition of several US units to the operational force to raise the number to around
150,000. According to Finlan (2014: 131), what was significant about the invasion
of Iraq was 'the critically small amount of ground forces used' (2014: 131). This was
to prove inadequate for phase IV operations after the Iraqi military was defeated
(See Chapter 6).

In what became 'Operation Telic', Air Chief Marshal Sir Brian Burridge was
appointed as 'UK Joint Force Commander' and was able to exercise influence over
the US campaign. Glen Torpy was appointed as 'Deputy Coalition Commander,

Air'; David Snelson as the 'Deputy Coalition Commander, Maritime' in Bahrain under US Admiral Timothy Keating (Interview with Royal Navy Rear Admiral, 2012); Robin Brims as the UK Land Component Commander and Graeme Lambe as the UK Special Forces Commander. British military personnel were put into the Strategic Planning Staff of US General Casey in Iraq (Interview with British Army Major-General, 2013). Amidst the diplomatic efforts that preceded the invasion, the UK did not wish to appear to prejudge the outcome and therefore held back from a logistical force build-up. This restricted the time that the British military had to get personnel and material into the theatre. It was compounded by the decision of Turkey to deny transit rights to the US 4th Infantry Division and British forces who had been expected to cross Turkey and enter Iraq from the north. The US did not lose hope of using Turkey as a gateway until March 2003 and this resulted in a shortfall in the forces that initially attacked Iraq (Barry, 2020: 115).

As in the first Gulf War, the British Army contributed the 1st Armoured division, comprised of 7 Armoured Brigade, 16 Air Assault Brigade and 3 Commando Brigade (Farrell, Rynning, and Terriff, 2013: 134). The UK provided over 46,000 personnel in the belief that this was the size of contribution necessary to obtain full consultation with the US (Foreign Affairs Select Committee, 2010). British forces were embedded in the US 1st Marine Expeditionary Force. The British focused on the taking and holding of the city of Basra and the oil fields in the south and released the US Marines from this task. By doing so, they avoided the arduous challenge of having to keep up with the two-pronged US formations that travelled for 300 miles up the Euphrates and Tigris rivers towards Baghdad. Despite having placed a premium on being interoperable with US formations in communications, command and control, and logistics, the tempo and speed of US operations would have presented difficulties for the UK (Ministry of Defence, 2003). Nevertheless, British airpower played a significant role in the western desert of Iraq and special forces contributed to ground operations.

Major General Robin Brims was cautious in taking Basra, laying siege to the city for 15 days. The British were more restrained than the US in the intensity of the artillery and tank fire and the air bombardment that they inflicted on Iraqi urban centres. Yet this should not detract from the achievement of US forces across the rest of the country. The US defeated the Iraqi military in three weeks and asserted their dominance, including within the capital Baghdad. Three of the major phases of the operation; the planning, the shaping of the battlespace, and the conduct of the major military operations had all been successful and with very low casualties.

British forces leased a US tracking system called the 'Force XXI Battle Command Brigade and Below' (Office of Force Transformation, 2005a). It had been trialled by the US 4th Infantry Division and created a secure digital network by linking satellites to air and ground sensors that enabled users to identify friendly and hostile units (Moreland and Mattox, 2009: 81; Mahnken, 2008: 209). It was installed on UK vehicles and aircraft to maximize information sharing, enhance situational awareness, and prevent the sort of 'blue on blue' errors that had plagued UK–US operations in 1991 (Interview with British Army Lieutenant General, 2015a). The incorporation of the system by the British military was an example of their attempt to use US technology that was at the forefront of operational techniques. But its attraction diminished when the US 1st Marine Expeditionary Force abandoned its use. The Office of Force Transformation (2005) judged that the 'Force XXI Battle Command Brigade and Below' provided an incremental, somewhat limited, contribution to improved coalition operations'.

Both the US Navy and the Royal Navy were optimistic that the 2003 war would result in a larger role for naval power than it had done in 1991. In preparation for the war, five US aircraft carriers and an amphibious task force that included *HMS Ark Royal* and *HMS Ocean* were assembled (Interview with Royal Navy Captain, 2014). There was an ease in the naval forces of the two countries in working together, including an established relationship between Sir Jonathan Band and the US Chief of Naval Operations. Yet the naval dimension of the conflict remained modest. An amphibious operation was mounted against the Al Faw Peninsula and it was significant only in that it demonstrated considerable confidence in the UK by placing a US Marine brigade temporarily under its command (House of Commons Defence Committee, 2017: para. 89).

Between the two navies the US Navy shared intelligence with the Royal Navy to an unprecedented extent. Even information that was officially not for release to other nationals was made available to selected Royal Navy officers, based largely upon personal relationships of trust (Interview with Royal Navy Rear Admiral, 2012). This included selective access to SIPRNet, the classified information distribution system used by the US Navy (Interview with Royal Navy Admiral, 2015). The US possessed an extensive array of satellite-based systems for optical, radar, and infra-red intelligence gathering and this was pooled with the UK. There was also some equipment that enabled Royal Navy ships to receive communications directly from satellites (Interview with Royal Navy Rear Admiral, 2012).

From the viewpoint of the RAF, the war of 2003 was fought very differently from the 1990–1991 conflict. The US-led coalition was eager to overcome Iraqi military forces with the greatest speed and the minimum collateral damage to infrastructure, such as the bridges over the River Euphrates. Instead of the sequential military actions that had characterized Desert Storm, combat operations in Operation Iraqi Freedom were conducted simultaneously (Mitchell, 2009: 103). The US Army and Marine Corps argued that they did not need to repeat the experience of the first Gulf War with a prolonged air campaign. They concentrated on 'simultaneity and speed' (Shimko, 2010: 147) and airpower became a support to the advance of the ground forces.

In the wars against both Afghanistan and Iraq, the US and the UK experienced conflicts in which they were able to rapidly overcome their adversaries. US conceptual thinking on transformation had worked in practice and empowered small interventionary forces to attain their objectives. If, in both countries, the US and the UK had funnelled in large numbers of ground forces after victory had been achieved, to stabilize the situations and undertake reconstruction, then the history might have been very different. But the US was unprepared for Phase IV operations after the kinetic phase (Cordesman, 2003) and the UK lacked the resources to materially change the situation. Barry (2020: 184) notes that General Tommy Franks was expecting to remove the majority of US combat forces from Iraq by September 2003. In Iraq, the security situation deteriorated quickly and a large-scale insurgency began to take hold. It was a highly complex and risk-laden situation and the ability of the US and the UK to work together suffered. Sir Jeremy Greenstock, who had replaced Sir John Sawers as the UK's highest political representative in Iraq, observed that, 'the strategic approach of the US, as our most capable partner by far, can be hard to mesh with' (quoted in Joint Doctrine Publication JDP 3-40, 2009: chapter 2).

In Afghanistan, ISAF controlled parts of the country but the Taliban was able to regroup and rebuild from across the border in Pakistan. It then began infiltrating back into the country after 2003 when US attention had switched to Iraq. In the face of these insurgencies in both Iraq and Afghanistan it became apparent that the US and UK lacked plans and sufficient personnel to respond effectively (Stewart, 2013: 79). This experience of fighting sustained counter-insurgency operations in Afghanistan and Iraq is the focus of Chapter 6.

Narratives

This has been the least demanding narrative. It has echoed the narrative of the Cold War that the UK and the US have to be prepared to confront and defeat any peer competitors that threaten the Western order. The means to achieve this is through the mobilization of resources to fight high intensity, inter-state conflicts. There has been continuity in using sophisticated platforms to prepare to fight and prevail against adversaries.

The UK perpetuated a discourse of support for US actions. The British have propounded stories of fighting 'side-by-side' with the US, with 'comrades in arms' and with having 'each others' backs' (Interview with former Chief of the Defence Staff, 2015). Such language is designed to bind both partners by shaping expectations based on mutual affection and respect.

The challenge for the UK in preparing for high intensity warfare has been to determine where it can add value to existing US capabilities. The UK has sought sufficient military capabilities to be able to stand alongside the US in all circumstances. Not only has the UK committed itself to be present, but it has sought to assume roles that the US takes seriously. This capacity has been a demanding one because it requires the US to be convinced and thereby willing to support the UK contribution in a way that helps realize its objective.

Yet a discourse can only go so far unless it is underpinned by tangible contributions. Many British military commentators have alluded to the fact that, as an ally, the US can take a practical and hard-headed approach to cooperation. General John McColl, for example, argues that there is no intrinsic 'special relationship' and that, 'Our influence as a junior partner depends on what we do' (2013: 118). The British agonized over what level of military commitment the US would regard as significant in each situation. They deemed that only an armoured division would secure a partnership role in the two conflicts against Iraq. Niche contributions, such as the provision of UK special operations forces, would be valued by US military commanders but would be insufficient to secure the second-in-command status that the UK sought.

Not only does the UK secure partnership with the US by the size of its contribution, it also eschews any substantive limitations on its forces. The US appreciates allies that commit to an operation without numerous red lines and caveats (Interview with former British Defence Attache to the USA, 2013). General Richard Dannatt opined that, 'credibility with the US is earned by being an ally that state(s) clearly what it will do and then does it effectively' (Quoted in Sengupta, 2009). The UK's contribution to specialness has been to contribute both substantial and highly trained forces willing to engage in combat. It has been an ally of the US willing to share in the full spectrum of risks. For example, whereas countries such as Germany placed restrictions on the ability of their forces in Afghanistan to operate in dangerous areas and at night, the UK was willing to engage in some of the hardest fighting of all.

The dangers inherent in such an approach are easily identifiable. Danchev (1997) has warned of the peril of 'mythicality' in the relationship: that the UK weaves a story to convince the US of its own strength and commitment and results in it deceiving itself. The UK has assumed tasks that are beyond its strength in order to please the US. Not only does that overburden the UK but it can result in US disillusionment when it realizes that the British military have been unable to deliver. Nicholas Witney, giving evidence before the Foreign Affairs Select Committee, contended that the UK's attempt to partner the US has been 'tested to destruction, first through Iraq and now through Afghanistan. We cannot afford it.' (Foreign Affairs Select Committee, 2010: Q67).

Conclusion

Although the disintegration of the Soviet Union in 1991 removed the likelihood of a high intensity war between East and West, the British armed forces were reluctant to relinquish these planning assumptions because they justified the purchase of weapon systems for traditional roles. In this the UK was aligned with the US military and it reinforced the thinking of those within the British armed services who were eager to preserve their capacity to operate alongside their larger ally. The British adapted American ideas about Network Centric Warfare and EBOs because they wanted to emulate the sorts of capabilities that the US military had pioneered. The purchase of military equipment from the US made it possible to operate with America in spite of pressure from periodic defence reviews.

The 1990 war against Iraq and the subsequent invasions of Afghanistan and Iraq provided opportunities to put UK intentions to the test. Interfacing UK air and naval power with that of the US was relatively straight forward but operating together with land power proved a far more difficult undertaking (Interview with British Army Lieutenant General, 2015). The relative success of the British Army in major land operations in Iraq in 1991 and then 2003 is testament to their skill and determination. The institutional relationship, carefully cultivated over many decades, smoothed this path and prevented differences of approach from growing into serious obstacles.

Having fostered a narrative of 'partnership', the UK felt the need to make major contributions to both conflicts against Iraq. This was an example of a path dependent response. Whilst the UK provision was welcomed, the US did not need the UK to provide such a level of effort. A House of Commons report noted that, 'the UK's significance to Washington has been more in providing political than military support' (Dodd and Oakes, 1998: 19). As a result, the UK did not come to enjoy the influence over American policy that it expected its contribution to justify. The subsequent Iraq War Chilcot Report argued that Britain went into Iraq in order to stay close to the US, but it failed to secure the influence it thought would result (House of Commons, 2016).

5

Operations Other than All-Out War

Introduction

The end of the Cold War had a dramatic effect on both the US and UK militaries. The operations for which they had been preparing, through NATO, disappeared. Charles Krauthammer christened it the 'Unipolar Moment' (1990) in which the US, as the sole remaining superpower, could impose a western-designed order. The US was now the world's policeman, protecting human rights, and capable of moving beyond the strictures of state sovereignty that had been imposed by the east–west confrontation. A new era of globalization and democratic enlargement was heralded, in which the values of the US and the UK could be spread throughout the world.

Contrary to expectations, this period has proved to be highly conflictual. States that were held together artificially during the Cold War were cut adrift from the patronage of major powers. Some, such as former-Yugoslavia, disintegrated whilst others underwent state failure. To these problems were added nuclear proliferation and the rise of violent sub-state actors such as terrorist groups. Western powers were faced with the conundrum of how to react in the face of these myriad challenges.

The tradition of thinking and consulting together ensured that the US and the UK approached these challenges in similar ways. They were able to adapt their relationship to the new environment and to act in concert. Yet there was no escaping the fact that these post-Cold War threats were different in nature from what had come before. The two countries no longer faced existential threats that put their own territories and societies at risk. Rather, they faced so-called 'wars of choice' where they could decide whether to become involved in regional conflicts. It also made the US and the UK more reluctant to incur casualties because it was harder to justify the loss of life to their own population for a cause that was not vital to national interests.

Rules

The removal of the conceptual framework provided by the Cold War left US and UK military forces in a position of uncertainty. They had been used to preparing for high-intensity, inter-state conflict. The risk of conflict between the superpowers

The Anglo-American Military Relationship. Wyn Rees, Oxford University Press. © Wyn Rees (2024).
DOI: 10.1093/oso/9780198884620.003.0005

had made it too dangerous to interfere in the internal affairs of sovereign states. Only classical peacekeeping had been possible, conducted under a UN mandate and approved by both sides. The UK had only occasionally been involved in UN peacekeeping whilst the US had avoided participation because it refused to place its forces under the control of another organization. The new era lifted the constraints on interventions and it became increasingly unacceptable for western countries to watch as neighbouring societies descended into ethnonationalist conflict.

New operational tasks, designated 'Operations Other Than War' (OOTW), were inherently unpredictable. There was a spectrum of possible contingencies: from delivering emergency humanitarian relief at one end, to making parties in a conflict cease fighting and enforcing peace, at the other. US and UK forces could be called upon to go up and down this spectrum, changing roles from peacekeeping to warfighting. Kretchik (2011: 227) notes that, 'War and OOTW were placed within separate categories but the overall emphasis remained war'. The military lacked both the doctrine and the weapons systems appropriate for these new tasks.

It was feasible that US and UK forces could be called upon to carry out more than one mission simultaneously within a conflict zone. US Marine Corps General Charles Krulak developed the concept of the 'three block' war (Annis, 2020). It was based on the assumption that in an urban environment across three blocks of a city, US forces could find themselves conducting multiple types of operations ranging from combat, through peace enforcement to economic reconstruction (Terriff, 2007: 149). The British Army were sympathetic to the concept of the three block war: they recognized that their armed forces had to be capable and psychologically prepared to conduct multiple types of operations concurrently (Mitchell, 2009: 2; Joint Doctrine Publication JDP 3-40, 2009).

Interventions were likely to be performed in highly complex political situations where the overall objective could either be unclear or could change in the course of the campaign. Western forces would have to be controlled in order to ensure that they retained the moral high ground. It would be important to show impartiality to all warring factions. The objective might not be the defeat of an opponent but to cause them to cease hostilities. The US and the UK experienced situations where they were attempting to use a mixture of diplomacy backed by the threat of force to coerce an actor to accede to their will. General Wesley Clark (2001: 254), the Supreme Allied Commander Europe, described his experience of the Kosovo campaign as moving from 'diplomacy backed by threat' to 'diplomacy backed by force' and eventually 'force backed by diplomacy'. At the same time it was important to appreciate that a conflict situation could escalate rapidly and result in a wider conflagration (Echevarria, 2011).

In the midst of this uncertain milieu, the US and UK militaries debated doctrine. The US Army had disliked the conceptual imprecision associated with OOTW since the Vietnam era (US Army Field Manual 100-5, 1993). US Army doctrine regarded OOTW as an alternative to large-scale military operations (US Army Field Manual 3.0, 2001) in which conflict was inherently limited and the all-out use of force was proscribed. This chafed against the Weinberger and Powell Doctrine that was agreed after Vietnam to determine criteria for future US involvement in foreign conflicts. The Weinberger and Powell doctrine called for clear national interests to be at stake; for recourse to force to be a last resort; that there must be an intention to prevail with clear military objectives; and that the operation had to enjoy public support and an exit strategy identified (Middup, 2011). Yet the types of post-Cold War operations in which US forces would be engaged did not provide the clarity demanded by the Doctrine. Neither would they afford the US the opportunity to employ its preponderant conventional capabilities.

The US faced a multiplicity of state and sub-state adversaries and would be required to perform a range of subsidiary tasks, such as counter drug operations (Egnell, 2009: 64). In the words of Serena (2011: 47), the US Army's adaptation would be 'inhibited by existing doctrine . . . established for an operational environment and enemies far different than those threatening US interests in the post-9/11 era'. According to Egnell (2009: 67), the 'uncompromising focus on conventional warfighting has left the US military ill-prepared for complex peace operations and post-conflict type settings'. The US Army Manual contained only a single paragraph on post-conflict operations (Kretchik, 2011: 241). As Chapter 4 demonstrates, the US military was focused on high-intensity warfare and equipment was procured accordingly.

The UK was eager to lead the way on adapting warfighting concepts to the new demands of the 1990s (Interview with US Army Colonel, 2014). US military dominance made it imperative, in British eyes, that they worked together in interventionary operations (Wither, 2006: 15). The British military felt that their own colonial history made them more culturally sensitive and therefore well suited to these tasks (Interview with US Army Colonel, 2014). They embraced the concept of 'peace support operations' (PSO) in which military forces provided a secure and stable environment into which other agencies could deliver reconstruction and security sector reform.

Yet there was also a lack of clarity in British military thinking towards these novel types of operations. The British were eager to assign forces for overseas operations and created a Permanent Joint Headquarters for this purpose. In 1998, they designed two Joint Rapid Reaction Forces to undertake expeditionary operations. But they were slower to reconfigure their force structures and develop new conceptual thinking. Griffin has noted how the British were unclear about the relationship between post-conflict stabilization planning and concepts of peace support and counter-insurgency (Griffin, 2011: 323).

There was an on-going dialogue throughout the 1990s between US and British military authorities regarding doctrinal developments (Interview with panel of

US Army Colonels, 2014). However, there were two principal, interrelated differences between the two sides. The first was that the US military was wedded to a warrior ethos that made them reluctant to prepare for anything less than high-intensity combat (Aylwin-Foster, 2005: 33). There was an assumption that forces trained for high-intensity conflict would be capable of moving up and down the conflict spectrum to deal with any contingency (US Army Field Manual 3.0, 2001). But this underestimated the self-control that troops would have to exercise when possessing, but not employing, overwhelming firepower. It also understated the potential complexity of operating with fragile coalitions and the difficulties of extracting forces from theatres once they had become engaged (Shimko, 2010: 105).

The US military was wedded to warfighting and regarded other roles as a distraction that could blunt their martial skills. According to Kagan (2006: 252), although OOTW missions were considered likely to be more frequent in future, 'none of the service visions really considered what the requirements of those missions might be'. Kagan's analysis is borne out by the policies that the US armed services pursued. The 'Army After Next' programme sought to focus on major military campaigns, rather than Phase IV operations, peace enforcement, or peacekeeping roles. Its architect, Major General Robert Scales contended that focusing on lesser types of conflict would detract from the Army's ability to carry out its core tasks (Jackson, 2007: 50; Mackinlay, 2004: 90). Similarly, the 'Joint Vision 2010' programme assumed that America would exert full spectrum dominance across all military operations (Mitchell, 2009: 21), but its military was paying relatively little attention to low-intensity conflict. This neglect of all except high-intensity missions was a criticism expressed by the White Commission in May 1995 in its report into the US armed forces (Hallion, 2011: 115)

A second and related difference was that, unlike the UK, the US was opposed to using its military forces for the purpose of nation-building. The US Army's vision was of utilizing its overwhelming power to achieve the military defeat of an adversary, followed by the rapid withdrawal of its forces from the theatre and the handing over of the situation to international peacekeeping forces or the UN. A strand of US thinking opposed the occupation of countries and the building of overseas empires. In President Clinton's National Security Strategy, it was envisaged that the US would conduct overseas interventions but would extricate itself rapidly from the country once the conflict was over (US National Security Strategy, 1994). Similarly, President George W. Bush's administration was firmly against the US military undertaking nation-building functions (Russell, 2013: 62). National Security Adviser, Condoleeza Rice, famously remarked that, 'the 82nd Airborne does not escort children to kindergarten' (Bellamy, 2003).

However, the US came to learn the lesson that it was easier to intervene in another country's internal affairs than it was for its forces to leave. In the words of former Chairman of the Joint Chiefs of Staff, Colin Powell, 'you break it (a country), you own it' (cited in Woodward, 2004). US Secretary of Defense Robert Gates argued that the US military came to recognize that it had no choice but to engage in nation building (2014: 267). The challenge of putting post-conflict societies back together, and preventing warring factions from resuming hostilities, was considerable. The military were not capable of achieving this alone: they had to work with a wide array of agencies such as the police, judiciary, and non-governmental actors. The US was able to call on National Guardsmen, who brought their experience from civilian life, but this was not cultivated methodically. Moreover, the US had to be willing to commit itself to police post-conflict societies for decades in order to prevent a return to violence. General Wesley Clark (2001) argued that even the US lacked sufficient resources to administer several countries simultaneously.

In contrast, the British military were less averse to the concept of nation-building than their US counterparts and regarded stabilization operations as the overarching framework in which other doctrinal precepts resided (DCDC, 2008). Whilst the diverse range of skills needed to rebuild post-conflict countries was acknowledged to be absent within NATO, many of these capabilities were present within the European Union. The British were open to the idea of the EU bringing complementary capabilities to bear and, if necessary, replacing NATO once the prospect of large-scale conflict had receded. Britain was cautious, however, in indulging the hope of the US military that they could intervene and then speedily withdraw from a country, leaving European military contingents to conduct the arduous nation building tasks. The British feared being left to pick up the pieces after a US intervention.

Inter-service relationships

The US Air Force (USAF) was the most adaptable to expeditionary operations alongside the Royal Air Force (RAF). Airpower has been the most widely used instrument for these types of operations. It was usually the swiftest to arrive in the theatre; it required the least political commitment; and it offered the capacity to rapidly inflict pain on an adversary. The risk was low because casualties from one's own side were rare, whilst precision attacks could limit collateral damage amongst the enemy (US Air Force Doctrine Document 1, 1997). The drawback was that airpower was rarely decisive and could not take and hold territory.

The RAF configured itself for expeditionary operations (RAF, 2009). It was sympathetic to the USAF approach that highly advanced strike aircraft could be the cutting edge of a military intervention and avoid the risk to land-based forces (Edmunds, 2010: 384). A key element was the provision of RAF strategic and tactical airlift capability to get ground troops and equipment into a theatre quickly. The lack of airlift capacity was a long-standing source of weakness amongst the armed forces of European countries (King, 2011: 174–5). In addition to its fleet of Hercules aircraft and Chinook helicopters, the UK acquired US C-17 heavy lift transports.

With its traditional close linkages to the US Navy and US Marine Corps, the Royal Navy found it relatively easy to cooperate on OOTW operations. The two navies were experienced in conducting policing missions and sanctions enforcement and they had no difficulty in agreeing rules of engagement. A good example of the new sorts of challenges was the co-ordinated response to drug trafficking in the Caribbean. With headquarters based in Key West, Florida, US drugs teams frequently worked on British vessels (Interview with former First Sea Lord, 2015). A Type 23 frigate with Royal Marines on board had the task of drug interdiction and intelligence collection within the Caribbean (Interview with Royal Navy Admiral, 2015a). The US Navy established an Expeditionary Combat Command in 2006 in recognition that it needed to be more focused on operations that fell short of peer competitor conflict. The US Marine Corps was the part of its armed services most attuned to the OOTW agenda because it embraced concepts such as fighting in urban areas and littoral regions (Terriff, 2007: 147).

Between the US Army and the British Army there were efforts to work out both doctrine and appropriate military capabilities. The US Army championed a new generation of fighting vehicles that were light enough, but with sufficient firepower and armour, to be capable of fighting heavily armed opponents in expeditionary operations. Within its 'Army After Next' programme, the US military created the Stryker Force (Serena, 2011: 44) based on a wheeled vehicle, with a range of possible armament configurations, and deployable in a C-130 Hercules aircraft. This was the Future Combat System (FCS) (Jackson, 2007: 58). The British Army mirrored this programme and sought to develop a Future Rapid Effects System (FRES), a family of armoured vehicles to replace the Warrior Infantry Fighting Vehicle. Like the US, the British struggled with trade-offs between weight and levels of protection as well as the degree of firepower. FRES was less ambitious: more lightly armoured and with a less complex transmission system, but it was 'benchmarked' against FCS (Farrell, Rynning, and Terriff, 2013: 152 and 184). There was prevarication over the specification of the vehicles and the Urgent Operational Requirement (UoR) demands for Afghanistan eventually knocked the FRES system off the agenda (Dannatt, 2011).

Yet despite efforts to cooperate over OOTW between the two sides, it was over ground forces that the greatest tensions emerged. In operations in both Bosnia and Kosovo, the interests of the UK and the US diverged and there were public tensions between them. This was unsurprising considering that the involvement of ground forces in each contingency operation carried with it the greatest risks in terms of political commitment and casualties. Both the UK and the US had to be clear about the objectives that they were pursuing and the exit strategy that would govern the withdrawal of their land forces.

Practices

The US and British militaries devoted considerable intellectual energy and resources to thinking about transformation and network centric operations (see Chapter 4). On the assumption of facing peer competitors, they were developing the next generations of combat aircrafts, ships, and submarines. Yet the post-Cold War conflicts in which they were engaged tended to be low intensity operations against inferior opponents. Insufficient attention was being invested to adapt military forces to conduct so-called 'Small Wars' (Serena, 2011: 45). Accordingly, 'A major mismatch soon developed between these Cold War legacy force structures and the post-Cold War missions' (Farrell and Bird, 2010: 36).

This made it difficult to undertake new types of post-Cold War operations. First, the force structures were inappropriate to the tasks that were being confronted. The policing of ceasefires and the implementation of agreements were being undertaken by forces configured for high-intensity conflict. Second, the absence of doctrinal thinking for these new types of activities made ad hoc developments necessary.

The First Gulf War demonstrated how anomalies could occur between high intensity conflicts and OOTW. Although the war was clearly a high intensity operation, it spawned a much more contained conflict which persisted through the rest of the 1990s. From April 1991, the US and the UK created a No Fly Zone (NFZ) above the 38th Parallel in 'Operation Northern Watch', to protect the Kurds of northern Iraq. In August 1992, a further zone was created below the 32nd Parallel in 'Operation Southern Watch' to protect the Shia marsh Arabs. These operations were increasingly dangerous for aircrews but gave the RAF valuable experience in operating routinely with the USAF. In 1998, US and UK aircraft executed 'Operation Desert Fox' in order to degrade Iraqi air defences that were engaging coalition aircraft enforcing the UN Security Council resolutions. The aircraft attacked 97 targets in a sustained three-day bombing campaign (Mahnken, 2008, 181). In addition to the Incirlik airbase in Turkey, the UK and the US utilized carrier-borne aircraft and the US Navy assisted the Royal Navy in developing laser designation techniques for precision air strikes. This experience was later to prove useful when conducting air operations in the 2003 Iraq war (Clarke, 2014: 232).

Despite anomalies like the No Fly Zone, the armed forces of the US and the UK sought in the 1990s to develop expeditionary capabilities. This was at the heart of the UK's 1998 Strategic Defence Review (SDR) in which Prime Minister Tony Blair declared that Britain would be a 'force for good' in the world, conducting liberal interventions (Centre for Defence Studies, 1998: 33). The Secretary of Defence, George Robertson, declared the need to 'go to the crisis, rather than have the crisis come to us' (Ministry of Defence, 1998: Introduction) by developing capabilities that would be suitable for operations alongside US forces. The Strategic Defence Review envisaged either one large-scale operation or two medium size operations (Dannatt, 2016: 233–234). Two new Queen Elizabeth class aircraft carriers became the centre piece of the procurement strategy and the interventionary capability. The UK predicated its stance on the US being involved: the 2003 Defence White Paper was explicit that the UK could only act in the context of an operation overseen by the US (Ministry of Defence, 2003). The added complexity was the diversity of thinking that was taking place within the US armed services. There was no unanimity about the priority that should be accorded to preparations for expeditionary operations and there was disagreement over how they should be carried out.

Bosnia

Two conflicts that shaped the debate about OOTW were the Balkan campaigns in Bosnia and Kosovo. The Bosnian case emerged in 1992 soon after the end of the Cold War and illustrated the complex operations that confronted the US and UK throughout the decade. Bosnia represented a challenge in determining the objectives to be pursued, because the US and UK had contending interests. This was compounded by the presence of UK forces on the ground, before a peace agreement was signed, whilst the US was absent. Bosnia showed how sharp Anglo-American divergences could arise in the context of Small Wars.

In Bosnia, a civil war ignited between three ethnic groups: Bosnian Serbs, Bosnian Muslims, and Bosnian Croats. The Bosnian Serbs were in the strongest position militarily because they were supported by neighbouring Serbia that had inherited the bulk of the equipment from the former Yugoslav Army. The US stayed on the sidelines, but criticized their European allies for promoting a 'level killing field' (Clarke, 2014). The US advocated lifting the UN arms embargo and striking the Bosnian Serbs, whom they identified as the principal aggressors. The Clinton administration condemned the UN–EU sponsored Vance–Owen Peace Plan on the grounds that it rewarded ethnic cleansing (Owen, 1996: 114). Meanwhile, the US was conducting its own secret diplomacy, shipping armaments to the Croats.

The British military operation in Bosnia began as an attempt to deliver humanitarian assistance in order to alleviate suffering and forestall a wider Balkan conflict (Major, 1995). The unwillingness of the US to support the European effort caused considerable British military resentment because it had an armoured infantry battlegroup and air assets deployed to the theatre (Farrell, Rynning, and Terriff, 2013: 126). According to the US Ambassador to the UK, 'The Americans chastised ... the British, for not doing more, and the Europeans criticized the Americans for not doing anything at all' (Seitz, 1998: 327). One commentator goes as far as to argue that the special relationship was in 'crisis' at this time (Dumbrell, 2013: 88), whilst another opined that it symbolized an absence of an 'overarching common threat' (Xu, 2017: 188). The Bosnian conflict placed great strains on the entire trans-Atlantic relationship and the UK was torn between its desire to preserve NATO and the needs of its forces in the Balkans.

A further source of tension at the trans-Atlantic level was the involvement of multiple states and international organizations in the Bosnian imbroglio. Thinking had emerged in Europe after the Cold War that called for a stronger European defence identity as an alternative to reliance on NATO. France was a supporter of this approach and argued that the newly forged EU should attempt to assert its leadership in the Bosnian crisis (Howorth, 2007). The British military were opposed to this approach and advocated continued reliance upon the US and NATO. The British armed services were sceptical that the EU possessed the political will or the capabilities to remedy major crises. They also wanted to preserve both their influence in NATO and their close collaboration with the US.

NATO provided a headquarters to coordinate European troop contributions under the United Nations Protection Force (UNPROFOR) mandate in Bosnia. It also enforced an air and sea blockade on the former-Yugoslavia and monitored UN declared 'Safe Havens' of six Bosnian cities. The UN was in overall charge of the operation under Yasushi Akashi, an envoy appointed by the UN Secretary General. The US became highly critical of the employment of NATO military capabilities through a decision-making process that ran through UN headquarters in New York. As US General Wesley Clark later commented, 'We wanted no repeat of the UNPROFOR experience in which a diplomat could insert himself into the chain of command and block military action' (Clark, 2001: 63).

The interaction of the UK and US militaries in the region was relatively smooth in comparison to the frictions in the high-level diplomacy. This was thanks in no small part to the personal relationship between the US Chairman of the JCS, John Shalikashvilli, and British CDS, Peter Inge (Interview with Royal Air Force Air Chief Marshal, 2012). The RAF and USAF cooperated closely in the maintenance of the No Fly Zone, 'Operation Deny Flight', from Gioia delle Colle in Italy. This was the first time that NATO had used airpower coercively. Royal Navy and US Navy vessels operated together in 'Operation Sharp Guard' to enforce the naval blockade of weapons (Interview with Royal Navy Vice Admiral, 2012). UK aircraft carrier *HMS Invincible* was stationed in the Adriatic Sea along with the *USS Theodore Roosevelt* (Interview with Royal Navy Admiral, 2012). The British military were clear that if a greater level of force was to be used to coerce the various factions into a peace agreement, then it was imperative that the strength and sophistication of the US military be harnessed to that task.

In the summer of 1995 the situation in Bosnia had deteriorated with the Bosnian Serbs overrunning the UN Safe Havens, and Croatian forces going on to the offensive in the neighbouring Krajina. The US had come to fear that long-term damage was being done to NATO's reputation by operations in Bosnia and therefore decided to act. Renwick argued that, 'Anglo-American cooperation was vital in ensuring that NATO was re-configured to play a crucial part' (2016: xxi). The

UK, France, and the Netherlands assembled a Rapid Reaction Force and the US indicated that it would provide up to 25,000 troops in the event of a ground war (Clark, 2001: 53). A US-led bombing campaign, 'Operation Deliberate Force', was unleashed upon the Bosnian Serbs in a careful interweaving of airpower and diplomacy. Close coordination took place between the air forces commanded by US Lieutenant General Michael Ryan and the land forces under British Lieutenant General Rupert Smith (Peach, 2014: 90). The Bosnian Serb leadership quickly sued for peace. Hallion (2011: 122) argues that the air campaign was the decisive factor but, according to Kagan (2006: 189), the USAF drew misguided lessons from the operation because they assumed that airpower had been more decisive than it actually was. This was to have significance in the subsequent Kosovo campaign when President Milosevic of Serbia did not capitulate so swiftly.

The cessation of hostilities in 1995 did not bring an end to all of the Anglo-American differences and lesson learning over Bosnia. The Dayton Accords mandated the creation of a 60,000 strong NATO Implementation Force (IFOR) in which the UK contributed 13,000 (Codner, 2014: 15). It was succeeded in the following year by the NATO Stabilisation Force (SFOR). What became clear was that the British and US armies differed in their interpretation over how to carry out peace enforcement duties (Garofano, 2004: 254). The US, determined to minimize the risk of casualties, placed a heavy emphasis on force protection and insisted upon travelling around Bosnia in heavily armoured vehicles or helicopters (Interview with US Army Colonel, 2014). Such an approach afforded little opportunity to interact with civilians and conveyed a sense of remoteness and hostility to the local population.

By comparison, the British adopted a more people-centred approach, patrolling on foot where possible so as to ensure contact with the people and to build an intelligence picture. It was fortunate for both sides that the level of violence was limited; otherwise differences of approach between the British and Americans might have been more stark. The British were able to exert influence over their US counterparts at both the tactical and operational levels in the midst of the joint effort to stabilize Bosnia. '[I]n the NATO operation in the Balkans, (the British) tactical contribution and our embedded staff had greater influence (than subsequently in Iraq)' (British Army, 2010: 82)

Bosnia also demonstrated that stabilization missions could become protracted commitments. Rebuilding a society, entrenching the rule of law, and preventing a return to violence was a generational undertaking (Interview with British Army Lieutenant General, 2021). The US was a reluctant participant in the Balkans and repeatedly indicated its desire to disengage its forces and hand over the situation to allies. In 2000, when the George W. Bush administration was preparing to enter office, it signalled its intention to withdraw its peace-keeping forces from the Balkans. The British government responded by threatening to pull-out because it feared being left to administer the commitment alone.

Kosovo

The Kosovan campaign had echoes of what had occurred in Bosnia. It was in a similar region of the Balkans and involved the same protagonist, President Milosevic of Serbia. The situation differed in the sense that the US was closely involved from the outset. US Secretary of State Madeleine Albright was in the vanguard of those Western countries trying to stop Belgrade from persecuting the Albanian minority in the province of Kosovo. When international diplomacy at a peace conference at Rambouillet, France, failed to achieve that objective NATO launched a military campaign. British ground forces were moved into the region and they were preparing to fight their way into Kosovo as part of a NATO intervention. However, they were confronted by a wave of Kosovar civilians who were being driven out of the territory by Serb militias. The British forces had to reconfigure their role from warfighting to building refugee camps (Interview with British Army Major-General, 2013). An air campaign commenced and the Alliance was confident it could rapidly bring President Milosevic to the negotiating table.

Yet the air campaign, 'Operation Allied Force', failed to result in Serbia's speedy capitulation. The fact that the US was providing around 70% of the airpower and the UK providing about 10% was illustrative of the centrality of the USAF to the operation (Mason, 2004: 48). US aircraft possessed all-weather and night-time capabilities and their precision weapons reduced the risk of civilian collateral damage. However, the reluctance of the US to incur casualties resulted in air strikes being conducted from a high altitude of 15,000 feet, which reduced their efficacy (Smith and Latawski, 2003), and meant that far fewer Serbian tanks and armoured personnel carriers were destroyed (Weiner, 2009: 107). Chairman of the JCS, Henry Shelton, claimed that 120 tanks and over 450 artillery pieces had been wrecked in air strikes, but when US ground forces entered the province there was little evidence to support these claims (Rayburn and Sobchak, 2019: 9). The campaign was increased in intensity with almost a doubling of the aircraft (Kagan, 2006: 191) and the adoption of a broader target list, including Serbian bridges, railway lines, and power stations. The US military saw this as attacking Milosevic's 'centre of gravity' (Clark, 2001: 241) but even then Belgrade resisted for a total of 78 days. Using airpower for purposes of denial to undermine Milosevic's military operations proved harder than the advocates of airpower theory had imagined (Pape, 1997: 97).

The inability to achieve their objectives led to Anglo-American military disagreement over the prosecution of the conflict. The British were sceptical that the air campaign would be sufficient and insisted that a ground force invasion was necessary to convince the Serbs of NATO's determination (Shimko, 2010: 225). President Clinton was unwilling to commit ground forces, fearing that the US people would find large-scale casualties unacceptable. The US Joint Chiefs began a military planning process and estimated that it might require a force of between

175,000 and 250,000 troops (Clark, 2001: 302). Up to 170,000 were likely to come from the US and 35,000 might come from the UK (Jackson, 2007: 53).

Anglo-American tensions over ground forces persisted into the aftermath of the conflict when peace enforcement arrangements were being finalized. As the withdrawal of Serb forces was being negotiated, the Russians saw the opportunity to arrive with a contingent of their troops to take Pristina airfield. The US SACEUR, General Wesley Clark, ordered his British subordinate, Lieutenant General Mike Jackson, to block the airfield and prevent the Russian action. Jackson refused to carry out the order on the grounds that it could start a conflagration with Russia: he referred the matter up the chain of command to the British Chief of the Defence Staff and the US Chairman of the JCS (Jackson, 2007: 272–273). Personality clashes could undermine even close operational cooperation.

The experience of Anglo-American disagreement over ground forces for Kosovo led the British military to relax their traditional opposition to the creation of a military capability within the EU. It had demonstrated that US–UK interests could diverge in practice. At Helsinki in 1999, the UK embraced the concept of a defence capacity to be created within the Union and military forces identified for possible tasks. The British continued to champion the primacy of NATO in defence because it believed that the Alliance 'amplified' its intimacy with the US (Ministry of Defence, 2015: 14). In UK eyes the EU could only undertake tasks such as security sector reform and rule of law missions and not warfighting.

Two other issues came to characterize US dissatisfaction with the Kosovo experience. The US had run the air campaign in Kosovo under NATO auspices but had suffered the constraints of conducting targeting strategy through a coalition process. In the words of a future US ambassador to NATO, the US had won an 'ugly victory' (Daalder and O'Hanlon, 2001). Military officers were assigned by coalition countries but frequently referred matters back to national capitals before carrying out orders. This made it necessary to keep a complex structure of national actors informed about military operations (Kiszely, 2008: 11). A French military officer had leaked NATO plans to Belgrade. This influenced US thinking in the case of Afghanistan as the US became averse to carrying out operations within an alliance framework that added little extra military value (King, 2011)

The other lesson the US derived from Kosovo was over the implications of nation building for both OOTW and high-intensity conflict. Once a peace was agreed over Kosovo, NATO inserted a force to implement the agreement—KFOR (Kosovo Force). NATO found itself taking over the running of the state: providing food and heating supplies; engaging with criminals and strong men who controlled the distribution of goods, as well as moulding the context in which future elections could occur. The US came to understand that it needed to ensure the coordination of the military with civilian agencies to administer the society. It also needed to harness the expertise of international organizations, such as the EU and UN, to help to rebuild Kosovo. The UN Mission in Kosovo (UNMIK) was designed for this purpose. This lesson was to prove pertinent to the US experience of intervention in Iraq in 2003 when the US did not enjoy the broad-based support of the international community.

Libya and Syria

OOTW that occurred after Afghanistan and Iraq need to be seen in the light of those conflicts. It was a fundamentally different context because the searing experiences of Afghanistan and Iraq made political and military decision-makers wary of committing Western ground forces to conflicts in Muslim countries. US President Barack Obama entered office in January 2009 on a platform that Iraq was the 'dumb war' that America should never have started, whilst Afghanistan was a crucial conflict in which it had to prevail. The stomach for America to lead in conflicts had disappeared and been replaced by a weariness over the country expending blood and treasure in foreign wars. This quickly became apparent in 2011 in the Arab Spring when civil conflict broke out in Libya and there was pressure for international intervention. The Libyan conflict exposed America's new-found reluctance to act: a White House spokesperson talked of 'leading from behind' (Lizza, 2011).

The difficulty for the British military was that they lacked a viable alternative framework for action in the absence of US leadership. Although the EU had developed a defence dimension since 1999, and conducted limited missions in the Balkans and Africa (Howorth, 2007), the British had resisted full involvement in the Common Security and Defence Policy (CSDP). The British military clung both to NATO and to America's position of leadership in European defence. An often overlooked aspect was that the US had played an active role in encouraging Britain's scepticism towards EU defence efforts (Rees, 2017).

The conflict in Iraq drove a stake into the heart of CSDP because the UK cleaved to the Bush administration in the face of Franco-German condemnation. CSDP required an Anglo-French partnership to provide a meaningful capability for small- to medium-scale operations in which the US stood aside. This was never given an opportunity to flourish. Instead, Britain and France developed a modest bilateral defence relationship within the 2010 Lancaster House Treaty that facilitated their cooperation in mutually advantageous areas such as the defence industrial sector. A positive development was the creation of an Anglo-French Joint Expeditionary Force for limited operations. The British military invested further in their relationship with France by assisting with the operation in Mali by providing Chinook helicopters, C-17 heavy lift aircraft, and limited numbers of ground forces.

The Libyan conflict resulted in the UK and France taking the lead. But rather than pursue this through CSDP, it was undertaken within a NATO framework, made possible by President Nicholas Sarkozy's return of France in 2009 to the Alliance's Integrated Military Structure. The US assisted the NATO operation by creating a permissive air environment in which Libyan air defences were attacked and degraded (Joint Doctrine Publication 0-30, 2017). It also provided command and control, surveillance, and intelligence assets (Richards, 2014: 313). The UK Defence Select Committee noted that, 'future operations will not be possible if the US is not willing or able to provide capabilities such as unmanned aerial vehicles, intelligence and refuelling aircraft' (Defence Select Committee, 2012: 8). France provided the greater part of the air power but the UK made important contributions, such as the Sentinel intelligence gathering platform and Apache attack helicopters. The two countries mounted largely independent military operations within a NATO framework (Interview with Royal Air Force Air Marshal, 2020). Critics of 'Operation Odyssey Dawn', such as Russia and China, later contended that the Western operation that removed the Gaddafi regime exceeded the UN Security Council mandate embodied in Resolution 1973.

Like Libya, the Syrian civil war was one in which no Western armed forces were eager to become involved, yet it differed from Libya in the sense that a more complex array of foreign actors became drawn into the violence. The government of Bashir Assad was fighting rebels across Syria and appealed to Iran and Russia for assistance. The conflict also pulled in the Islamic State in the Levant (ISIL), or Daesh, which established a caliphate in the city of Racca, as well as the Kurds in Northern Iraq and Southern Turkey.

In 2013, the administration of President Barack Obama had warned the Syrian regime that the use of chemical weapons against the rebels was a red-line that would result in retaliatory action by US forces. However, when the Syrian government forces used chemical weapons in September, the US drew back from conducting airstrikes because of a lack of support from its allies. The British Prime Minister David Cameron had been approached by the US but had failed to obtain backing for airstrikes within the House of Commons. The lack of UK military support was a factor in the Obama administration retreating from its intended course of action. Such an event had practical consequences on the military relationship, as British planners at US Central Command were requested to withdraw from participation in Syrian issues after the Parliamentary vote (Interview with British Army Lieutenant General, 2015).

In September of the following year, the US launched a coalition against ISIL/Daesh. The aim was to arrest the expansion that the group had achieved in both Syria and Iraq and to reduce the size of the territory under its control. Turkish and Syrian Democratic Front (SDF) forces provided the ground element along with small contingents of US and British special forces. The US, UK, France, and other countries provided the air power in 'Operation Inherent Resolve'. UK airstrikes, as part of 'Operation Shader', were undertaken by Tornado and Typhoon aircraft from the sovereign base on Cyprus. The RAF estimated that it killed over 4000 militants in these strikes (Fisher, 2020: 13).

Narratives

Narratives relating to OOTW were difficult to fashion because both the British and American armed services were unsure of the way forward in the post-Cold War environment. There was a lack of clarity about what they were trying to do and uncertainty about what demands would arise in interventionary operations. The need to assemble coalitions of countries made it imperative to assert the legitimacy of the mandate under which operations were conducted. Whether carried out under the auspices of NATO or through ad hoc coalitions, the UK–US bilateral relationship formed the nucleus of Western actions. According to former US Ambassador to NATO, Robert Hunter, the US valued the UK's global perspective (Foreign Affairs Select Committee, 2009) and its willingness to participate in operations outside of the European theatre. British Prime Minister Tony Blair played a leading role, through his speech to the Economic Club in Chicago, in constructing a 'Doctrine of International Community' to justify Western military intervention (Blair, 1999). Blair argued that sovereignty was not unbounded and that states had obligations to act within moral constraints, otherwise the international community was justified in considering armed intervention to protect human rights (Fiddes, 2017: 131).

When potential interventions arose, what the US required were allies that would commit themselves to contingency operations. This is precisely what the British military were prepared to do. They offered substantial combat power even when the mission was ill-defined and the doctrine was untested. Not only would the British make the second largest contribution after the US, but they would ensure that these forces were of the highest quality. The British chose some of their brightest and best officers for secondment or to be embedded in operational roles within US structures (Interview with British Defence Attache, 2014). The impact of these officers was multiplied by the fact that they were granted greater latitude by their American hosts. With its hierarchical and centralized approach (Aylwin-Foster, 2005: 32), the US granted disproportionate influence to British officers. US General David Petraeus complimented the contribution of British personnel on his staff in Iraq, 'the lead writer of our Joint Comprehensive Plan was a brilliant British colonel. In fact, for my tenure of MNF–I [Multinational Forces Iraq], our lead campaigners were British officers' (quoted in British Army, 2010: 81).

In addition, the British made a point of embracing roles and desisting from imposing constraints on their involvement. They allowed their forces to be sent into conflict zones or employed at night. The British assisted the US in bringing other countries into the coalition and served as the liaison with allied states. One of the roles of the British military, as second in command, was to listen to the views of partner countries and ensure their continuing support (Interview with Royal Navy Admiral, 2015).

Conclusion

Path dependency was not possible in OOTW because much of the experience was new and the UK and the US found themselves in unpredictable situations. The UK was not a rule-taker in the OOTW domain because the 'rules of the game' were fluid. There was more pulling and hauling in this aspect of the Anglo-American military relationship and therefore greater opportunity for UK entrepreneurship to shape the debate. It took the British military several years to switch their own defence strategy from one focused on the defence of Europe, with heavy armoured regiments, to a contingency-based posture based around mobile brigades (Terriff and Osinga, 2010: 197). The 1998 Strategic Defence Review was the working-out of that altered mindset. The British military were eager to exploit the influence they were able to exert on their American counterparts.

It is a tribute to the resilience of the military relationship that their two armed forces proved able to adapt to the challenges of peacemaking, peace enforcement, and peacekeeping. The institutionalized relationship aided the process of adjusting to change and facilitated new patterns of collaboration. Personal relationships between British and American officers smoothed this process. The British military were prepared to engage in difficult issues and, led by both Conservative and Labour governments, developed policies where Washington was unenthusiastic. This was a phase of the Anglo-American relationship where the UK was pushing for change and the US were hesitant. Nevertheless, the US valued the contribution that the UK made to these types of operations and, in turn, the British helped the US to 'expunge an entrenched Cold War mentality' (Kretchik, 2011: 263).

The process was not without its frictions. Transitioning from the predictability of the Cold War to the vagaries of post-Cold War 'wars of choice' was difficult. There were tensions between the US and British militaries over the political objectives to be pursued, the size and nature of the forces to commit, the intensity of force to be employed, and the level of casualties that were tolerated. OOTW exposed differences in the way the US and the UK approached conflicts as well as the importance they attached to organizations such as the UN (Interview with Royal Air Force Air Chief Marshal, 2012). In the case of crises in the Balkans and Libya, the British military were to be found calling for a more substantial engagement than even the US was willing to provide. The British were pressing for more ground forces and for a more sustained post-conflict presence than the US.

What was striking about many of these conflicts was the US reluctance to lead. Because the US saw no interests of their own at stake, they were lukewarm about involvement. In Bosnia and Libya, the US either hung back or let their allies take the lead. Haass (1997) describes this as the 'reluctant sheriff' syndrome. The experiences of becoming involved further chastened the US and they emerged determined not to intervene elsewhere. In the case of Syria, they chose to use only air power and let local forces undertake the ground campaign. The UK believed it was necessary that the US acted as the glue to keep Western powers together. A key way to influence the US was to be alongside it in its interventions around the world. Prime Minister Tony Blair argued that 'the price of influence is that we do not leave the US to face the tricky issues alone' (quoted in Danchev, 2003: 18).

6

Insurgency and Low Intensity Conflict

Introduction

Low-intensity, or counter-insurgency (COIN) conflict, became one of the defining experiences of the Anglo-American military relationship during the conflicts in Iraq and Afghanistan. The high intensity conflicts against the Taliban in 2001 and the Iraqi Army in 2003 were followed by protracted insurgencies. These involved coalition forces confronting a mixture of irregular forces, ranging from Taliban and former Iraqi soldiers, to militiamen and foreign jihadists. Whilst the main fight for each country was over, US and UK forces experienced ambushes, hit and run operations, and the use of improvised explosive devices (IEDs), in Iraq up to the time of the US withdrawal in 2011 and in Afghanistan until 2014. US and British Army servicemen became caught up in a civil war between the Sunni and Shia communities in Iraq, as a major shift of power took place towards the Shia. In Afghanistan, having driven the Taliban from government, the insurgency was focused on unseating the pro-western Karzai regime. Thus began the period of the so-called 'Forever Wars' where Anglo-American forces suffered casualties at the same time as trying to pacify the two countries and conduct reconstruction.

Insurgencies are not inevitable outcomes of post-conflict situations. The invasions of both Afghanistan and Iraq were carried out by small, technological forces fighting against much less well-armed adversaries (see Chapter 4). Yet the very nature of those victories set the stage for the ensuing insurgencies. The ease with which the US and the UK achieved their objectives bred complacency and left both sides with in-theatre military forces that were inadequate to the task of stabilizing and policing entire countries (Shimko, 2010: 162). The insurgencies in Afghanistan and Iraq required high numbers of troops in the theatre, something that did not exist in the aftermath of either conflict. In Iraq, the US and the UN had anticipated a humanitarian crisis involving shortages of food and medical supplies but this did not come to pass. The expectation had been that coalition forces would be received as liberators, that democracy would take hold, and that invasion forces could speedily withdraw. Instead, the cessation of combat operations was accompanied by chaos and looting, yet the US reduced the inflow of troops to Iraq who might have stabilized the situation. Similarly, the British Chief of the Defence Staff (CDS), Sir Michael Walker, did not order a review of force levels in Iraq in the summer of 2003 or spring of 2004 (House of Commons, 2016: 94 and 96).

The Anglo-American Military Relationship. Wyn Rees, Oxford University Press. © Wyn Rees (2024).
DOI: 10.1093/oso/9780198884620.003.0006

The mistakes made in the preparations for the war against Iraq were exacerbated by decisions made in its aftermath. Paul Bremer, Head of the Coalition Provisional Authority (CPA), issued edicts in May 2003 that fundamentally altered the dynamics of the situation. Bremer decided to postpone handing back power to Iraqi leaders; to extensively de-Baathify the Iraqi government, and to disband the Iraqi Army, leaving a reservoir of armed but unemployed men who were rapidly co-opted into the insurgency. These errors were compounded by the 'fratricidal' relationship that existed between the CPA and the US military commander in Iraq, Lieutenant General Ricardo Sanchez (Rayburn and Sobchak, 2019: 322; Synnott, 2008: 20). The insurgency arose principally in urban centres around Baghdad, in the Sunni Triangle in the north that included Anbar province and the region of Saddam's home town of Tikrit.

The warfighting stages of both conflicts had convinced indigenous forces that engaging with the US and UK militaries in a head-on confrontation would result in defeat. Consequently, those hostile to a Western occupation were motivated to resist it asymmetrically (Galula, 1964). Once this resistance gained momentum, it drew in fighters from abroad who were eager to make common cause against Western troops and it spawned the emergence of al-Qaeda in Iraq (AQI). It was fuelled by arms and explosive device technology from Iran that supported Shia militant groups. In the words of Foreign Secretary William Hague (2010), 'Our armed forces are currently involved in fighting . . . wars-amongst-the-people'.

In the case of Afghanistan, the US and the UK became engaged against a largely rural insurgency. The routing of the Taliban led the US to switch attention to the emerging conflict with Saddam Hussein's Iraq. This hiatus made it possible for the Taliban to regroup in Pakistan—in the Federally Administered Tribal Areas— and then infiltrate back across the border and commence their campaign. The coalition forces occupied the urban centres and the insurgency drew strength from exploiting sanctuaries in Pakistan. Simpson described the Afghan Taliban as a 'fragmented franchise organisation' (2012: 52 and 75), whilst General David Richards described them as a mix of 'hard line militant Islamists . . . drug barons and alienated tribal chiefs' (Richards, 2009). Two of the most potent elements were the Haqqani network and the group led by Gulbuddin Hekmatyar.

Rules

It was evident from the early stages of the Iraqi insurgency that both the US Army and the British Army lacked robust and well-practiced doctrine for COIN. 'The US military has . . . viewed insurgency warfare as unglamorous, unwanted and diverting' (Egnell, 2009: 59), a view confirmed by the fact that the US Army Manual in 1986 had contained only seven paragraphs on the subject (Kretchik, 2011: 212). The US historical experience of COIN has been an unhappy one, having been associated with failure in Vietnam. State-building tasks were also viewed as inappropriate distractions for military forces (see Chapter 5). The US Army went on to regard COIN with disdain, seeing it as an aberration from its core mission (Finlan, 2014: 80). The rebuilding of the US military after Vietnam was based on the expectation of high intensity conflict against a peer adversary such as the Soviet military (Long, 2016).

Countering an insurgency campaign is hugely complex. Hammes (2005: 189) contends that insurgencies are examples of 'fourth generation warfare' in which actors employ an information age strategy designed to change the minds of Western decision-makers by inflicting disproportionate costs. Such wars are fought across all dimensions: namely 'political, economic, social and military'. In both Afghanistan and Iraq, the US and UK found themselves trying to co-ordinate a multiplicity of objectives that included trying to defeat insurgents, conduct reconstruction and development operations, train local security forces, and lay the foundations for handing political control to local forces. In the words of Serena (2011: 58), military operations of this nature called for 'unparalleled dexterity'. There were notable differences between the British and American approaches that resulted in tension between the two sides.

Whilst US doctrine acknowledged the need for a politico-military strategy in Phase IV, it tended to treat stabilization as part of COIN and accorded primacy to its military (Pounds, 2013: 226). Although kinetic operations were recognized to be one among several components of a successful strategy, there was a tendency to resort to search and destroy missions. With their technological superiority, US military culture remained wedded to the use of overwhelming numbers and the application of firepower (Mackinlay, 2004: 90). British Brigadier Aylwin-Foster was on attachment to US forces in Iraq during the insurgency and he wrote that the US Army's strategic culture was bureaucratic, overly hierarchical, and wedded to offensive operations (2005: 28). Security was regarded as a vital pre-condition before other aspects of policy and the work of other agencies could be delivered. This rendered US doctrine 'better focused for the guerrilla stage of an insurgency' (Pounds, 2013: 229) and less appropriate for the rebuilding phase. Amidst the complications of an insurgency, the military needs to be both capable and willing to move up and down the spectrum of conflict to suit the prevailing circumstances. They must be committed to building close relationships with the security forces of the host nation and be prepared to hand over control to indigenous security forces as quickly as practicable.

The British recognized that the military was just one component of the overall effort and not necessarily the most important part. After combat, Phase IV operations would quickly come to dominate and this would be the longest phase, involving political, economic, and social reconstruction. The UK appreciated that the political objective was the foremost consideration: the military defeat of the Taliban was secondary to winning the support of the population through delivering improved services (Farrell, Rynning, and Terriff, 2013: 164). Stabilization had to focus on reconstruction, even when the legitimacy of state structures might be in question. In the words of Defence Secretary Robert Gates, 'Kinetic operations should be subordinated to measures to promote participation in government, economic progress to spur development and efforts to address grievances' (quoted in Joint Doctrine Publication JDP 3-40, 2009: chapter 4). The US perpetuated the divide between the military and civilian agencies and accorded its military the lead role (Egnell, 2009: 75).

The US lacked appropriate doctrine for moving from high intensity combat to Phase IV stability and COIN operations (Serena, 2011: 66). The US culture of kinetic operations and the targeting of insurgents made them psychologically ill-suited to transitioning to Phase IV. The ethic within the US military was that their forces could prevail against any adversary and it was misguided to place constraints upon them (Interview with British Army Major-General, 2013). By contrast, the ethos of the British Army enabled it to transition swiftly from a war-fighting stance to one more appropriate for post-conflict operations (Egnell, 2011: 298). There were echoes here of the old argument that Britain brought intelligence and sophistication to the Anglo-American relationship whilst the US provided the money and the brawn.

The British were more open than the US to a multi-agency approach in Phase IV operations. A multi-agency approach requires the subordination of the military effort as soon as a tolerable level of security has been achieved (Joint Doctrine Publication JDP 3-40, 2009). As a superpower, the US had less experience of building consensus with international governmental organizations and was predisposed to act alone. The US military was reluctant to cede primacy to other actors and it was not until November 2005 that the US Department of Defense published Directive 3000.5 in which it recognized the need for multi-agency operations to deal with complex emergencies. By contrast, in the case of Afghanistan, the UK supported early participation by NATO, the UN, and the European Union. The UK had experience of working in conflict zones with coalition partners and with multilateral organizations. It recognized the need to work cooperatively amongst a group of member states in order to move a post-conflict country forward. In Iraq, the UK welcomed the involvement of the United Nations (Synnott, 2008: 35), despite US misgivings, but the initiative was undermined by the bombing of UN headquarters in Baghdad in August 2003. The British military accepted that their role was to create a secure environment in which civilian agencies could engage.

The British took this a stage further and developed the so-called 'Comprehensive Approach' in which all coalition agencies, military and civilian, had to be aligned with the political objective (House of Commons, 2010). The challenge for the UK in implementing the Comprehensive Approach was to get its various government departments to act in concert: the military, the Foreign and Commonwealth Office, and the Department for International Development (DfID).

By giving one overall responsibility, the other departments risked drawing back and leaving it to the lead agency. The Post-Conflict Reconstruction Unit (PCRU) was created across the three departments in 2004 in an attempt to transcend this organizational stove-piping. The UK Ministry of Defence (MoD) produced a Joint Discussion Note in 2005 entitled 'The Comprehensive Approach'. It was followed in March 2007 by a Joint Doctrine Note and became a part of defence doctrine in August 2008. Based on the experiences in both Iraq and Afghanistan, it was recognized that inadequate resources had been devoted to the PCRU and a new version was created in 2007, the Stabilisation Unit. This became an influential part of a broader NATO development (see Chapter 5).

Inter-service relationships

Conducting COIN campaigns in Iraq and Afghanistan was the responsibility of the British Army rather than the other two services. Between the British Army and the US Army, COIN proved to be a source of antagonism. Mumford (2017) makes the case that contending approaches towards COIN strategy had long been a cause of tension, rather than amity, in the Anglo-American relationship. The British were able to draw on COIN experiences from their colonial history, such as in Kenya, Malaya, and Oman (Porter, 2010: 362). In the case of Northern Ireland, they had obtained extensive experience of confronting a determined adversary (Interview with British Army Lieutenant General, 2021). Nagl (2005) argued that the campaign in Malaya was a role model for good COIN practice as the focus had been upon the civilian population, the British were successful in isolating the insurgents and operations had been underpinned by intelligence. Yet historical hostility towards the British Empire made the US Army reluctant to learn from the experience of their ally (Long, 2016).

There was a sense within the British Army that their structure and training were better adapted to the requirements of a COIN campaign than their US counterparts. The regimental system was judged to be more appropriate to COIN warfare because lessons learned at a local level could rapidly percolate into doctrine (Mackinlay, 2004: 90). Furthermore, the more decentralized command structure of the British Army and its lesser reliance on technology rendered it more nimble in responding to threats. The UK concept of mission command was one in which senior officers set the objective and then subordinates were left to determine how to achieve it. According to Egnell, 'the idea behind mission command is to increase and improve the ability to deal with fluid and disorderly situations' (2011: 24) and this contrasted with the more hierarchical approach of the US armed forces (Kiszely, 2013: 125).

Whilst the British Army believed it was more historically experienced in COIN and better suited to its demands, there was limited opportunities for the

cross-fertilization of ideas with the US. The two armies were responsible for separate areas in both Iraq and Afghanistan and the tempo of operations left few
openings for the two sides to compare approaches. With American forces experiencing more violence in the north of Iraq early on in the campaign, the British
were confirmed in their view that they were pursuing a superior approach in the
south. As the intensity of the insurgency increased in the north, General David
Richards, Assistant Chief of the General Staff, suggested that British troops from
Basra could be sent to Baghdad to assist with urban patrolling and with working
with the Iraqi police. However, the Chiefs of Staff rejected such an initiative, fearful that their resources would be stretched (Richards, 2014: 174). In October 2004
a British regiment of the Black Watch moved to Camp Dogwood, near Baghdad, to
support US forces during the US Marine Corps offensive in Fallujah. Apart from
this deployment, British forces remained in the south and this added to US Army
resentment of the British.

Practices

Iraq

The tensions between the differing priorities and operational concepts of the US
and the UK towards COIN and stability operations were quickly evident in Iraq.
These contrasting approaches existed within a political context in which the US
supplanted the Office for Reconstruction and Humanitarian Assistance (ORHA)
with the CPA as an interim governing structure under UN Security Council Resolution 1438. Despite the UK arguing for a swift handover of political power to
Iraqi authorities, and transferring power to Iraqi governors within their areas of
control, the US deferred the holding of elections (Greenstock, 2016). It was clear
from an early stage that there would be strains between the two countries over their
approaches to post-war Iraq and that the UK would enjoy only limited influence.
For example, there was not even a clear reporting line from the CPA to Whitehall.
British criticism of the US began to increase, albeit it was voiced privately rather
than in public.

    Long notes that, 'The US Army's actual conduct of COIN in Iraq from 2003 to
2006 seldom matched the written doctrine' (2016: 180). US commanders prosecuted the conflict according to traditional organizational ideas and resorted to
overwhelming force to counter insurgent activity. This was true of the Fourth
Infantry Division and the Eighty-Second Airborne Division located in Anbar
Province (Egnell, 2011). Most notoriously, the US Marine Corps used intense violence in its operation Vigilant Resolve to clear Fallujah of insurgents in the summer
and autumn of 2004—a policy that was driven primarily by US political leaders

(Barry, 2020: 206–207). This included the regular use of air strikes and heavy artillery. Such operations alienated the bulk of the population who either fled as refugees or stayed in their homes and risked being killed. It incurred the criticism of British commanders (McColl, 2013: 116). Richards noted that, 'the US Army is trying to turn around a culture that is built on the very successful "warrior" ethos' (2014: 260). The US was determined to take on, defeat, and clear insurgents from areas under their control.

US military culture was unsuited to the restraint necessary for the effective application of COIN principles in Iraq. Civilian reconstruction was subordinated to military operations and, as the insurgency increased in ferocity, non-military efforts became sidelined. A tolerable level of security for US forces was unobtainable. In certain provinces to the north of Baghdad, the US found themselves engaged in ferocious combat. The US also had to operate as a strategic reserve to support coalition partners that were under pressure in other parts of the country. In August 2004, for example, the US deployed a Stryker battalion from Mosul to Multi-National Division Centre South (MNDCS) to help deal with unrest there (Graham, 2013: 104). Improving local services was made difficult by the chronic insecurity in the country. In contrast, the British made efforts to improve the lives of Iraqi civilians. In the words of Garfield, 'the British approach to stability and reconstruction . . . achieved some success in Iraq, ensuring greater stability, fewer casualties, less alienation and more reconstruction' (quoted in Egnell, 2011: 144).

British forces regarded their US allies as heavy-handed. Wither (2006: 51) cites a House of Commons Foreign Affairs Committee report that criticized US forces for being wedded to kinetic responses. One reason that explains the different approaches was that British forces did not place the same premium as their US counterparts on 'clearing' the enemy from a locality (US Army Field Manual 3-24, 2006). For the British, it was acceptable to disrupt insurgent actions within the area of operations rather than kill or capture them. The British military saw their role as providing security in order that other agencies, focused on political dialogue and development, could be empowered to operate within the contested space (Joint Doctrine Publication JDP 3-40, 2009: 58).

A second reason was that, under Operation Telic, the British did not control such violent areas of Iraq as the Americans. In Multinational Division South East (MNDSE), they had been given the southern districts of Basra, Maysan, al-Muthanna, and Thi Qar. This was a region of Iraq that had experienced persecution under Saddam so there was initial goodwill towards the British occupiers. Even though there had been limited British preparations for Phase IV operations (House of Commons, 2016: 86), the Army were initially able to patrol in Basra in berets rather than helmets. They were careful to avoid the use of intensive firepower in military operations and prided themselves on a low-key approach. With the departure of Spanish forces in April 2004, the US invited UK forces to extend their area of control to include parts of the central region but this was declined (Rayburn and Sobchak, 2019: 266).

A third reason was that US agencies had their own competing visions of the task in Iraq and they were reluctant to work to a single, coordinated plan. When Robert Gates replaced Donald Rumsfeld as US Secretary of Defense, he was frustrated to find that the Pentagon was devoting only part of its energies towards the conflicts in Iraq and Afghanistan (Gates, 2014: 122). The earlier emphasis on transformation and technology were in tension with COIN's emphasis on the human and cultural dimensions of conflict (Weisner, 2013). Gates insisted that the US armed forces prioritize the ongoing conflicts and pushed through procurement programmes, such as mine-resistant ambush protected (MRAP) vehicles, that were essential to troops operating in both theatres.

British criticism of their ally's operations caused friction with the US military. American commanders thought that the British were under-estimating the severity of the violence that was occurring (Elliott, 2015: 109). Nevertheless, it helped in October 2004 to prompt an overhaul of US COIN doctrine that was undertaken in cooperation with British advisers (Wither, 2006: 52). Both militaries came to place greater emphasis on the need to win over the civilian population as well as train local partners with whom to share security responsibilities. This new thinking was taught at the COIN Centre for Excellence at Taji, near Baghdad, to US officers that were taking over command of units within Iraq (Alderson, 2013: 288).

In 2005, General David Petraeus led a team at Fort Leavenworth that delivered in the following year a new blueprint for US COIN strategy: Field Manual 3-24 (Interview with British Army Brigadier, 2014); Interview with US Army Colonel, 2014). With the help of advisers such as David Kilcullen (Nacos, 2016: 248), and cooperation from the US Marine Corps, the new strategy devoted considerably greater attention to the need to protect the Iraqi civilian population, as the operation's revised centre of gravity. This had the effect of bringing US and UK doctrine into closer alignment (Joint Doctrine Publication JDP 3-40, 2009: 55). It recognized that support from civilians was essential to the success of the coalition campaign, and that it could only be obtained by incentivizing them to assist the security forces. To this end the US would only use minimum force and would conduct operations that were intelligence-led. Intelligence would provide an understanding of the conflict as well as information about how to target the adversary. It would be obtained by moving US forces out of their fortified compounds and dispersing them to live in police stations and guard houses amongst the population. They were encouraged to patrol locally and to provide greater security reassurance to the people. The aim was to separate the insurgents from the population and to facilitate an increase in development activity such as the re-building of infrastructure, schools, and medical facilities. FM 3-24 became the 'coalition strategy for Iraq in 2007' (Finlan, 2014: 194).

Growing US tensions with the UK

After April 2004, the British sectors came to experience higher levels of violence, sparked by the conflict that American forces were experiencing in the north. The honeymoon period that the UK had enjoyed in the south of Iraq came to an end and a period of intense and brutal violence commenced. In areas such as Maysan and Basra, Shia militias were asserting their control and the most powerful was the 'Mahdi army', or Jaish al-Mahdi (JAM), led by the cleric Moqtada al-Sadr. The British Army found itself under constant attack, its patrols ambushed on the streets and its bases shelled by mortars.

After the invasion, the British had drawn down to only a brigade. By the time of the upsurge in Shia violence there was a presence of a mere 8600 personnel, resulting in inadequate British forces to carry out extensive COIN operations (Egnell, 2011: 142). Had a larger force been available and a more robust strategy adopted, the conflict with the Shia militias might have been resolved at an early stage (British Army, 2010: 75). The UK was slow to acknowledge the rising levels of violence and adapt its equipment to the increasing threat. Inadequate force protection, such as soft-skinned Land Rovers and insufficient body armour, resulted in mounting casualties and declining morale. Without the requisite resources, the British Army were restricted to their operational bases. They appeared too eager, in the eyes of their ally, to hand over responsibility to Iraqi security forces.

Under the leadership of Major General Richard Shirreff, attempts were made between October 2006 and the spring of 2007 to regain the initiative by instigating 'Operation Sinbad' (Fairweather, 2011). Sinbad was a toned-down version of 'Operation Salamanca', a more ambitious and kinetic plan that was never carried out (British Army, 2010: 49). A source of British weakness was the inadequate development of the Iraqi security forces to the point where they would have been confident of their ability to combat the militias. The British had failed to follow the US example of embedding their forces within Iraqi army units (Elliott, 2015: 110). There were also weaknesses within the Iraqi police. The British had lacked a gendarmerie style training force that would have been more appropriate to the threat (Stewart, 2013: 86). The police had been infiltrated by forces influenced by Iran and were highly sectarian. Operation Sinbad was a determined effort, albeit with limited forces, to reverse the decline in the UK's control of Basra and its surrounding regions.

The US perception was that the British were slow to adapt to the changing situation (Barry, 2020: 323) and had abdicated responsibility for providing security because of a lack of both the resources and the political will to overcome the JAM (Foreign Affairs Select Committee, 2010). The sense of US dissatisfaction was exacerbated by two factors. First, in February 2007 the British announced they were reducing their troop presence to just 5000. Second, in 'Operation Zenith', the British pulled out of Basra city and relocated to a base at the airport. The British rationale was that they had become targeted by Shia militias that were fighting for power. The Army saw themselves as caught up in the middle of a fight that was not their own and reached an accommodation with the Shia militias after a period of sustained fighting. The contrast between the strategic direction of the US and the UK was stark. Whilst the US was preparing for a 'surge' of over 40 000 extra troops designed to assert control, the UK had removed its contingent to a position of relative seclusion (Dannatt, 2016). The US suspected that the British action was a precursor to withdrawal from Iraq altogether (Strachan, 2013a: 332).

A gulf had emerged between the UK and the US in Iraq. The UK failed to obtain the influence over strategic policy that it had expected its contribution to the war merited (Interview with British Army Lieutenant General, 2015). Part of that failure reflected US dominance in the politico-military decision-making of the coalition. British commanders conducted operations in their area of responsibility that were distinct from the broader US campaign plan (Fry, 2014: 234). Yet part of the failure can also be ascribed to the British military that failed to exploit its command positions within the US structure. In April 2004, the US had divided its command in Iraq. Multinational Forces Iraq (MNF–I) remained as the overall coalition headquarters based in the Green Zone in Baghdad, with a British deputy. In addition, a Multinational Corps Iraq (MNC–I) was created at Baghdad Airport, with a British officer as one of the three deputies under an overall US commander. According to Lieutenant General Andrew Graham, 'From a British perspective, establishing British deputies to both four- and three-star levels of command improved the UK's capacity to influence, engage, monitor and contribute' (2013: 98). However, the British did not capitalize on the influence they could have exerted on the Americans at the strategic level and failed to appreciate that the US was focused on Baghdad and the overall campaign in Iraq (Interview with British Army Lieutenant General, 2021; Synnott, 2008: 41). The British remained focused on their own tactical concerns in the south (Elliott, 2015: 179). According to a senior British officer alongside General Casey, 'there were close links between Permanent Joint HQ and CENTCOM in Tampa but there was remarkably little interest in what we were doing in Baghdad' (Parker, 2013: 134).

This lack of influence was evident as the US military began their 'surge' of additional forces into Iraq. Because the US viewed the British as in the process of extricating themselves from Basra, this major change in US strategic posture was undertaken, 'with no apparent prior consultation with the UK' (Shaw, 2013: 176). President Bush had taken a surprise decision based on a case made to him by retired General Jack Keane and contrary to the advice of his Army Chief of Staff, General Peter Schoomaker (Robinson, 2008: 27). Under the command of General David Petraeus, the US Army was told its troops had to live amongst the Iraqi population to build relationships with them and to generate locally derived intelligence. The White House regarded America's credibility to be at stake in Iraq and it was unwilling to leave the country amidst a perception of defeat. The US government committed greatly increased resources to stabilize the situation.

It would be misleading to convey the impression that the British military had no influence upon broader US strategic policy. Two examples illustrate the fact that British ideas were taken seriously and helped to shape the direction of US thinking. One was in 2007 when Sunni tribes in the central region of Iraq were lured away from the jihadists at the centre of the insurgency. The Central Intelligence Agency (CIA) and Britain's Secret Intelligence Service (SIS) had developed contacts amongst the tribal leaders (Urban, 2010) and it had become evident that many of them had grown disaffected by the brutality of Al-Qaeda in Iraq (AQI). Lieutenant General Graeme Lambe, Deputy Commander MNF-1, was instrumental in convincing General David Petraeus that contacts should be initiated with some of the Sunni tribes in order to bring them over to the side of the coalition (Robinson, 2008: 177). The US was willing to embrace this British initiative as it gave senior American officers the potential to disavow the outreach effort if it failed (Interview with British Army Lieutenant General, 2012). The US Marine Corps developed cooperation with the Hamza Brigade in Anbar Province and with representatives of the Anbar People's Council in Ramadi. Local militias were recognized, trained, and paid by the US and these forces helped to drive out Al-Qaeda elements from their localities. The so-called 'Anbar Awakening' was a significant plank in turning around America's faltering position in the country and it owed much to the initiative of the British.

The other example was the activities of US Joint Special Operations Command (JSOC) under the command of General Stanley McChrystal. It was responsible for conducting special operations on an industrial scale against high value insurgent targets, including AQI operatives led by Musab al-Zarqawi. The British Special Air Service and Special Boat Service played a major role in these operations (Urban, 2010). They operated by maintaining blanket surveillance, by monitoring the mobile telephone network, and then conducting night-time raids (Interview with British Army Lieutenant General, 2015a). Operations included the targeting of high profile jihadis and insurgent commanders, the disrupting of their operations, and the gathering of intelligence. The British and the Americans worked well together, based on high levels of trust and mutual respect.

In spite of these successes, US military concerns about the weak British position in the south of Iraq continued. Eventually it came to a crisis in March 2008 when the Iraqi Prime Minister, Nouri al-Maliki, decided to intervene in Basra to counteract the Shia militias. Maliki initiated this intervention in the south without consulting the British, whom he disliked, or the Americans (Interview with British Army Major-General, 2012). His action forced the hand of US commanders in Baghdad who were unwilling to risk the failure of the Iraqi government. They moved resources in Maliki's support, including Military Transition Teams (MiTT) that trained the Iraqi Army, predator drones, and attack helicopters. Although the

British provided artillery support, their lack of involvement was symptomatic of the low level of contact with their US counterparts (British Army, 2010: 6). The so-called 'Charge of the Knights' proved to be a successful episode from the viewpoint of the Iraqi and American governments because it drove the JAM out of the city. But it threw a pall over the British role in Basra (Porter, 2010: 368). It reflected a long-standing Anglo-American divergence over the merits of confronting and seeking to defeat the militias (Rayburn and Sobchak, 2019: 302). The British subsequently pulled their forces out of Iraq.

Afghanistan

There were two military missions operating simultaneously in Afghanistan after the initial defeat of the Taliban: 'Operation Enduring Freedom' in the east in which US forces continued to hunt al-Qaeda, and the NATO International Security Assistance Force (ISAF) designed to stabilize the country. European states involved in ISAF had expected their role to involve armed peacekeeping and development but, after the resurgence of the Taliban in 2005, they found themselves being drawn into COIN operations (Gates, 2014: 203). Many countries were unprepared to put their forces at risk and pressed to operate in relatively peaceful parts of the country or imposed caveats upon how their forces were employed. The British chose to provide unrestricted support to the US-led mission. From December 2002, Britain led the ISAF based upon its framework nation role in the Allied Rapid Reaction Corps (ARRC). The British had sought to have ISAF placed under the command of CENTCOM but this had been vetoed by both Donald Rumsfeld and the German government (Barry, 2020: 85).

Afghanistan presented a difficult challenge for the US and the UK. It was a desperately poor country, ravaged by decades of civil war and without a government capable of exerting authority over the entire territory. There was no politico-security framework to whom Western militaries could handover control. Security agencies were lacking, there was no army or police force that was capable of operating effectively and corruption was rampant. Anglo-American efforts at security sector reform to create a centralized, Western style army and police force proved problematic. Furthermore, judicial structures within society were either missing or in their infancy. There was little functioning court system outside of some of the major cities. Even regional governors were often former warlords or enjoyed political power due to their links with the Karzai government. This meant that UK and US forces needed to counter the insurgency whilst simultaneously building the organs of government and security.

The US and UK had a poor understanding of Afghan society when they intervened. The armed forces of both countries appreciated the need for a strong cultural understanding of the target society (Interview with former Chief of the

Defence Staff, 2015), but neither really comprehended the complexities of the Afghan tribal system nor what motivated people to fight. US forces operated for 12- or 15-month tours of duty whilst British forces only stayed for 6 months (British Army, 2010: 4). The result was that UK brigade commanders entered the theatre with a short window of time in which to implement their own ideas. This militated against a long-term, consistent strategy and encouraged high profile initiatives. It was not until they became bogged down in protracted insurgencies that the US and the UK immersed themselves in studying Afghan society. The US developed a Foreign Military Studies Office (Joint Doctrine Publication JDP 3-40, 2009: chapter 3) and subsequently recruited anthropologists to assist their understanding of the context in which they were operating.

The British took the decision to move into Helmand province in 2006 with the aim of extending the Afghan government's area of control. 16 Air Assault Brigade were the lead unit and were followed subsequently by 3 Commando Brigade of the Royal Marines. The British Army were eager to make a bigger contribution and, with the Canadians securing the lead role around Kandahar, the UK undertook responsibility for Helmand. UK Secretary of Defence John Reid said that he would be satisfied if the British brigade never fired a shot in the province. The naivety of this approach, in the face of large-scale and intense opposition, was reflected in the despatch of a half strength brigade of 3150 soldiers (Farrell, 2009: 574). Helmand had only been quiet prior to 2006 because the government in Kabul had not attempted to exercise any substantive control over the province (Simpson, 2012: 53).

According to General Richard Dannatt, Prime Minister Tony Blair 'over-committed' when he agreed to go into Helmand in addition to Iraq, seeking to be a 'dependable ally' of the US (2016: 296). But the British military bear some of the responsibility for the advice they gave. They were reluctant to say 'no' to politicians. It was poor judgement on the part of senior military leaders that the UK attempted to prosecute two long-term, medium-sized operations simultaneously. According to Maciejewski (2013: 162), it was being driven by officers 'who thought Afghanistan was merely a way out of Basra' and those that yearned for a 'redemptive mission' after the experience of Iraq (Fry, 2014: 231). The 'British High Command gave its support to wars without ensuring that the wider Whitehall elite had a clear understanding of what was involved' (Elliott, 2015: 217). It became necessary to speed up the drawdown in Iraq in order to provide more troops for Helmand.

As well as off-setting the disappointments of the campaign in Iraq, the intervention in Helmand was driven by a desire to impress the US and preserve a 'can-do' approach. The British military wanted to demonstrate that it was an ally capable of assuming more significant roles. Riley commented that the Afghanistan campaign was as much about '(their) bilateral relations with the US, as anything else' (2013: 246) and Cowper-Coles, (2017: 11) the former British Ambassador to Afghanistan, concurs. It soon became apparent, however, that Helmand was a major COIN campaign (Farrell, Rynning, and Terriff, 2013: 124) and that the British would be painfully over-extended. The situation had been significantly under-estimated and General Richard Dannatt described the Army as 'running hot' trying to conduct concurrent COIN operations in both Afghanistan and in Iraq (Norton-Taylor, 2006).

The COIN strategy adopted by the US and British in Afghanistan had similarities. Both sides sought to 'Clear' the environment of insurgents, 'Hold' the territory and then 'Build' through reconstruction efforts. The British were successful in the 'Clear' phase but lacked the necessary numbers of troops to 'Hold' territory. This enabled the Taliban to return and resume their control after the British forces departed. The 'Build' phase was even more problematic as there was an insufficiently secure environment to facilitate civilian-led reconstruction (Dannatt, 2011). It was both hard to protect the agencies undertaking the economic effort and to ensure the work continued after the projects were completed (Joint Warfare Publication 3-50, 2004).

The British strategy was the idea of an 'ink blot': to occupy small parcels of territory and then join these up over an extended period of time, to develop 'Afghan Development Zones'. Small units were based in platoon houses throughout Helmand, supplemented by special forces personnel, to demonstrate a British presence. To the British Army's horror, these forces became the target for sustained Taliban attack and it became challenging to resupply them, other than by helicopter. The loss of any of these outposts would have inflicted a military setback with broader political ramifications for the Anglo-American relationship (Barry, 2020: 374). The British Army found itself in a major conflict, unable to operationalize its COIN doctrine that sought to focus on governance and development (Egnell, 2011: 302).

The Anglo-American operating strategy evolved in the face of the insurgency. The US was using sweeps of territory by large military units. In the British case, far-flung platoon houses were abandoned and forces operated from some of the towns and villages in the province, occasionally taking control of those urban centres in which the Taliban were entrenched. The British conducted regular patrols and contended with IEDs, ambushes, and sniper fire. Both the UK and the US had insufficient forces on the ground. US force levels were as low as 10,000 in 2002 and, with preparations for the invasion of Iraq, attention was diverted from the Afghan theatre. Even up to 2008, when the insurgency was at its most intense, US force numbers never exceeded 32,000 (Long, 2016: 209). UK troop numbers in Helmand went from an initial 3000 to 7000 and then to 10, 000 (Strachan, 2013: 335). Both countries had to rely on tactical air support to extricate forces from firefights when they were at risk of being overwhelmed and depended too heavily on the kinetic use of air power to offset inadequate numbers of ground troops.

There were several areas of persistent tension between British and American commanders, some that were unique to Afghanistan and others that were also common to Iraq. One that figured centrally in the case of Afghanistan was the huge problem of poppy cultivation along the banks of the Helmand valley. Poppy growing was the staple crop for farmers and it presented a problem in terms of the funds it generated to finance opposition to British forces (Simpson, 2012: 107). The British Army found itself conducting a counter-narcotics campaign that was at odds with its focus on 'hearts and minds' (Elliott, 2015: 159). The British had helped remove the head of opium cultivation, the Helmand Governor Sher Mohammed Akhundzada in 2006 (Chandrasekaran, 2012: 46) but subsequently proved reluctant to acquiesce to the US strategy of crop eradication until there was an alternative crop for the livelihood of farmers (Interview with British Army Major-General, 2012). In American eyes, the UK wilfully ignored the problem of opium, whose production had continued to increase despite British forces on the ground (Chin, 2007: 210). For their part, the British military feared that farmers that had been dispossessed of their livelihoods would enlist in the Taliban (McColl, 2013: 110).

A second source of tension were the attitudes of the British and the Americans towards reconstruction and development. Colonel Nick Carter, a British officer embedded as the chief planner in US military headquarters, had played a major role in designing the concept of Provincial Reconstruction Teams (PRTs). He had conceived of it as a means to bring practical help and skills to local people across Afghanistan. The UK pioneered a model in the north of the country of a fully civilian PRT, amidst a fairly benevolent environment (Farrell, Rynning, and Terriff, 2013: 165). In Helmand, there were even US military and civilian advisers in the UK PRT in Lashkar Gah (Defence Select Committee, 2011: paragraph 53). In comparison, the US PRTs were mostly military-led and were endowed with resources on a scale that far surpassed those of the British. A USAID report on PRTs in Afghanistan stated that, 'PRT culture, people, and resources were predominantly military' (Long, 2016: 216). This made it harder for other agencies to work with US PRTs because many non-governmental organizations and charities were afraid of compromising their neutrality by working with the US military.

The UK enjoyed limited influence over its US ally in Afghanistan (Interview with former British Ambassador to Afghanistan, 2012). As in the case of Iraq, this owed much to the fact that British command structures led to a focus on the British Army's campaign in Helmand rather than the broader campaign plan across the whole of the country (Interview with British Army Lieutenant General, 2015). Despite having British Lieutenant General Nick Parker double hatted as Deputy Commander of ISAF (DCOMISAF) and National Contingent Commander of British forces, as well as a Senior Civilian Representative in Kabul (Defence

Select Committee, 2011: paragraph 54), attention tended to remain on the tactical level (Interview with former Commander of British Land Forces, 2015).

This can partly be explained by the fact that the British Chief of Joint Operations was running the operation from London and the theatre commander was answering to the CDS, rather than interacting with the US senior commander in Kabul (Interview with British Army Lieutenant General, 2015a). Frontline commanders were taking direction from officers based in the UK. 'In contrast to the commanders of the US-led coalitions, who were located "forward" … Operational command was held back in the UK' (Elliott, 2015: 219). The US expressed concerns that their British allies were too focused on Helmand and were insufficiently contributing to the debates about the overall Afghanistan strategy (Interview with former Chief of the General Staff, 2014).

By 2007, after the surge in Iraq, the situation was improving there whilst it was deteriorating in Afghanistan. But the US did not have the numbers to increase the mission in Afghanistan until a drawdown had occurred in Iraq. Hence it was not until 2010, after Iraq was being wound down, that President Obama ordered a surge in Afghanistan. It was accompanied by a withdrawal date of 2014, as Obama was determined not to become bogged down in the country (Renwick, 2016: 400). The setting of a date for withdrawal was against the advice of the Secretaries of State and Defense, as well as numerous commentators, on the grounds that it gave the Taliban the message that the US commitment was time-limited. General David McKiernan had wanted an extra 30,000 troops but Obama was cautious in authorizing this number. In 2009, McKiernan was replaced by General Stanley McChrystal, who was appointed as both the US national commander and the senior officer within ISAF. With America's surge and 10,000 extra European troops, the US finally had the capacity to conduct manoeuvre operations. Yet it was telling that McChrystal came rapidly to call for substantial extra US forces (Strachan, 2013: 225).

With the US surge, there was a deployment of US 2nd Marine Expeditionary Brigade to Helmand Province. Around 20,000 Marines went to Helmand and this substantially increased the combat power available. General David Richards acknowledged to the Defence Select Committee that there had been tensions between British forces and the US Marines (Defence Select Committee, 2011: 36). The US Marines brought with them 20-times the number of helicopters that the UK forces had been operating (Farrell, 2017: 263; see also Cornish and Dorman, 2011: 341). In the words of Chandrasekaran (2012: 211), 'The Marines were bent on expansion; the British were intent on retrenchment'.

After 2014 ISAF forces began to drawdown as the strategy changed to providing training, Operation Resolute Support, for the Afghan National Army and the Police. Indigenous forces took on the lion's share of fighting the Taliban whilst the US and the UK provided air support. During the Presidency of Donald Trump, the US opened up negotiations with Taliban representatives in Doha and the US presence in the country dwindled to below 3000 personnel. When President Biden assumed office in 2021, he ordered the pull-out of all US forces in the summer. Without a US contingent, the British announced their departure from Afghanistan and a hasty and chaotic airlift marked the withdrawal of the Western presence in the country.

Narratives

A key element in the UK narrative of the special military relationship with the US has been the expertise of its armed forces. When operational tasks arose, the British military wanted their US counterparts to trust them with the conduct of a mission. Based on their past experience of COIN operations, the British military was confident that it could dominate in their sectors in Iraq and Afghanistan and could be relied upon to carry out their task. They even hoped that their American allies would emulate their practice and that this would enhance their standing in the relationship. It was made clear to US planners that the British were willing to sacrifice in the execution of their partnership with the US (Porter, 2010: 375).

However, this narrative proved counterproductive because the British Army over-promised to the US and then under-delivered. In the words of Griffin (2011: 318), it led to a, 'loss of confidence in the robustness of the doctrinal foundations supporting British military operations'. The privileged relationship that the UK had enjoyed with their US counterparts was based on the added value that they could contribute to US-led coalition operations. When the US came to see its ally as weak and unable to live up to its reputation, the narrative that the British military had cultivated was seen as hollow (Hendershot, 2013: 68).

Not only was British experience and expertise in COIN called into question, but doubts arose in US minds as to whether the UK shared its intent. Operations in the south of Iraq demonstrated that the British were reducing the size of their forces, their footprint was diminishing, and they were entering into secret agreements with the Shia militias. At a time when the US was surging its forces, the British had withdrawn to the relative safety of Basra airport (Interview with US Army Colonel, 2014). This undermined one of the key elements in the Anglo-American military relationship, namely that the UK was reliable and willing to share risk. US Army General Jack Keane, who had conducted an assessment of the situation in Iraq for the Bush administration, later lamented that the American government had suffered a crisis of confidence in the UK.

The US Army was critical of the British Army for not using decisive force against the Shia militias. For example, US political and military authorities were dismissive of the less confrontational approach that Major General Andrew Stewart, the British commander, pursued towards the Shia militias in the South East sector. They went as far as to call for his replacement (McColl, 2013: 112). Stewart was of the view that the British lacked the resources to enter a full-scale fight against the militias (Rayburn and Sobchak, 2019: 300). He contended that, '(the Americans) found it difficult when ... (the British) did not deploy that (warrior) ethos to the same extent that they did' (Stewart, 2013: 87). This reflected the differences in strategy and culture between the British and American forces. The British believed that they had adopted the correct course by managing the sectarian conflict, training the Iraqi forces to take the lead, and switching to an 'Overwatch' stance.

In Afghanistan, a UK–US relationship built on trust and reputation dissolved into recriminations. The US criticized the lack of resources that the UK invested in the Helmand campaign: it is telling that their nickname for British forces was 'the borrowers', based on the extent of the military material that was loaned (Interview with former Commander of British Land Forces, 2015). In 2006, the British had pulled out of Musa Qala as part of a deal with tribal leaders, only to have to retake the town a year later from the Taliban. In 2009, the UK refused to contribute to President Obama's surge (Chandrasekaran, 2012: 213) and the British Army were eager to hand over responsibility for Afghan towns like Sangin and Lashkar Gah to the US (Interview with US Army Colonel, 2014). Even when it came to withdrawal, in August of 2021, there were strains in Anglo-American relations (Economist, 2021: 28). The Biden administration refused British requests to prolong their presence at Kabul airport and this resulted in a proportion of supporters amongst the Afghan population being left behind.

Unlike previous cases such as Suez, where US criticism was directed at the British political class, on this occasion American ire was focused on the British armed forces (Interview with former Chief of the Defence Staff, 2015). US General Dan O'Neill, commander of ISAF, was highly critical of the British mission in Helmand. When the US Marines entered Helmand their perception was, after the experience of Basra, that they were coming to the rescue of the British (Dannatt, 2016: 309). In many cases US criticisms were unjustified and, after they had suffered casualties of their own, the US military realized that the UK had faced a much more formidable enemy than had previously been acknowledged (Farrell, 2017: 358).

What is evident is that Anglo-American narratives may not be similar and may be expressed in different ways. As the weaker partner in the relationship, the UK has always been careful about voicing any criticisms of the US. In both campaigns in Afghanistan and Iraq, the UK was critical of US policy but it expressed its view in private, 'sotte voce'. In the words of Tony Blair's foreign policy adviser David Manning, UK criticism is never conducted in public (Manning quoted in Dumbrell, 2004: 441). But the US, with less to lose, has not been as constrained in its criticism of the UK. The US military did not show the same reluctance as their British counterparts when it came to criticizing the role played by their allies.

Conclusion

Institutionalism was placed under unprecedented strains by the experience of COIN campaigns in Iraq and Afghanistan. Regardless of all of the collaboration and embeddedness of British forces with the US, the two campaigns caused serious fissures to be exposed between the two countries. On the one hand, this is not so surprising as both sides under-estimated the tasks and found themselves fighting in protracted campaigns that pressured their militaries. On the other hand, they took responsibility for different sectors of Iraq and Afghanistan yet there were still divergences. The US was dismayed by the failure of the British to overcome the militias in the south of Iraq and the Taliban in Helmand. The trust they had in the British military and its ability to deliver on its objectives was dented. In return, the British were disillusioned that the US was so unappreciative of the sacrifices that they had endured.

It was evident to the US that the British military had lacked the capacity to prosecute the two campaigns simultaneously. The blame had to be shared with the Blair and Brown governments that had resourced these military operations inadequately. The British narrative was complacent and could not be seen through to the end. Iraq and Afghanistan exposed how two medium-scale operations exceeded the capacity of the British Army (Bailey, 2013: 21). In the words of Porter, the campaigns served to 'accelerate a long-term process: the eclipse of British power in American eyes' (2010: 358). It threw a pall over the ability of the UK and US to work together on future operations (Interview by telephone with former British Army Liaison Officer to the US Training and Doctrine Centre, 2019).

As well as the overall resource envelope allocated to the British armed forces in the two theatres, two other factors caused tensions within the Anglo-American military relationship. One was the lack of agility demonstrated by the British Army when counterinsurgency doctrine proved to be inadequate. Having focused hitherto on high intensity conflict, an insurgency found the British unprepared both doctrinally and in terms of equipment and training. The US military quickly recognized the weaknesses of their own strategy, allocated substantial resources to reconceptualize it and implemented a new approach. Their thinking rapidly overtook British ideas that were based on COIN doctrine from 1995 (Alderson, 2013: 285). Attempts by the British to mirror the US changes between 2006 and 2007 failed to materialize. This reflected an internal tussle within the British Army's Development, Concepts and Doctrine Centre for jurisdiction over revisions to doctrine (Farrell, Rynning, and Terriff, 2013: 167). This inability to adapt in a timely fashion contrasted the British and American approaches (Foley, Griffin, and McCartney, 2011: 259).

A second factor was the apparent lack of will that senior levels of the British Army demonstrated in Iraq and Afghanistan. Despite Elliott's assessment that, 'the

UK's pre-eminent policy objective for the decade was to support its 'special relationship' (2015: 150), the UK lacked resolve at crucial times. The British were insufficiently focused on victory and unwilling to devote the necessary level of effort (Interview with British Army Lieutenant General, 2015a; Foreign Affairs Select Committee, 2010: paragraph 62). In the face of the US surges, the UK was winding down its involvement and heading for the exit. The result was that the UK lost credibility in the eyes of its ally. Major-General Mungo Melvin, summed up the result in Iraq, 'the US and the UK got in together, acted individually and left separately' (quoted in Elliott, 2015: 122).

7

The Nuclear Relationship

Introduction

Most analysts agree that one of the core features of the special relationship is the field of nuclear cooperation. It is significant because it involves the ultimate weapons of international security and the very survival of the state. By any standards, the US–UK nuclear relationship has been special: Simpson (2013: 241) describes it as the 'jewel in the crown' of their defence cooperation. Thirteen years after the US suspended cooperation with the UK, it began to share its most intimate nuclear secrets with its ally. From 1960 to the present day, the US committed to furnishing the UK with a strategic nuclear delivery vehicle. In the words of Michel (2009: 147), 'there exists no other program where the United States has worked so intimately with another country for such an extended period of time'.

For the UK government, nuclear weapons offered a means to facilitate cooperation with the US as well as to influence its strategic thinking (Wynn, 1994: 324). With the nuclear 'sword' at the heart of Western strategy during the first two decades of the Cold War, the UK regarded it as essential that it contributed a proportion of the nuclear offensive. Along with US nuclear bases in Britain, this country had to play a role in order to justify US consultation.

There has been a continuity to nuclear cooperation that has marked it out from other aspects of Anglo-American military relations. Since the early 1960s, the UK has not needed to discern the direction in which the US was heading nor worry about questions of interoperability. Rather, the UK wanted US nuclear assistance and sought to ensure that a reliable missile system was made available. The UK accepted the vulnerability that resulted from being a dependent ally and the independence that was being sacrificed. It pledged its weapons to NATO but reserved their right to be launched by a British prime minister in the event of a supreme national emergency.

However, the very possession of a deterrent indicated an ambivalence in the UK's attitude towards the US. An independent nuclear force signalled a desire for a hedge against uncertainty and the UK's unwillingness to rely entirely upon its ally. Whilst ostensibly confident in the US guarantee to defend the continent, the UK force was a form of insurance, both nationally and for other NATO members, against a diminishing US commitment to European defence. By threatening to use its independent nuclear power, the British state might act as a trigger on a US president reluctant to risk his own country's population (Kandiah and

The Anglo-American Military Relationship. Wyn Rees, Oxford University Press. © Wyn Rees (2024).
DOI: 10.1093/oso/9780198884620.003.0007

Staerck, 2005). A nuclear capability provided a second centre of decision-making that complicated an adversary's strategic calculations (Ministry of Defence, 2006: 18). Although the UK has made it clear it would only use nuclear weapons in extremis, it has not spelt out precisely what would constitute such a situation.

The UK military never regarded US nuclear assistance as inevitable: rather, as something that it would need to work for and justify. The size of their nuclear effort meant that US administrations did not treat the UK nuclear contribution as a necessary component of their strategic posture. This was recognized by the UK. As early as 1955, Reginald Maudling, Minister of Supply, noted that Britain's contribution to the western deterrent would be 'political' in nature rather than 'military' (TNA, DEFE 7/964, 1955). Nuclear weapons were about developing a relationship with the US that would give the UK access to nuclear capabilities to ensure its own security. The UK has striven to be regarded by the US as a worthy partner and has walked a tricky path between its contribution to the broader western deterrent and the perceived needs of its own national security.

Institutionalism is more central to the nuclear relationship than other areas of the military relationship. The extent of the cooperation between the two sides and the sensitivity of the issues have served to knit the two nuclear establishments together in a unique way. It has been conducted by a community of military officers, officials, and scientists that have been insulated from the vagaries of the political relationship. Trust has been at its heart, although Baylis and Eames (2023: chapter 14) trace persistent strands of ambiguity within the cooperation resulting from subtly differing interests. In spite of the sophistication and secrecy of the technology, since the early 1960s the relationship has been remarkably cooperative. However, for the analyst, tracing this reality is more difficult because of the opacity of nuclear relations and the dearth of official material released.

Rules

In order for the UK to enter into nuclear collaboration with the US, it required a nuclear weapon and delivery capability of its own. When the UK possessed an independent airborne deterrent, it was content to allow US Thor Intermediate range missiles onto its soil under a dual-key arrangement. But when it chose Polaris as its national deterrent, the UK insisted that its own warheads be fitted to the missiles so that it could use the weapons independently. Since the end of the Cold War, this requirement has been less pressing due to the risk of nuclear conflict receding.

The type of deterrent has been an important issue for the UK because it has faced the challenge of trying to maintain its credibility within the context of superpower technological rivalry. Having mastered the physics of producing workable fission and fusion bombs, the UK struggled to keep up with the speed of change and the cost of delivery systems. Although missile technology appeared to offer a solution, the UK was a relatively small island and placing land-based missiles in hardened silos risked creating an attractive first-strike target. Thus the advent of US submarine-launched missiles offered a solution to several British problems. Polaris and later Trident submarine-based missiles presented invulnerable second-strike platforms that were far removed from UK shores. Acquiring this US technology resolved the dilemma of the UK falling behind the superpowers.

UK policymakers came to the view that trying to preserve a purely national nuclear programme risked undermining a global defence policy. What the UK sought was access to US nuclear know-how, thus avoiding research and development costs as well as duplication of defence effort. They believed that they could secure this by demonstrating such a level of nuclear proficiency that the US would enter into a cooperative partnership. The possession of a nuclear capability became a way to demonstrate to the US that the UK was a worthy ally with whom to share nuclear information (Baylis and Stoddart, 2012: 340).

The July 1958 Agreement on the Uses of Atomic Energy for Mutual Defence Purposes (MDA) has remained the legal basis for the close nuclear relationship between the two countries. This agreement facilitated the transfer of technology and the exchange of personnel. It also included the sharing of secret information, such as defence from nuclear attack and the mechanisms for carrying US nuclear bombs on RAF aircraft (Simpson, 1983: 114–115). The MDA fundamentally transformed US attitudes (Horne, 1986: 89), making it possible to transfer nuclear materials to countries that had made 'substantial progress' of their own and were capable of making a contribution to mutual security. It accorded the UK a special nuclear status and gave it unique insights into US nuclear thinking. It was agreed that the UK could receive highly enriched uranium and tritium, whilst supplying the US with plutonium in return (Simpson, 1983: 131). The MDA was updated every five years to preserve its relevance and in 1984 this was extended to ten-year updates.

The MDA was also important in making it possible for the UK to receive advice from the US on the configuration of its warhead designs. It was able to benefit from the larger-scale programme and the engineering expertise of the US. This made it possible for the UK to accede to the moratorium on nuclear testing because it could have confidence in the reliability of its designs (Simpson, 2013: 247). Yet the UK continued with its own warhead development. To have relinquished this would have amounted to a further aspect of dependency on the benevolence of its ally.

The Polaris Sales Agreement (PSA) of 1963 laid out the terms for the purchase of the missiles (Gill, 2014: 48). The PSA itself was updated and amended in the move to the next generation of missiles (Foreign Affairs Select Committee, 2010: paragraph 133). In January 1979, Prime Minister James Callaghan secured an undertaking from the Carter administration that the Trident nuclear missile system would be made available to the UK and this was formalized by the government of Margaret Thatcher (Hennessy, 2007: 326). In March 1982, the British Government announced it would purchase the more advanced Trident D5 system rather than the C4.

There have been differences in the nuclear strategies of the two powers. British planning was more modest than that of its superpower ally and was based on a concept of 'nuclear sufficiency'. The UK has always maintained that its nuclear forces represent a 'minimum deterrent': a means to dissuade a potential aggressor from using nuclear weapons against the country and as a contribution to the larger Western deterrent. This saw expression in a 'counter-value' strategy in which a small number of Soviet cities were held at risk. One consideration regarding the size of the deterrent was its ability to strike certain time-urgent Soviet targets, or those that might be of greater importance to the UK than to the US (TNA, AIR 8/2400, 1958). Calibrating the size of the deterrent was primarily determined by what the US would consider a significant contribution (Clark, 1994: 232) and by a minimum number of targets whose destruction would likely deter Soviet planners. A force of 144 bombers was judged to be a meaningful contribution to the Western deterrent (TNA, DEFE 5/70 Annex to COS, 1956). British targeting was coordinated with the US rather than integrated into the US war plan. By the early part of the next decade, the Macmillan government had reappraised the number of targets within the Soviet Union that it wanted to be able to target and there was a reduction in the ambitions for the UK force (Clark, 1994: 389–390 and 394).

This contrasted with a US strategy that intended to attack both counter-value and 'counterforce' targets, namely enemy nuclear forces. US thinking was driven by two factors. One was the increasing accuracy of US nuclear systems, such as Minuteman and Peacekeeper Intercontinental Ballistic Missiles (ICBMs) and Trident Submarine Launched Ballistic Missiles (SLBMs) that made it possible to destroy hardened Soviet targets. The other was the growing parity between the US and the USSR that encouraged a movement away from city targeting to decrease the likelihood of US population centres being destroyed.

With the end of the Cold War, the UK Trident force was de-targetted as a way of signalling improved East–West relations. In 1998, the UK also decommissioned their tactical nuclear weapons, such as the WE-177 bombs. These had been fitted to Tornado aircraft for both land attack and for maritime operations. In their place, Trident submarines were accorded a 'sub-strategic' role in which they could be utilized to strike pin-point military targets. This mission was never clarified but it could have involved nuclear retaliation against a chemical or biological weapons attack. Accordingly, some of the warheads were reduced to a 10-kiloton, rather than the usual 100-kiloton, explosive yield in order that they could be employed more discriminatingly (Ritchie, 2009: 81). The UK was decreasing its overall nuclear stockpile but according itself a wider range of options as to how nuclear weapons could be used.

In 2007, the Labour Defence Secretary Des Browne revoked this sub-strategic role (Stoddart and Baylis, 2012: 509–510). He announced that Trident would not be used against military targets during a conflict and re-committed the UK to solely counter-value targeting. There was a reduction in the numbers of warheads on a smaller number of missiles.

UK and US government thinking changed in the post-Cold War years as a result of the evolving international environment. Fears of confrontation with the Soviet Union were replaced by concerns over nuclear proliferation and, post 9/11, the risk of nuclear materials falling into the hands of terrorist groups. Fortunately for the UK, the US did not view its provision of Trident to the British as contrary to non-proliferation norms (Doyle, 2018: 1176). This was based on the under-standing that the UK would not share its nuclear capabilities with third countries. Extensive consultations between the two sides over nuclear issues ensured that they held common threat perceptions regarding nuclear proliferation (Foreign and Commonwealth Office, 2003).

Concerns about the spread of weapons of mass destruction resulted in antago-nistic relations with Iraq, Iran, Libya, and Syria. It was over the fear of a clandestine Iraqi weapons programme that the US and UK went to war with Saddam Hussein in March 2003. The British government, with the acquiescence of the US, also took the lead in convincing Libya's Muammar Gaddafi to cease his attempt to acquire a nuclear capability (Blair, 2010: 391). This followed the interception of a ves-sel destined for Libya that was carrying nuclear components. In relation to Iran, the US and UK have pursued a long-term project to prevent it from weaponizing its uranium-enrichment programme. The UK became one of the three Euro-pean countries (the E-3 along with France and Germany) to negotiate the Joint Cooperative Plan of Action (JCPOA) in 2015.

Russian strategic rearmament after 2007 marked a shift in Anglo-American back to the risk of great power conflict. Not only has Russia began to modernize and expand its strategic nuclear arsenal but China has started to enlarge its nuclear armoury. Both countries present a challenge to a Western-led international order. Russia took the step of issuing veiled nuclear threats following its invasion of Ukraine in February 2022 whilst China's nuclear posture may be influenced by its determination to regain Taiwan in the future.

Practice

The priority for the British has been to preserve commonality with US develop-ments, within the constraints of affordability. When the Nassau agreement was reached the UK was initially offered the Polaris A2 missile (Nailor, 1988: 16). This was later superseded by the A3 and the UK chose to upgrade to the latter system, although it was only in development, to ensure it maintained commonality with a US system.

The UK chose to purchase an American system and then adapt it over time as the technology evolved. The benefit was that Britain would preserve a weapon that was compatible with the US but would not need to keep pace with US technological developments. When the US moved to a successor missile, Poseidon, with its Multiple Independently Targeted Re-entry Vehicle (MIRV) technology and greater accuracy, the UK chose not to request the new capability. The US had not offered the missile to the UK and the decision was taken that a new missile was not needed at that time. It is interesting to note that the Royal Navy, with the support of the US Navy, pressed unsuccessfully for Poseidon on the grounds that it would preserve the closest possible relationship (Baylis, 1984: 173).

Instead of requesting purchase of Poseidon, with or without MIRV technology, the UK chose instead to develop the Chevaline system domestically. Chevaline was a project to redevelop the Polaris warhead to design decoys and dummies that would evade missile defences and ensure its penetrability to the target. The UK wanted to be able to strike important targets in the Soviet Union, particularly Moscow (the so-called 'Moscow criterion'), as well as a number of major population centres, as the core of its strategy. The UK was focused on a national targeting strategy in which the capability to destroy Moscow was vital, rather than as part of an integrated targeting plan with the Americans (Stoddart and Baylis, 2012: 498). Moscow was protected by an anti-ballistic missile system whose size was limited by the 1972 Anti-Ballistic Missile Treaty.

Chevaline was an ambitious project that put the British back into the role of trying to develop superpower-level nuclear technology. One of the three warheads on the A3 Polaris warhead was replaced with penetration aids. The system was operational in 1982, after Margaret Thatcher had become prime minister. Nevertheless, it proved to be a salutary experience as the cost of the 'Antelope' and 'Super Antelope' (Jones, 2019, Volume II) research programmes multiplied approximately threefold to £1 billion and took nearly a decade to complete (Hennessy, 2007: 322). The complexity of Chevaline demonstrated the risks of pursuing a nuclear programme independently of the US. The Trident system eventually replaced Polaris/Chevaline and offered an integral ability to penetrate the Soviet Union's anti-ballistic missile system.

Interdependence has meant in practice that the UK obtains missiles from the US whilst building its own submarines and warheads. In the case of Polaris, there were four Resolution class submarines. The US decommissioned its Polaris submarines at an earlier stage than the UK and replaced them with Poseidon. The British kept Polaris for longer and extended its service life from 20 to 25 years. America demonstrated good faith by reopening the rocket motor production line to assist the UK Polaris programme (Callahan and Jansson, 2008: 133). The last of the UK Polaris submarines was withdrawn in 1996. The decision to purchase the Trident system necessitated both a new submarine and a warhead. The UK chose to upgrade from Trident C4 to Trident D5 as the latter was the programme that the US was introducing. Opting for D5 enabled the UK to benefit from the skill and resources of the US nuclear community to address and overcome any future challenges. It enabled the Royal Navy to operate closely together with its US counterpart over a common system.

The UK considered other nuclear options when replacing Polaris and Trident. Options included an air-delivered deterrent and cruise missiles on either dedicated submarines or on existing hunter-killer submarines. Cruise missiles were seriously considered but even these required high levels of dependence on the US, for the provision of the missiles as well as the satellite information integral to their guidance. The attraction of cruise missiles was their much lower unit cost than ballistic missiles. However, they had two drawbacks. The first was their vulnerability to air defences and therefore the need for large numbers of them to be procured. The second was their relatively limited range that reduced the areas from which they could be deployed. This would have reduced the sea area in which submarines would have been able to operate. The UK government chose to remain with the US ballistic missile option.

The benefits for the UK have been considerable. Britain was able to deploy a strategic nuclear deterrent, as sophisticated as that of the US, at a fraction of the cost that would have been incurred by developing the missile technology indigenously. The US levied only a 5% contribution towards the research and development costs. In the Polaris programme, the cost of running the system amounted to about 2% of the defence budget. In the case of moving from the purchase of Trident C4 to D5, the US agreed that a fixed research and development levy of $116m would be imposed. This had the effect of insulating the UK from further cost increases as the system was brought into operation (Doyle, 2017: 889). Furthermore, US advanced engineering techniques and its devotion of larger resources reduced future risks to the programme. The US provided reactor fuel (Mackby and Cornish, 2008: 16) and there was collaboration on the W76 warhead where the UK based its design on a model that contained components purchased from the US.

This is not to deny that reliance on the US has involved drawbacks for the UK. One drawback has been the foreclosing of other co-operative nuclear relationships and opportunities. The bilateral relationship that the UK has pursued with the US has precluded closer cooperation with France (Interview with former First Sea Lord, 2012). The American MDA limited nuclear sharing to those countries that had made substantial progress of their own and Washington was zealous in ensuring that Britain was prevented from sharing with France. The potential for Britain to work with France existed throughout the period and President Charles de Gaulle reacted to the UK decision to purchase Polaris by refusing its application to join the European Economic Community. The UK did talk to France in the

1970s about nuclear systems but its room for manoeuvre was constrained by the US preventing classified information or nuclear materials being shared with third parties. In particular, this limited the sharing of commercial reactor technology for nuclear submarines that the French government was interested in acquiring. US Admiral Rickover had made clear to Chief Scientific Adviser Sir Solly Zuckerman that the UK was barred from sharing any submarine propulsion knowledge with the French government.

The US was aware that helping the UK with its nuclear forces impacted negatively on its relations with France, yet the American government wanted to monopolize decisions relating to sharing nuclear secrets. The US conducted its own nuclear relations with France in the 1970s that were aimed at assisting it with complex technologies (Baylis and Eames, 2023: chapter 8). It was ironic that the UK was perturbed at this Franco-American liaison. They feared that it undercut what they might offer to France as well as detracting from the uniqueness of the UK–US relationship.

The Lancaster House agreement of 2010 was an attempt to improve the nuclear relationship between France and the UK. Although the British were mindful of jeopardizing their cooperation with Washington (Clark 1994: 429), there were efforts to improve Anglo-French nuclear cooperation. The Teutates Treaty was an attempt to systematize collaboration on matters of mutual nuclear interest. One aspect has been cooperation on hydrodynamics research through the French facility at Valduc (Burt, 2016: 182). This focused on maintaining the reliability of their respective nuclear stockpiles and was made possible by the fact that this innovative area of technology was outside the US–UK nuclear field (Xu, 2017: 132).

A second drawback was that the British acquired capabilities beyond what they considered necessary. Whilst assessing the possible replacement of Polaris in the 1970s, the Cabinet sub-committee viewed Trident D5 as a more capable system than the UK required. Trident D5's 6500 mile range exceeded British needs; its number of warheads was greater than the UK's minimum deterrent posture and its costs were greater than planned (Stoddart and Baylis, 2014: 146). However, the need to preserve commonality with the US led the UK to buy the American system.

The UK addressed the superior capability of D5 by never exploiting its full potential. While the D5 missile was capable of carrying up to 12 nuclear independently targetable and manoeuvrable re-entry vehicles (MARV) on 16 missiles, the UK chose to deploy only a limited number of warheads on 8 operational missiles. This gave the UK a total of 48 warheads on each submarine (Stoddart and Baylis, 2012: 508). In 2010, the decision was announced to further reduce the number of warheads, so that each submarine would carry no more than 40 warheads (Ministry of Defence, 2010: 38). This would result in a UK stockpile of only 160 warheads, an approach consistent with the 'nuclear zero' espoused by the Obama administration in which nuclear weapons would be eradicated.

Subsequently, the UK chose to reverse course and increase its nuclear stockpile. This reflected a perceived change in the international security environment following Russia's decision to upgrade its nuclear forces and China's decision to significantly expand its strategic nuclear capabilities. In the UK Integrated Defence and Security Review of 2021, it was announced that the UK would increase its stockpile up to a ceiling of around 260 warheads (Ministry of Defence, 2021).

Institutional relationships

The institutional aspect of the nuclear relationship has been particularly important. It has involved a small community of people within a highly specialized and secretive domain. These elites have represented a transatlantic epistemic community, a group of people whose common specialist knowledge has brought them together across an international boundary. Groups from the UK side have interacted with their American counterparts on the basis of trust. The UK has made stringent efforts to prevent anything from impacting on the relationship or undermining those bonds. There have been three communities within the UK responsible for perpetuating cooperation.

The first of these communities has been the military involved in the running of the nuclear deterrent. The Royal Air Force (RAF), with its elite V-bomber crews, was the original purveyor of the deterrent and never wanted to relinquish the role to the Royal Navy. The RAF was aware that their bombers could reach Soviet territory ahead of those of America's Strategic Air Command. They could have destroyed enemy air defences, to pave the way for the US bomber force, or they could have attacked airfields and missile sites that might launch attacks on the UK homeland. These two competing demands diminished once the Soviets possessed ballistic missiles and invulnerable second strike capabilities. The RAF remained part of the US nuclear war plan and was allocated both military and counter-value targets.

At first the Royal Navy was indifferent to the idea of taking responsibility for the deterrent. The Navy feared that it would detract from their existing conventional priorities and in particular they were anxious that Polaris would impact on the submarine building programme (Boyes, 2019: 109). After all, a new branch of the Royal Navy had to be created and trained for the nuclear role and this risked bleeding talent from the surface and sub-surface forces, but the Navy came to embrace the submarine-based nuclear force and grew into strong advocates of Polaris. As the submarines became operational from 1969, the two navies developed a close pattern of cooperation on nuclear issues that has continued to the present day.

The US Navy and the Royal Navy were able to build upon existing bonds of cooperation that stretched back to World War II. Under the guidance of Hyman Rickover, the US Navy provided an S5W nuclear reactor from Westinghouse for

Royal Navy submarines. The link between senior officers in both navies became the channel through which the Royal Navy was inducted into Polaris. From October 1958, Rickover authorized the admittance of a British liaison officer into the US Navy Special Projects Office that managed the Polaris programme (Jones, 2019, Volume 1: 38). First Sea Lord Louis Mountbatten argued to Admiral Arleigh Burke that in the development of Polaris, 'We must make common cause' (quoted in Clark, 1994: 286). In January 1961, Admiral Burke invited a team from the Royal Navy to visit and make an assessment of the implications of running their own Polaris submarines (Clark, 1994: 382).

The possession of strategic nuclear weapons tied the Royal Navy and US Navy together, in 'strategic targeting . . . communications and . . . submarine operations' (Eberle, 1986: 156). Nuclear propulsion benefited from the exchange of officers between the two sides. The UK was also provided with the inertial navigation system, the fire control system, and the specialized steel for the hulls of the submarines (Marsh, 2013: 181). The relationship has been strengthened by continuity: the Royal Navy has not switched between modes of delivery but has remained wedded to a US system.

With the introduction of Trident, the collaboration between the two navies was enhanced. Like Polaris, the UK built the Vanguard class of submarines at Barrow in Cumbria and attached their own warheads from the Atomic Weapons Research Establishment at Aldermaston (AWRE). The 60 Trident II D5 missiles were not purchased but rather leased from a pool held by the US Navy. Cooperation has also woven the UK into a host of arrangements with the US. For example, the submarines were armed with the Trident missiles at King's Bay Georgia. A small number of these missiles were used to undertake test firings off the coast of Florida before the Trident fleet was considered trained and mission ready. But these missiles do not need to be serviced for many years and thus the dependence on the US for facilities was reduced between Polaris and Trident (Stoddart and Baylis, 2014: 165). The submarines then exercise and obtain their operational readiness off that same coast before transiting to their patrol area. Both sides conduct long patrols and British crews compare themselves against the crews of US Ohio class submarines.

As well as undertaking the nuclear deterrent mission, the two submarine services have grown close in a further dimension. Both sides have wanted to put the adversary's strategic missile submarines, SSBNs, at risk. During the Cold War, unlike Western submarines, Soviet SSBNs remained in protected 'bastions' or sanctuary areas close to shore where they could be protected by naval assets and land-based aircraft (McGwire, Booth, and Connell, 1975). British and American hunter-killer submarines, SSNs, sought to hunt these vessels in order to be capable of destroying them in the event of war before they could launch missiles against Western cities (Interview with former First Sea Lord, 2015). In the post-Cold War period, identifying the sonar signatures of Russian and Chinese SSBNs has remained a priority for UK and US SSNs (Interview with Royal Navy submarine Captain, 2012). UK and US vessels conduct surveillance, intelligence gathering and shadowing of ballistic missile submarine movements. The ability of the Royal Navy to conduct such operations has earned it credibility in the eyes of the US Navy and standing tasks are shared between the two navies (Interview with Royal Navy Admiral, 2015)

Cross-national lobbying has been a feature of the Anglo-American relationship, especially where major defence programmes or essential roles have been at stake. Within the inter-service competition for providing the nuclear deterrent, in both countries, the Royal Navy and the US Navy worked together. Sir James Eberle commented that, 'in fighting the Air Force Department, the Royal Navy continuously enlisted the direct and indirect support of the USN' (1986: 156). There have been two principal risks for the UK in such situations. One has been that it becomes immersed in US debates that do not reflect UK national interests. The other is that the RN becomes entangled in internecine rivalries between the US armed services.

The second community responsible for the Anglo-American nuclear relationship has been the senior military officers and civilian officials managing policy within the Ministry of Defence and the Pentagon. Officers and officials have administered the deterrent programme and supervised the acquisition of successor systems. They have criss-crossed the Atlantic, ensuring that the nuclear weapon systems remain fit for purpose and coordinating how they would be used under the terms of the US Single Integrated Operational Plan (SIOP). Xu (2017: 126) refers to meetings of principal level officials every 18 months and subordinate level officials every 6–9 months. This network of officials has been the backbone of the special nuclear relationship as well as its institutional memory. Because of the commonality between US–UK weapon programmes and their long operational lives, British individuals have forged their careers working in cooperation with American counterparts.

At the heart of the liaison between the UK and US nuclear establishments were the project management organizations tasked with bringing both Polaris and Trident into service. The UK set up the Polaris Executive to replicate its US forerunner. According to May and Treverton (1986: 176), 'The British Polaris Executive and the American Special Projects Office . . . worked hand in hand'. A Joint Steering Task Group was created between the two governments to coordinate the respective construction programmes and address any problems that arose (Nailor, 1988: 69). The benefit for the UK was enormous as they were able to avoid some of the pitfalls experienced by the US organization. In the case of Polaris, the institutional relationship was in its relative infancy. By the time of Trident in the 1980s, it was possible to see an institutional relationship that was mature and experienced. Franklin Miller (2008: 176) refers to, 'an enduring web of relationships amongst key policy officials' that discussed all manner of nuclear issues related to both countries.

Two examples illustrate the close policy cooperation that has been achieved. The first stems from the fact that the US has agreed to furnish the UK with the successor system to the Trident D5. Prime Minister Tony Blair reported to the House of Commons in 2006 that agreement had been reached in principle with the George W. Bush administration to participate in the US life extension programme for the D5 missile. The US has agreed to ensure that the configuration of the future missile compartment on its replacement for the Ohio class SSBN will be compatible with the next generation of British missile-carrying submarines (Interview with Counsellor for Defence Policy and Nuclear Issues, 2014). It would have been impossible to proceed with the UK submarine programme unless agreement had been reached that D5 missiles, and their successors, would match the new design. Only 8 missile tubes will be fitted on the new submarines compared to 16 on the Vanguard class. The US has gone out of its way to ensure the UK remains in the strategic nuclear field (Till, 2010: 48).

Another example is the effort that is invested in so-called 'water space management'. The mission of ballistic missile submarines is to leave their base and then become untraceable for the period of several weeks that they are on operational patrol. Although there have always been fears over a potential technological breakthrough in satellite monitoring of submarines, this has not occurred so far. Consequently, the Royal Navy and the US Navy de-conflict their ocean patrol zones in the Atlantic Ocean, for a period up to two years in advance (Interview with Royal Navy submarine Captain, 2012). This is to avoid the danger of their submarines operating in the same area, with the risk of collision or misidentification. In 2009, a French and a British ballistic missile submarine collided in the Atlantic (Till, 2010: 48). The fact that the whereabouts of each others' missile firing submarines is shared between the two communities is testament to the huge amounts of trust that have been built up.

The third specialist community that has interacted across the Atlantic has been nuclear scientists and engineers. This community of nuclear experts and practitioners served to bind together the scientific and the military actors of the two sides. This process, overseen by the US Department of Energy's National Nuclear Security Administration, experienced a long gestation and is described as 'unique' between the two countries (Edelman, 2010: 33). Britain's independent development of fission and fusion bombs and the V-bomber programme were essential prerequisites for convincing the US government to share nuclear secrets in the latter half of the 1950s. The two sides came to exchange information on their warhead designs that proved to have immense value to the UK. The value of this was evident in the warheads that were developed for the Polaris and Trident programmes. Weapon design teams at Lawrence Livermore, Los Alamos, and the Sandia laboratories worked closely with their UK counterparts at AWRE (Simpson, 1983: 223). Baylis and Eames (2023: chapter 9) cite the example of a nuclear test in the 1970s that was conducted jointly by AWRE and Lawrence Livermore.

Most of the interactions were between government laboratories, but there have also been transatlantic links between commercial companies engaged in nuclear projects. These have included submarine links between the US Electric Boat Company and BAE Systems; over missiles with Lockheed Martin, and over nuclear reactors between Westinghouse and Rolls Royce. Richardson (2008: 145) cites the example of the two countries coming together over the next generation fusing mechanisms for their respective nuclear stockpiles. Due to its larger programme, the US has enjoyed substantially more advanced engineering designs. As the former Director of the Lawrence Livermore Laboratory noted, 'the UK did not have the resources (of the US) . . . they had to think of clever ways to get the job done more efficiently' (Foster, 2008: 277).

On the basis of regular contacts between the two sides a series of Joint Working Groups (JOWOGs) were created that became responsible for facets of the nuclear programme (Kandiah and Staerck, 2005: 38). Xu (2015: 122) records that 17 JOWOGs were instigated on matters ranging from nuclear materials and computer technology; 5 focused on warhead design; and 5 sub-groups dealing with matters such as electrical components and manufacturing systems. These groups have been expanded as new technologies have developed. For example, a Joint Re-entry System Working Group (JRSWG) was created to address the multiple warheads on the Polaris missile (Nailor, 1988: 24).

The UK scientific community has been able to contribute valuable skills and expertise to the US. In light of the Comprehensive Test Ban Treaty, both sides have needed to find ways to guarantee warhead safety in the absence of underground testing. The way forward has been arrived at through modelling and the combination of laser technology and advanced computer analysis. Project Orion at the AWRE has delivered high-powered lasers (Burt, 2016: 179), while supercomputers have facilitated the modelling of nuclear explosions (O'Nions, Anderson, and Pitman, 2008: 183). This has been important because, through scientists working together, 'complementary (US-UK) capabilities (have) emerged' (Simpson, 2013: 258)

Ongoing programmes have helped to generate collaborative momentum within the relationship. A permissive environment had been created for Anglo-American nuclear collaboration but it was predicated on the UK having a development programme, such as Polaris or Trident, on which the US could offer advice and expertise. The same was true at the start of the nuclear age when the McMahon Act had forced the UK to construct a weapon of its own (Baylis and Eames, 2023: chapter 3). It has been harder to sustain patterns of cooperation in the absence of major programmes. Stocker (2004) notes that after the introduction of Polaris, the British became aware that the nuclear relationship with the US was at risk of atrophying. In the words of a deputy under-secretary (policy) in the MoD, 'we must make some effort to keep our weapon system credible, as much to impress our allies as our potential enemies' (Stocker, 2004: 134). The Chevaline project, for example, helped to reenergize the scientific and military relationship between the two nuclear weapon communities (Stocker, 2004: 138).

The military, policy-making, and scientific communities all illustrate the fact that trust, mutual respect, and personal contacts have been at the heart of the nuclear relationship (Simpson, 2013: 241–242). Friendships built up over extended periods of time have oiled the wheels of cooperation and provided the confidence to share national security secrets (Miller, 2008: 176).

The replacement for Trident

Having celebrated 50 years of 'Operation Relentless', the Continuous at Sea Deterrence mission (Joint Doctrine Publication 0-10: UK Maritime Power, 2017), the UK is proceeding with a new generation of submarine development to replace Trident. Due to the long lead times, a 'Main Gate' decision was taken and ratified in Parliament in July 2016. A Trident Alternatives Review had been conducted three years earlier at the behest of the Conservatives' coalition partners and had affirmed that a ballistic missile system was the most cost-effective option (Williams, 2016: 112). A decision to extend the life of the existing Trident submarines was taken in 2010 (Ministry of Defence, 2010a) with the result that the first of the new Dreadnought class is due to be operational in 2028. The last of the existing Vanguard submarines will be phased out by 2032. The cost of bringing four Dreadnought class vessels into service is predicted to be £31 billion, spread over a decade (Ministry of Defence, 2015: 36).

The Dreadnought submarines will carry a new warhead on the existing Trident missiles. The UK has been working with the US on its 'Reliable Replacement Warhead' (RRW) programme (Foreign Affairs Select Committee, 2010: para 134). The 2010 Strategic Defence and Security Review indicated that the decision about the new warhead could be deferred because the Trident missile is not due to be replaced by the US before 2042. It is likely that the UK will ultimately produce a warhead derived from the designs of the RRW.

Narratives

There has been considerable debate over whether the UK is an independent nuclear power or whether it has sacrificed this goal and entered into a dependent relationship with the US. Authors such as Navias have referred to a policy of 'independence in concert' in which the UK has sought to make a nuclear contribution, in the context of US leadership of western nuclear strategy (Navias, 1991: 107). The US policy of extended nuclear deterrence over Western Europe provided a framework in which debates about the UK nuclear contribution resided. There was never an expectation on the UK side that it would be involved in a nuclear war in which the US was absent. Although a weapons programme requires a submarine platform, a missile, warhead, and fissile material, the irreducible requirement of 'independence' for the British government has been, in the eyes of Michael Quinlan, a former senior MoD civil servant, the ability to initiate the use of its nuclear weapons in defence of its vital interests (Callahan and Jansson, 2008: 127–128).

Critics have frequently been harsh. Leader of the Opposition, Harold Wilson, famously derided the 'so-called British, so called independent, so-called deterrent' (quoted in Croft, 2001: 72). More recently, analysts have contended that the deterrent can at best be described as 'semi-independent', because it is reliant on the US for its missiles and it is vulnerable to that assistance being withdrawn over a period of time (Wallace and Phillips, 2009: 270). The UK has been willing to rely upon the US because it has regarded its ally as benign, and because it has built a relationship of trust.

Nuclear weapons have played a vital part in the UK–US military narrative. The UK believed that deterrence was the best way of assuring the security of the country from nuclear attack. There were doubts about the continuation of the deterrent by opposition parties. The Labour Party argued in the 1970s that they would not continue the nuclear deterrent, despite conducting studies on how a successor system might be developed. The Thatcher administration of the 1980s was clear that it wanted to preserve Britain's status as a nuclear power beyond the life of Polaris and Chevaline.

So, for the UK military, the relationship with the US became a delicate balancing act. The British sought to convince the US that they were a partner worthy of special cooperation, with whom it should share its nuclear secrets. In return the US provided the UK with a deterrent that underpinned its great power status. The deterrent was a source of prestige with which to stand alongside the US (Ritchie, 2007: 393). Baylis and Stoddart (2012: 343) note that the nuclear relationship with the US was an important part of British identity and that the UK needed the ultimate weapons to enable it to stand alone, as it had done in 1940. According to Simpson (1983: 46), 'not for the first time . . . British nuclear weapon activities were justified not on the basis of the need to deter an enemy, but on the diplomatic need to have bargaining power in relation to a friend (the US)'.

The British military saw nuclear weapons as a means for Britain to influence global affairs and preserve its great power status. There was a fear that discontinuing the deterrent would be perceived as signalling British decline in the eyes of the Russians, but more importantly, in the eyes of the US. If America's allies were relinquishing their defence burdens, this might lead the US to retreat from its transatlantic defence obligations. This led to a complex dimension to the Anglo-American military relationship in terms of the balance between nuclear and conventional forces. For its part, the UK realized that it could put pressure on the US by threatening to reduce its conventional forces if nuclear assistance was not forthcoming. In return, the US pressured their ally to sustain conventional defence spending in return for American nuclear generosity.

The US has increasingly wanted to share the responsibility of being a nuclear power and valued the role that that the British military could play. It has seen the British possession of nuclear weapons as part of a shared identity that has deflected opprobrium from the US. If the UK were to relinquish its nuclear deterrent, it would raise questions as to why the US could not follow a similar path. At a NATO meeting in Brussels in 2016, US Defense Secretary Ashton Carter said that it was important that Britain preserved Trident due to its role in NATO deterrence and the 'outsized role on the global stage' that it allowed it to play (BBC News, 2016).

The UK's nuclear status has become a part of its contribution to the Western-led international order. In a letter between the defence secretaries of the Carter and Thatcher governments the US declared that it 'attaches significance to the nuclear capability of the UK' (quoted in Stoddart and Baylis, 2012: 506). The US appreciated that the UK has been sharing the nuclear burden of the West. It has also understood that the principal risk to the British deterrent is the cost of successor generations of systems. 'The key to understanding the Anglo-American military relationship in nuclear energy is the acceptance by both states that it is in their mutual interest for Britain to have a technically effective strategic deterrent at minimum cost' (Simpson, 2013: 226).

Conclusion

The Anglo-American nuclear relationship is a classic illustration of institutionalism. Despite personal relationships between heads of state varying in intensity, the institutional relationship has kept the US and the UK together. It is strong because it is made up of the various strands of the military, policymaking, and scientific communities. All three communities have cooperated together, they have built trust over a period of time, and they have brought new systems into operational service. When critical junctures have arisen, such as the transition from Polaris to Trident or the follow-on system to Trident, the two sides have been committed to continuing their path-dependent relationship. When challenges arise, 'officials . . . instantly know who to talk with' (Xu, 2017: 43).

The post-Cold War Anglo-American nuclear relationship has experienced stability and relative smoothness. This contrasts with the early friction in nuclear matters in the 1950s and 1960s. The US attitude towards the UK deterrent stabilized and became consistent. Both sides acknowledged a mutual interest in perpetuating the UK as a nuclear power (Interview with former First Sea Lord, 2015). Williams (2016: 108) goes as far as to describe the successor to Trident as the 'barometer' of the special relationship.

Dependency, however, has not been without its concerns. Whilst the UK has provided some reciprocity to the US in terms of bases for its submarines, in early warning, and in the contribution of British scientists to certain nuclear technologies, at heart the relationship has been fundamentally unequal. It has rendered the UK vulnerable to potential changes in US policy. The US had never used the deterrent as a means of pressure, but having relinquished a national nuclear programme, the UK would find it enormously difficult and costly to develop and deploy its own delivery system. Wallace and Phillips (2009: 270) argue that this awareness of dependence has underpinned British support for post-Cold War US interventions.

8

Conclusion

This study has explored how, since the end of the Cold War, the British armed forces have maintained a close relationship with their US counterparts. During times of peace and conflict, all three of the armed services have worked assiduously to cooperate with American forces. It has not been a single relationship, but rather a patchwork of different ones, conducted between several specialized communities. The Royal Navy submarine community, for example, have interacted closely with their counterparts in the US Navy, whilst the relationship between special forces has been particularly significant. Some of these interrelationships have been more robust than others and levels of intimacy have varied over time.

The British armed forces have actively cultivated cooperation with the US military. By embedding their personnel in US structures and conducting a constant dialogue, the British military has sought to understand American doctrine and planning and be apprised of its direction of travel. This effort to be institutionally 'plugged in' to the US military in peacetime has sought to facilitate the ability to transition smoothly to a wartime posture. This book has sought to investigate how links are maintained at various levels and how they pertain to different sorts of capabilities and issue areas. Personal friendships between officers, civil servants, and scientists of the two countries have played a particularly important part in sustaining the vibrancy of the overall relationship.

By drawing upon the theory of historical institutionalism, this study has shown how patterns of interaction over time have made the military relationship a key part of UK–US relations. Whilst it is subordinate to, and much less visible than, the interchanges between the two governments, it has contributed and helped to foster a broader political relationship. During periods of tension between leaders of the two countries, the continuation of a regular defence dialogue and practical cooperation between conventional and nuclear forces has been a source of strength.

Regular collaboration and exercises have provided the means for the British military to practice working with the US armed services. Key events, such as the end of the Cold War, the War on Terror, and the conflicts against Iraq, have represented 'critical junctures' and tests for the relevance of the military relationship. The UK has invested considerable effort at such moments to adapt past patterns of working together to be able meet new demands (Marsh, 2013: 189). Drawing upon earlier experience and accumulated trust has made that possible. Whilst the technological transformation of UK forces has been less ambitious than its superpower ally and

The Anglo-American Military Relationship. Wyn Rees, Oxford University Press. © Wyn Rees (2024).
DOI: 10.1093/oso/9780198884620.003.0008

the overall size of forces has been reduced, the British military have striven to make themselves the most significant contributors to US-led operations (Interview with British Army Lieutenant General, 2015).

The British have also constructed a narrative designed to convince the US of their worth. They have emphasized their history of steadfast support. American leaders have been given the confidence to treat the UK as their ally of first choice. This has generated path dependence within the relationship: the US has considered the UK its most reliable partner. The strategic nuclear relationship is testimony to the success of this approach and has been consistent and intimate for some sixty years.

It was a widespread assumption that the special relationship would wither following the end of the Cold War. McKercher described it as having 'lost its strategic relevance' with the disappearance of the Soviet threat (2017: 108). This study refutes that view. The post-Cold War era brought different, but important, strategic challenges of its own. Although it was characterized by American hegemony, the period was one in which an unprecedented number of conflicts occurred and the US was in need of coalition allies. As the British responded to these demands, it gave new purpose to Anglo-American military cooperation.

The hazard throughout the post-Cold War period, from the UK's perspective, has not been overbearing American power but the risk of its absence. The UK has been anxious that the US could withdraw from multilateralism and its existing commitments. It might choose to do this on the grounds that its Western allies were either not worth supporting or were capable of ensuring their security alone. In UK eyes, the loss of US leadership risked leaving the West rudderless and jeopardizing its own investment in partnering Washington. As a result, the UK was eager to convince America that there was support for its interventions around the world and a contributor that could be depended upon.

Post-Cold War conflicts, including the War on Terror, varied in their scale and nature (Dumbrell, 2004: 440). The two wars against Iraq were high-intensity and interstate, whilst the conflicts in the Balkans and against Libya were more circumscribed operations. The British and American militaries were required to traverse the spectrum of conflict, responding to war and peace-making and peace enforcement demands. There was a lack of doctrine for many of these tasks and their armed forces had to improvise. These unpredictable operations drew their militaries together. The high level of institutionalization between them ensured that common approaches were taken and that the US valued British judgement.

Even though the British military were eager to partner with the US, the disparity in size and strength inevitably led to pressures. Maintaining expeditionary capabilities and preserving interoperability with US forces imposed a strain on Britain's defence budget (Development, Concepts and Doctrine Centre, 2007). Post-Cold War defence reviews—with the exception of the 1998 Strategic Defence Review— amounted to Treasury efforts to reduce spending. Pressure was particularly acute after the financial crisis of 2008 and led to the defence reviews of 2010 and 2015. Defence spending fell below 2% of gross domestic product (Michta, 2019: 65) and in 2010 Army personnel were reduced from 95,000 to 82,000 (Wither, 2006). This resulted in fears within the US defence establishment of the loss of mass in the British armed forces. Former US Secretary of Defense, Robert Gates, questioned whether the UK could remain, 'a full spectrum partner', capable of acting alongside the US in all circumstances (BBC News, 2014; McCourt, 2014, 170). Even senior British officers contended that cuts had undermined the country's position as a leading military ally of America. General Sir Nicholas Houghton, for instance, cautioned that cuts to the British Army had resulted in the creation of a 'hollow force' (Houghton, 2013), while General Richard Barrons warned of Britain becoming 'Belgium with nukes' (Haynes, 2018: 4).

Over the last thirty years, the British military has wrestled with a dilemma. Would it be more cost effective, but still politically effective, to offer specialized capabilities to US operations, such as air-to-air refuelling, special forces, or mine counter-measures vessels (Foreign Affairs Select Committee, 2010)? Such an approach could be justified on the grounds that a major operation would always be conducted in concert with the US. The Defence Secretary, Ben Wallace, broke with tradition in January 2020 when he questioned whether the UK could always assume it would operate in conjunction with the US or that the US would always want to be involved. There have been those that have argued that by undertaking specialized roles, the UK could offer more value to the US and reduce the burden of defence spending. Clarke opined that it would be, 'Better to be capable of doing a job in a US-led coalition, even if it is less prestigious . . . but be trusted to accomplish it well.' (Foreign Affairs Select Committee, 2010: para. 92). A former senior Army officer questioned whether an 'empowered' brigade might be more value than a division that was largely hollow and lacked capability (Interview with former Chief of the General Staff, 2014).

It is clear that reputational damage has occurred when the British promised to provide a capability but then proved unable to deliver on that commitment. Those were the lessons of British deployments in both Helmand and southern Iraq, and they resulted in harsh criticisms by senior US officers and politicians. A similar sort of risk could emerge if UK cuts in defence spending render its armed forces incapable of carrying out major roles. The US might lose the trust that they could depend on the British in an emergency.

The UK has chosen to preserve a balanced military capability—a 'United States Lite' option (Elliott, 2015: 238). It has done so on the grounds that being able to mount the full breadth of operational tasks has been part of what has made the UK special. A high-end capability, albeit of modest size, was judged to be the most attractive contribution to US operations (Lindley-French, 2015). In doing so it has locked the UK into a demanding operational posture. If it had chosen instead to adopt unbalanced forces, there was a fear that it could have resulted in even greater reliance on the US. There were concerns that the UK risked entering into an increasingly vulnerable relationship.

Nevertheless, operating alongside the US in various sorts of operations has led to tensions with the UK. War has exposed differences in strategic culture as well as in priorities between the two sides. For example, British and US militaries took contending approaches to Phase IV operations in Iraq and Afghanistan. Similarly, the US rethought its counter-insurgency doctrine in Iraq and left the British military struggling to align with its practice. Trust within the relationship was weakened. It is a testament to the underlying strength of the institutional relationship that such differences did not undermine the entire pattern of cooperation. Challenges and criticisms were absorbed without the entire edifice of military to military relations being jeopardized.

In spite of participating in US-led coalition operations, the UK did not perceive itself to obtain substantial influence over US policy (Wallace and Philips, 2009; Dumbrell, 2004: 448). Former UN ambassador Jeremy Greenstock (2016: 409) expressed disappointment that a strong military contribution paid few political dividends. Porter (2010: 372) differentiates between benefits and influence: he argues that the UK obtained benefits from working with the US, but not influence over its policy, because the US is too powerful. Whilst the UK obtained privileged access to US thinking, this did not necessarily translate into influence (Interview with former Commander of British Land Forces, 2015). This book bears out that assessment. The British military were successful in achieving close collaboration with their American counterparts but there was a failure to translate this into political sway at the theatre or strategic level (Interview with British Army Lieutenant General, 2015). The British military chose to focus on their region of responsibility and there was political reluctance from Whitehall to shoulder a larger responsibility for the outcome of the Iraqi and Afghan conflicts. This complements the view of Niblett (2007: 639) that the special relationship tends to operate at the tactical level rather than the strategic level.

The UK Parliament's Foreign Affairs Committee predicted that Britain's ability to influence the US would decline following the end of the wars in Iraq and Afghanistan (Foreign Affairs Select Committee, 2009). On one level this was prescient as cessation of the two operations has reduced Anglo-American military interchange. The relationship benefits from active projects on which to build momentum. Yet on another level the then Labour Foreign Secretary David Milliband was correct in asserting that the relationship would continue (Foreign Affairs Select Committee, 2010a). As this book has demonstrated, the Anglo-American military relationship has shown the ability to adapt to meet new security threats.

As well as the risks of overextension, success or failure for the British military has too often been measured in terms of US judgement. British armed forces have tended to view their relationship with America as an end in itself, rather than as a means to an end. The military have not been exempt from the tendency within the wider British state to weigh themselves through American eyes. This has resulted in the UK preserving roles and capabilities that it can no longer afford and delaying cuts for fear of earning US criticism. It has perpetuated an artificial sense of the UK as a global power that must put US interests first.

This tendency to defer to American priorities has stemmed from one of the achievements of the special relationship, namely British military intimacy with its thinking. Sharing in US threat assessments and being party to its planning processes has led to the British identifying too readily with their ally's priorities. UK policy, and that of its military planners, has suffered from being captured by the ideas and world view of the US. In the words of Xu (2017: 27), it has reflected the British state's 'consistent willingness to pay the price' to keep the US committed to the relationship.

A further drawback of Anglo-American cooperation has been the opportunity cost. Britain has paid a price in terms of denying itself closer bilateral cooperation with European countries, such as France (Gomis, 2011). Through the Lancaster House Treaty and the subsequent Sandhurst agreement, France and the UK signalled their intention to work more closely together. In particular, the UK has identified the benefits of nuclear cooperation with France but it has been constrained by the provisions of existing cooperation with America. Leaving the European Union and affirming the centrality of the US in UK defence aspirations has made it harder to build on cooperation with Paris and other European countries.

The UK needs to be clear-eyed about what serves its own interests, rather than just the interests of the US. Menon (Menon, 2010: 11) argues that Britain, 'must be willing to recognize genuine differences of interest with the United States', and should not shrink from making self-interested calculations (Foreign Affairs Select Committee, 2009: 7). For example, there was little British strategic interest in the 2006 decision to increase its commitment in Helmand and the Army gave poor advice to ministers (Kennedy, 2012: 70). The UK should be more robust in acknowledging that disagreements can occur with Washington without prejudicing the overall relationship. Witney contends that policy should not be driven by considerations of what would make the US take the UK seriously (Foreign Affairs Select Committee, 2010: Evidence 23).

Looking to the future

According to a senior British Army officer giving evidence to Parliament, 'It will continue to be in the UK's national interest to remain strategically relevant to the US' (Defence Select Committee, 2011). While this book supports that view, the future of Anglo-American military relations will depend upon the wider political and strategic context in which the special relationship operates. There are a host of issues that could shape that context and determine the challenges that the British armed forces will face. These issues include the threat environment, the strength of the UK economy, and the alignment of US and UK foreign interests.

A divergence in transatlantic interests has long been a trend identified by commentators (Foreign Affairs Select Committee, 2009). Tensions within US–European relations at the time of the 2003 War against Iraq contributed to a prolonged malaise that reached a nadir with the Trump administration. The US has consistently expressed dissatisfaction with the level of defence spending by its European allies, accusing them of free-riding. During his election campaign President Donald Trump increased the pressure by calling NATO 'obsolete' and threatened to reduce US force levels in Europe. The UK tried to set an example by increasing defence expenditure. There was an uplift in defence spending under Prime Minister Boris Johnson to 2% of GDP. Substantially enhanced spending would provide the British armed forces with more capabilities that they could offer to the US and help to convince its elites that Europe intended to pull its weight.

Divergence in transatlantic relations has impacted disproportionately upon the UK. This is because of its traditional attempt to play a transatlantic interlocutor role and the fallout from Brexit. Since Brexit the UK has less influence with the US: it no longer speaks on behalf of Europe and it cannot constrain developments in the EU's Common Security and Defence Policy (Defence Select Committee, 2018b, Nuland). The significance of this, however, should not be exaggerated. Whilst an EU member the UK was always lukewarm about defence integration and contributed only token forces to CSDP missions. As Marsh (2018: 16) has argued, EU defence was never at the heart of the special relationship: the British always championed the primacy of NATO. The British military placed a much higher priority on cooperation with the US than with the EU.

One factor that has caused a diminution in US attention to Europe was its 'pivot' to Asia. This initiative began under President Barack Obama and was intensified under Presidents Trump and Biden. The US signalled its intention to devote greater attention to strategic and economic developments in the Indo-Pacific rather than the Euro-Atlantic area. America sees China as the greatest long-term threat to its interests because of Beijing's economic prowess, its security crackdown in both Hong Kong and Xinjiang, and its ambition to incorporate Taiwan (Ministry of Defence, 2021). The US has strengthened its military capabilities in recognition of the fact that Pacific Command faces a more hostile environment for its carrier battlegroups and surface vessels the closer they come to the Chinese mainland. America has also sought to revitalize security cooperation with major regional allies such as Japan, South Korea, and Australia.

In its Integrated Review, the UK responded to America's Indo-Pacific strategy by designating China as one of its principal threats, alongside Russia (Ministry of Defence, 2021: 62). This UK 'tilt' towards the theatre reflected its desire to offer a relevant military contribution to the US. The first operational deployment of the new aircraft carrier *HMS Queen Elizabeth* was made to the Pacific in April 2021, including the hosting of US Marine Corps F-35Bs on its flight deck. The Royal Navy also announced that a Littoral Response Group will be permanently deployed to the region along with a complement of Royal Marine Commandos. This will form the kernel of an interventionary capability that can be supplemented by special forces or other naval vessels as the need arises.

Yet because of its location and limited resources, the UK can never be a major Indo-Pacific actor (Magill and Rees, 2022: 91). The British armed forces lack the numbers and the reach to sustain a significant presence. Where the UK has a role to play is in encouraging regional actors to more actively support the US. The Australia, United Kingdom, and United States (AUKUS) announcement in September 2021 was demonstration of the constructive part open to London (BBC, 2021). The UK and the US entered into a pact with Australia to provide it with the technology to build eight nuclear-powered, hunter-killer submarines. Although this replaces an earlier French deal with Australia, it offers a way for the Australian Navy to access nuclear powered vessels with greater speed and range than they could otherwise possess. Such partnerships provide the UK with a valuable opportunity to assist the US.

It has been the return of Russia as an aggressive great power that has reinforced Anglo-American future relations. President Vladimir Putin's seizure of Crimea in 2014 and his subsequent invasion of Ukraine in February 2022 have exposed the continuing threat that Russia poses to European security. While the Integrated Review focused attention on the long-term challenge posed by China, the invasion of Ukraine showed the UK that its principal effort must remain the deterrence of Russia. Once more Russia has become the glue that draws the two sides of the Atlantic together against a shared threat. With the US diverting resources and attention to the Indo-Pacific region, there is a need to arrive at a division of labour.

The British military are well placed to rise to that challenge and share America's burden. The UK will be able to exploit its traditional focus on NATO as its primary contribution to the military relationship with America. This will maximize the UK's status and enable it to operate to the closest possible extent with Washington. A British battlegroup and airpower assets already reinforce Estonia, combat engineers are situated in Poland, and additional naval forces have been despatched to the north Atlantic. The UK has provided substantial military equipment and training to Ukraine. In addition to NATO, the UK has signalled its intention to remain active in the Persian Gulf. A new British naval base, *HMS Juffair*, has been acquired in Bahrain, the home of the US 5th Fleet.

Great power threats will evolve and the Anglo-American military relationship will need to adapt to meet them. In the contemporary world, high technology developments present a major challenge. Artificial intelligence, directed energy weapons, nano technologies, quantum computing, space-based systems, and the manipulation of cyberspace are all emerging domains. They add further pressure to budgets by creating new realms for military competition. In addition to space technologies, Britain has been investing heavily in defensive and offensive cyber capabilities. A National Cyber Force was launched by the UK in November 2020 and brings together the capabilities of the Ministry of Defence, the Government Communications Headquarters (GCHQ), and the intelligence services (Niblett, 2021). The US is looking to the UK to cooperate on innovative technologies. Yet there are also limits to the resources that the UK can muster because its research and development spending is several orders of magnitude smaller than that of the US.

The British military wants to remain close to the US. Britain's post-Cold War investment in high-intensity warfighting capabilities in the Euro-Atlantic area is valuable to America. Operations Other Than War and counter insurgency, whilst dominant during the conflicts in Iraq, Afghanistan, and Libya, have now been eclipsed by the risk of war with Russia or with China. After the salutary experiences of expeditionary operations in the 1990s and 2000s, Britain and America are reluctant to become drawn into other regional conflicts. Yet it would be a foolish analyst that predicted that such operations could never re-occur.

The Anglo-American relationship will continue because US hegemony has been eroded and it will need allies that are willing to undertake substantive roles. The British military have proven their willingness to serve as a reliable partner, to invest resources, and provide leadership in military operations. It has deployed personnel of high quality that have made significant contributions to coalition operations across the world.

The British military will be able to leverage their institutional linkages with the US armed services to perpetuate cooperation in the future. Past patterns of routinized consultation and planning will give each side the confidence to combat new threats. The British and US armed services will draw upon friendships and trust between officers and officials that have been built up over a considerable time. The US military will look first to their British allies to assist them in confronting both conventional and nuclear challenges. Military cooperation will remain a vital element of the wider special relationship.

Bibliography

Books

Badsey, S. Grove, M. and Havers, R. (2005) *The Falklands Conflict Twenty Years On: Lessons for the Future*, Taylor and Francis, London.

Bailey, J., Iron, R. and Strachan, H. (2013) (eds) *British Generals in Blair's Wars*, Ashgate, Farnham.

Bankcroft, J. (ed) *US-UK Relations at the Start of the 21st Century*, Nova Science Publishers, New York.

Barry, B. (2020) *Blood, Metal and Dust: How Victory Turned into Defeat in Afghanistan and Iraq*, Osprey, Oxford.

Bartlett, C. (1972) *The Long Retreat. A Short History of British Defence Policy 1945–70*, Macmillan, London.

Bartlett, C. (1992) *'The Special Relationship': A Political History of Anglo-American Relations since 1945*, Longman, London.

Baylis, J. (1984) *Anglo-American Defence Relations 1939–1984: The Special Relationship*, Palgrave Macmillan, Basingstoke.

Baylis, J. (1997) *Anglo-American Relations since 1939: The Enduring Alliance*, Manchester University Press, Manchester.

Baylis, J. (1995) *Ambiguity and Deterrence: British Nuclear Strategy 1945–1964*, Clarendon Press, Oxford.

Baylis, J. and Eames, A. (2023) *Sharing Nuclear Secrets: Trust, Mistrust and Ambiguity in Anglo-American Nuclear Relations since 1939*, Oxford University Press, Oxford.

Billière, P. de la (2008) *Storm Command: A Personal Account of the Gulf War*, Harper Collins, London.

Blair, T. (2010) *A Journey*, Random House, London.

Boyes, J. (2019) *Blue Streak: Britain's Medium Range Ballistic Missile*, Fonthill, Warwickshire.

Burk, K. (2009) *Old World, New World*, Grove Press, New York.

Campbell, D. (1984) *The Unsinkable Aircraft Carrier: American Military Power in Britain*, Michael Joseph, London.

Cassidy, R. (2004) *Peacekeeping in the Abyss: British and American Peacekeeping Doctrine and Practice after the Cold War*, Praeger, Westport.

Chandrasekaran, R. (2012) *Little America: The War within the War for Afghanistan*, Bloomsbury, London.

Childs, N. (2009) *The Age of Invincible: The Ship that Defined the Modern Royal Navy*, Pen and Sword Books, London.

Clark, I. (1994) *Nuclear Diplomacy and the Special Relationship. Britain's Deterrent and America 1957–1962*, Oxford University Press, Oxford.

Clark, W. (2001) *Waging Modern Wars: Bosnia, Kosovo and the Future of Combat*, Public Affairs, New York.

Codner, M. and Clarke, M. (2011) (eds) *A Question of Security: The British Defence Review in an Age of Austerity*, I. B. Tauris, London.

Cowper-Coles, S. (2012) *Cables from Kabul: The Inside Story of the West's Afghanistan Campaign*, Harper Collins, London.

Croft, S., Dorman, A., Rees, W. and Uttley, M. (2001) *Britain and Defence 1945–2000: A Policy Re-evaluation*, Longman, Harlow.

Daalder, I. and O'Hanlon, M. (2001) *Winning Ugly: NATO's War to Save Kosovo*, Brookings Press, Washington DC.

Danchev, A. (1986) *Very Special Relationship: Field Marshal Sir John Dill and the Anglo-American Alliance, 1941–44*, Brassey's, London.

Danchev, A. (1997) (ed) *On Specialness: Essays in Anglo-American Relations*, Palgrave Macmillan, Basingstoke.

Dannatt, R. (2011) *Leading from the Front*, Corgi, London.

Dannatt, R. (2016) *Boots on the Ground. Britain and her Army since 1945*, Profile Books, London.

Darby, P. (1973) *British Defence Policy East of Suez, 1947-68*, Oxford University Press, Oxford.

Davis, B. (1990) *Qaddafi, Terrorism and the Origins of the US Attack on Libya*, Praeger, New York.

Deutsch, K., Burrell, S., Kann, R., Lee, M., Lichterman, M., Lindgren, R., Loewen-heim, F., and Wagenen, R. von, (1957) *Political Community and the North Atlantic Area: International Organization in Light of Historical Experience*, Greenwood Press, New York.

Devereux, D. (1990) *The Formulation of British Policy Towards the Middle East, 1948–1956*, Macmillan, Basingstoke.

Dickie, J. (1994) *Special No More: Anglo-American Relations: Rhetoric and Reality*, Weidenfeld and Nicolson, London.

Dobson, A. (1995) *Anglo-American Relations in the Twentieth Century: The Politics and Diplomacy of Friendly Superpowers: The Politics and Diplomacy of Superpowers*, Routledge, London.

Dobson, A. and Marsh, S. (2013) (eds) *Anglo-American Relations: Contemporary Perspectives*, London, Routledge.

Dockrill, S. (1988) *British Defence since 1945*, Basil Blackwell, Oxford.

Dockrill, S. (2002) *Britain's Retreat from East of Suez: The Choice between Europe and the World?* Palgrave Macmillan, Basingstoke.

Dorman, A. (2009) *Blair's Successful War: British Military Intervention in Sierra Leone*, Ashgate, Aldershot

Dumbrell, J. (2001) *A Special Relationship: Anglo-American Relations in the Cold War and After*, Palgrave Macmillan, London.

Dumbrell, J. (2006) (Second edition) *A Special Relationship: Anglo-American Relations from the Cold War to Iraq*, Palgrave Macmillan, London

Duke, S. (1987) *US Defence Bases in the United Kingdom: A Matter for Joint Decision,* St Antony's, Macmillan Series, Basingstoke.

Eden, A. (1960) *Full Circle*, Cassell, London

Elliott, C. (2015) *High Command. British Military Leadership in the Iraq and Afghanistan Wars*, London, Hurst and Company.

Egnell, R. (2009) *Complex Peace Operations and Civil–Military Relations. Winning the Peace*, Routledge, London.

Fairweather, J. (2011) *War of Choice: The British in Iraq 2003-9*, Jonathan Cape, London.

Farrell, T., Rynning, S. and Terriff, T. (2013) *Transforming Military Power since the Cold War: Britain, France and the United States, 1991–2012*, Cambridge University Press, Cambridge.

Farrell, T. (2017) *Unwinnable: Britain's War in Afghanistan, 2001–2014*, The Bodley Head, London.

Finlan, A. (2014) *Contemporary Military Strategy and the Global War on Terror. UK and UK Armed Forces in Afghanistan and Iraq 2001–2012*, Bloomsbury, New York.

Freedman, L. (2005) *The Official History of the Falklands Campaign, Volume 2, War and Diplomacy*, Routledge, London.

Fukuyama, F. (1992) *The End of History and the Last Man*, Free Press, New York.

Fursdon, E. (1980) *The European Defence Community. A History*, Macmillan, London.

Futter, A. (2016) (ed) *The United Kingdom and the Future of Nuclear Weapons*, Rowman and Littlefield, London.

Galula, D. (1964) *Counterinsurgency Warfare: Theory and Practice*, Praeger Security International, Westport.

Gamble, A. (2003) *Between Europe and America: The Future of British Politics*, Palgrave Macmillan, Basingstoke.

Gates, R. (2014) *Duty. Memoirs of a Secretary at War*, Alfred Knopf, New York.

Giegerich, B. (2006) *European Security and Strategic Culture. National Responses to the EU's Security and Defence Policy*, Nomos, Baden-Baden.

Gill, D. (2014) *Britain and the Bomb: Nuclear Diplomacy 1964–1970*, Stanford University Press, Stanford.

Gowing, M. (1974) *Independence and Deterrence: Britain and Atomic Energy, 1945–52, Volume 1. Policy Making*, Macmillan, Basingstoke.

Greenstock, J. (2016) *Iraq: The Cost of War*, Arrow Books, London.

Grove, E. (1987) *Vanguard to Trident*, Bodley Head, London.

Grove, E. (1991) *Battle for the Fiords. NATO's Forward Maritime Strategy in Action*, Ian Allan, London.

Haass, R. (1997) *The Reluctant Sheriff: The United States after the Cold War*, Brookings Press, Washington DC.

Healey, D. (1989) *The Time of My Life*, London, Penguin.

Hiro, D. (2003) (Second edition) *Desert Shield to Desert Storm: The Second Gulf War*, Authors Choice Press, New York.

Howorth, J. (2007) *Security and Defence Policy in the European Union*, Palgrave Macmillan, Basingstoke and New York.

Ikenberry, J. G. (2001) *After Victory: Institutions, Strategic Restraint and the Rebuilding of Order after Major Wars*, Princeton University Press, Princeton.

Jackson, M. (2007) *Soldier: The Autobiography*, Bantam Press, London.

Johnson, A. (2014) (ed.) *Wars in Peace: British Military Operations Since 1991*, Royal United Services Institute, London.

Johnson, R. Haaland Matlary, J. (2019) (eds) *The United Kingdom's Defence after Brexit: Britain's Alliances, Coalitions and Partnerships*, Springer, Switzerland.

Jones, M. (2019) *The Official History of the UK Strategic Nuclear Deterrent, Volume 1: From the V-Bomber Era to the Arrival of Polaris, 1945–1964*, Routledge, London.

Jones, M. (2019) *The Official History of the UK Strategic Nuclear Deterrent, Volume II, The Labour Government and the Polaris Programme 1964–1970*, Routledge, London.

Kagan, F. (2006) *Finding the Target. The Transformation of American Military Policy*, Encounter Book, New York.

Kampfner, J. (2003) *Blair's Wars*, Free Press, London.

Keohane, R. (1989) *International Institutions and State of Power: Essays in International Relations Theory*, Westview Press, Boulder.

King, A. (2011) *The Transformation of Europe's Armed Forces: From the Rhine to Afghanistan*, Cambridge University Press, Cambridge.

Krasner, S. (1983) (ed) *International Regimes*, Cornell University Press, Ithaca.

Kretchik, W. (2011) *U.S. Army Doctrine. From the American Revolution to the War on Terror*, University Press of Kansas, Lawrence.

Kydd, A. (2005) *Trust and Mistrust in International Relations*, Princeton University Press, Princeton.

Lewis, A. (2018) (Third edition) *The American Culture of War. The History of US Military Force from World War II to Operation Enduring Freedom*, Routledge, New York.

Lindley-French, J. (2015) *Little Britain? Twenty-First Century Strategy for a Middling European Power*, CreateSpace Publishing Platform, Scotts Valley.

Long, A. (2016) *The Soul of Armies. Counterinsurgency Doctrine and Military Culture in the US and UK*, Cornell University Press, Ithaca.

Louis, W. and Owen, R. (1988) (eds) *The Suez Crisis and its Consequences*, Clarendon Press, Oxford.

Louis, W. and Bull, H. (1986) (eds) *The 'Special Relationship': Anglo-American Relations since 1945*, Clarendon Press, Oxford

Lowndes, V. and Roberts, M. (2013) *Why Institutions Matter: The New Institutionalism in Political Science*, Palgrave Macmillan, Basingstoke.

Mackby, J. and Cornish, P. (2008) (eds) *US-UK Nuclear Cooperation after Fifty Years, CSIS and Chatham House*, CSIS Press, Washington DC.

Mahncke, D., Rees, W. and Thompson, W. (2004) *Redefining Transatlantic Security Relations: The Challenge of Change*, Manchester University Press, Manchester.

Mahnken, T. (2008) *Technology and the American Way of War*, Columbia University Press, New York.

McGwire, M., Booth, K. and Connell, J. (1975) (eds) *Soviet Naval Policy: Objectives and Constraints*, Praeger, New York

McInnes, C. (1996) *Hot War, Cold War. The British Army's Way in Warfare 1945–95*, Brassey's, London.

McKercher, B. (2017) *Britain, America and the Special Relationship since 1941*, Routledge, London.

Menaul, S. (1980) *Countdown: Britain's Strategic Nuclear Forces*, Hale, London.

Miller, R. (1995) (ed) *'Seeing off the Bear: Anglo-American Air Power Cooperation during the Cold War'*, Joint Meeting of the Royal Air Force Historical Society and the Air Force Historical Foundation, Air Force History and Museums Program, Washington DC.

Miskimmom, A., O'Loughlin, B. and Roselle, L. (2013) *Strategic Narratives: Communication Power and the New World Order*, Routledge, London.

Mitchell, P. (2009) *Network Centric Warfare and Coalition Operations: The New Military Operating System*, Routledge, London.

Mumford, A. (2017) *Counterinsurgency Wars and the Anglo-American Alliance: The Special Relationship on the Rocks*, Georgetown University Press, Washington DC.

Nagl, J. (2005) *Learning to Eat Soup with a Knife: Counterinsurgency Lessons from Malaya and Vietnam*, Chicago University Press, Chicago.

Nacos, B. (2016) (Fifth edition) *Terrorism and Counterterrorism*, Routledge, Abingdon.

Nailor, P. (1988) *The Nassau Connection: The Organisation and Management of the British Polaris Project*, Her Majesty's Stationery Office, London.

Naughtie, J. (2004) *The Accidental American*, Macmillan, London.

Navias, M. (1991) *Nuclear Weapons and British Strategic Planning 1955–1958*, Clarendon Press, Oxford.

Owen, D. (1996) *Balkan Odyssey*, Indigo, London.

Peters, G. (2019) (Fourth edition) *Institutional Theory in Political Science: The New Institutionalism*, Bloomsbury, London.

Posen, B. (1984) *The Sources of Military Doctrine: France, Britain and Germany between the World Wars*, Cornell University Press, Ithaca.

Rayburn, D. and Sobchak, F. (2019) (eds) *The US Army in the Iraq War, Volume 1. Invasion, Insurgency, Civil War,* US Army War College Press, Strategic Studies Institute, Carlisle Barracks, PA.

Renwick, R. (2016) *Fighting with Allies: America and Britain in Peace and War*, Biteback Publishing, London.

Renz, B. (2018) *Russia's Military Revival*, Polity, Cambridge.

Richards, D. (2014) *Taking Command*, Headline, London.

Richardson (1996) *When Allies Differ: Anglo-American Relations during the Suez and Falklands*, Basingstoke, Macmillan.

Riddell, P. (2003) *Hug them Close: Blair, Clinton and the Special Relationship*, Politico, London.

Ring, J. (2001) *We Come Unseen: The Untold Story of Britain's Cold War Submariners*, John Murray, London.

Robb, T. (2013) *A Strained Partnership? US-UK Relations in the Era of Détente 1969–77*, Manchester University Press, Manchester.

Robinson, L. (2008) *Tell Me How This Ends. General Petraeus and the Search for a Way Out of Iraq*, Public Affairs, New York.

Sanders, D. (1990) *Losing an Empire, Finding a Role: British Foreign Policy since 1945*, Macmillan, Basingstoke.

Sapolsky, H., Friedman, B. and Green, B. (2009) (eds) *US Military Innovation since the Cold War. Creation without Destruction*, Routledge, London.

Schwarzkopf, N. (1992) *It Doesn't Take a Hero*, Bantam Books, London.

Scott, W. (1995) (Fourth edition) *Institutions and Organizations: Ideas, Interests, and Identities*, Sage, London.

Seitz, R. (1998) *Over Here*, Phoenix, London.

Seldon, A. (2008) *Blair Unbound*, Packet Books, London.

Self, R. (2010) *British Foreign Policy since 1945. Challenges and Dilemmas in a Changing World*, Palgrave Macmillan, London.

Serena, C. (2011) *A Revolution in Military Adaptation: The US Army in the Iraq War*, Georgetown University Press, Washington DC.

Shimko, K. (2010) *The Iraq Wars and America's Military Revolution*, Cambridge University Press, Cambridge.

Simpson, E. (2012) *War from the Ground Up. Twenty-first Century Combat as Politics*, Hurst and Company, London.

Simpson, J. (1983) *The Independent Nuclear State: The United States, Britain and the Military Atom*, Macmillan, Basingstoke.

Smith, R. (2005) *The Utility of Force. The Art of War in the Modern World*, Penguin, London.

Smith, M. and Latawski, P. (2003) *The Kosovo Crisis*, Manchester University Press, Manchester.

Snyder, J. (1977) *The Soviet Strategic Culture: Implications for Nuclear Options*, RAND, Santa Monica.

Stocker, J. (2004) *Britain and Ballistic Missile Defence, 1942–2002*, Frank Cass, London.

Stoddart, K. and Baylis, J. (2014) *The British Nuclear Experience: The Roles of Beliefs, Culture and Identity*, Oxford University Press, Oxford.

Strachan, H. (2006) (ed) *Big Wars and Small Wars. The British Army and the Lessons of War in the Twentieth Century*, Routledge, Abingdon.

Strachan, H. (2013) *The Direction of War. Contemporary Strategy in Historical Perspective*, Cambridge University Press, Cambridge.

Stromseth, J. (1988) *The Origins of Flexible Response: NATO's Debate over Strategy in the 1960s*, Macmillan, Basingstoke.

Svendsen, A. (2010) *Intelligence Cooperation and the War on Terror: Anglo-American Security Relations after 9/11*, Routledge, London.

Synnott, H. (2008) *Bad Days in Basra. My Turbulent Time as Britain's Man in Southern Iraq*, I. B. Tauris, London, New York.

Terriff, T. (2002) (ed) *The Sources of Military Change: Culture, Politics, Technology*, Lynne Reinner, Boulder.

Terriff, T., Karp, A. and Karp, R. (2007) (eds) *Global Insurgency and the Future of Armed Conflict. Debating Fourth Generation Warfare*, Routledge, London.

Terriff, T., Osinga, F. and Farrell, T. (2010) (eds) *A Transformation Gap? American Innovations and European Military Change*, Stanford Security Studies, Stanford.

Urban, M. (2010) *Task Force Black*, Abacus, London.

Warden, J. (2000) *The Air Campaign: Planning for Combat*, iUniverse, New York.

Weigley, R. (1960) *The American Way of War: A History of United States Military Strategy and Policy*, Indiana University Press, Bloomington.

Weisner, I. (2013) *Importing the American Way of War? Network Centric Warfare in the UK and Germany*, Volume 48, Nomos, Baden-Baden.

Wells, A. (2017) *A Tale of Two Navies. Geopolitics, Technology and Strategy in the United States Navy and the Royal Navy, 1960–2015*, Naval Institute Press, Maryland.

Wheeler, N. (2018) *Trusting Enemies: Interpersonal Relationships in International Conflict*, Oxford University Press, Oxford.

Winand, P. (1993) *Eisenhower, Kennedy and the United States of Europe*, St Martin's Press, New York.

Woodward, B. (2004) *Plan of Attack*, Simon and Schuster, New York.

Wynn, H. (1994) *The RAF Strategic Nuclear Deterrent Forces: Their Origin, Roles and Deployment 1946–1969. A Document History*, Her Majesty's Stationery Office, London.

Xu, R. (2017) *Alliance Persistence within the Anglo-American Special Relationship: The Post-Cold War Era*, Springer Nature for Palgrave Macmillan, Switzerland.

Young, H. (1998) *This Blessed Plot: Britain and Europe from Churchill to Blair*, Macmillan, London.

Articles

Aldrich, R. (2004) 'Transatlantic intelligence and security cooperation', *International Affairs*, 80, 4: 731–753.

Ashton, N. (2005) 'Harold Macmillan and the "Golden Days" of Anglo-American relations revisited, 1957–63', *Diplomatic History*, 29, 4: 691–723.

Aylwin-Foster, N. (2005) 'Changing the army for counter-insurgency operations', *Military Review*, LXXXV, 6, November-December: 2–15.

Baylis, J. and Macmillan, A. (1993) 'The British Global Strategy Paper of 1952', *Journal of Strategic Studies*, 16, 2: 200–226.

Baylis, J. and Stoddart, K. (2012) 'The British nuclear experience: The role of ideas and beliefs', (Part 1), *Diplomacy and Statecraft*, 23, 2: 331–346.

Baylis, J. and Wirtz, J. (2012) 'The U.S.-UK "Special Military Relationship": Resetting the partnership', *Comparative Strategy*, 31, 3: 253–262.

Boot, M. (2003) 'The new American way of war', *Foreign Affairs*, 82, 4: 41–58.

Cebrowski, A.K. and Gartska, J.H. (1998) 'Network centric warfare. Its origins and future', *Proceedings of the US Naval Institute*, 124, 1: 28–35

Chin, W. (2007) 'British counter-insurgency in Afghanistan', *Defence and Security Analysis*, 23, 2: 201–225.

Coker, C. (1992) 'Britain and the New World Order: The special relationship in the 1990s', *International Affairs*, 68, 3: 407–422.

Cornish, P. and Dorman, A. (2011) 'Dr Fox and the philosopher's stone: The alchemy of national defence in the age of austerity', *International Affairs*, 87, 2: 335–353.

Danchev, A. (1996) 'On specialness', *International Affairs*, 72, 4: 737–750.

Danchev, A. (2003) 'Greeks and Romans: Anglo-American relations after 9/11', *Royal United Services Journal*, 148, 2: 16–20.

Danchev, A. (2005) 'How strong are shared values in the transatlantic relationship?' *British Journal of Politics and International Relations*, 7, 3: 429–436.

Dawson, R. and Rosencrance, R. (1966) 'Theory and reality in the Anglo-American alliance', *World Politics*, 19, 1: 21–51.

Doyle, S. (2017) 'A foregone conclusion? The United States, Britain and the Trident D5 Agreement', *Journal of Strategic Studies*, 40, 6: 867–894.

Doyle, S. (2018) 'Preserving the global nuclear order: The Trident agreements and the arms control debate, 1977–1982', *The International History Review*, 40, 5: 1174–1190.

Dumbrell, J. (2004) 'The US-UK "Special Relationship" in a world twice transformed', *Cambridge Review of International Affairs*, 17, 3: 437–450.

Dunn, D. (2008) 'The double interregnum: UK-US relations beyond Blair and Bush', *International Affairs*, 84, 6: 1131–1143.

Dunne, T (2004) '"When the shooting starts": Atlanticism in British security strategy', *International Affairs*, 80, 5: 893–909.

Edelman, E. (2010) 'A Special Relationship in jeopardy', *The American Interest*, July-August: 25–34.

Edmunds, T. (2010) 'The defence dilemma', *International Affairs*, 86, 2: 377–394.

Egnell, R. (2011) 'Lessons from Helmand, Afghanistan: What now for British counterinsurgency?' *International Affairs*, 87, 2: 297–315.

Farrell, T. (2008) 'The dynamics of British military transformation', *International Affairs*, 84, 4: 777–807.

Farrell, T. (2009) 'Improving in war: Military adaptation and the British in Helmand Province, Afghanistan 2006–2009', *Journal of Strategic Studies*, 33, 4: 567–594.

Feldman, M., Sköldberg, K, Brown, N. R. and Horner, D. (2004) 'Making sense of stories: A rhetorical approach to narrative analysis', *Journal of Public Administration Research and Theory*, 41, 2: 147–170.

Foley, R., Griffin, S. and McCartney, H. (2011) '"Transformation in contact": learning the lessons of modern war', *International Affairs*, 87, 2: 253–270.

Freedman, L. (1986) 'The case of Westland and the bias to Europe', *International Affairs*, 63, 1: 1–19.

Gavin, F. (2015) 'Strategies of inhibition: US grand strategy, the nuclear revolution and proliferation', *International Security*, 40, 1: 9–46.

Goodman, M. (2015) 'The foundation of Anglo-American intelligence sharing', *Studies in Intelligence*, 59, 2: 1–12.

Griffin, S. (2011) 'Iraq, Afghanistan and the future of British military doctrine: From counter-insurgency to stabilization', *International Affairs*, 87, 2: 317–333.

Hammes, T. (2005) 'War evolves into the fourth generation', *Contemporary Security Policy*, 26, 2: 189–221.

Hall, P. and Taylor, R. (1996) 'Political science and the three New Institutionalisms', *Political Studies*, XLIV: 936–957.

Hall, P. and Thelen, K. (2009) 'Institutional change in varieties of capitalism', *Socio-Economic Review*, 7, 1: 7–34.

Helmke, G. and Levitsky, S. (2004) 'Informal institutions and comparative politics: A research agenda', *Perspectives on Politics*, 2, 4: 725–740.

Hood, F. (2008) 'Atlantic dreams and European realities: British foreign policy after Iraq', *European Integration*, 30, 1: 183–197.

Joffe, J. (1984) 'Europe's American Pacifier', *Foreign Policy*, 54: 64–82

Johnston, A. (1995) 'Thinking about strategic culture', *International Security*, 19, 4: 32–64.

Keohane, R. (1988) 'International institutions: Two approaches', *International Studies Quarterly*, 32, 4: 379–396.

Kennedy, G. (2012) 'Anglo-American strategic relations and maritime power today', *Journal of Transatlantic Studies*, 10, 1: 68–83.

Krauthammer, C. (1990) 'The unipolar moment', *Foreign Affairs*, 70, 1: 23–33.

Lowndes, V. (1996) 'Varieties of new institutionalism: A critical appraisal', *Public Administration*, 74, 2: 181–197.

Mackinlay, J. (2004) 'Review essay. Counter-insurgency: The US-UK tensions', *The Royal United Services Journal*, 149, 5: 88–90.

Magill, P. and Rees, W. (2022) 'UK defence policy after Ukraine: Revisiting the integrated review', *Survival*, 64, 3: 87–103.

Marsh, S. and Baylis, J. (2006) 'The Anglo-American "Special Relationship": The Lazarus of International Relations', *Diplomacy and Statecraft*, 17, 1: 173–211.

Marsh, S. (2018) 'The US, Brexit and Anglo-American relations', *Journal of Transatlantic Studies*, 16, 3: 272–294.

Marsh, S. (2019) 'Anglo-American relations and the past present: insights into an (ongoing) mythologisation of the special relationship', *Journal of Transatlantic Studies*, 17, 3: 310–340.

McCourt, D. (2014) 'Has Britain found its role?' *Survival*, 56, 2: 159–178.

Niblett, Robin (2007) 'Choosing between America and Europe: A new context for British foreign policy', *International Affairs*, 83, 4: 627–641.

North, D. (1991) 'Institutions', *Journal of Economic Perspectives*, 5, 1: 97–112.

Oliver, T. and Williams, M. (2016) 'Special relationships in flux: Brexit and the future of the US–EU and US–UK relationships', *International Affairs*, 92, 3: 547–567.

Pape, R. (1997) 'The limits of precision guided air power', *Security Studies*, 7, 2: 93–114.

Porter, P. (2010) 'Last charge of the knights? Iraq, Afghanistan and the Special Relationship', *International Affairs*, 86, 2: 355–375.

Rachman, G. (2001) 'Is the Anglo-American relationship still special?' *The Washington Quarterly*, 24, 2: 7–20.

Rees, W. (2017) 'America, Brexit and the security of Europe', *British Journal of Politics and International Relations*, 19, 3: 558–572.

Rees, W. and Davies, L. (2019) The Anglo-American military relationship: Institutional rules, practices and narratives', *Contemporary Security Policy*, 40, 3: 312–334.

Reynolds, D. (1985–1986) 'A "Special Relationship"? America, Britain and the international order since the Second World War', *International Affairs*, 62, 1: 1–20.

Ritchie, N. (2009) 'Deterrence dogma? Challenging the relevance of British nuclear weapons', *International Affairs*, 85, 1: 81–98.

Ritchie, N. (2007) 'Replacing Trident: Britain, America and nuclear weapons', *Contemporary Security Policy*, 28, 2: 384–406.

Ritchie, N. (2011) 'Rethinking security: a critical analysis of the Strategic Defence and Security Review', *International Affairs*, 87, 2: 355–376.

Rumsfeld, D. (2002) 'Transforming the military', *Foreign Affairs*, May-June: 20–32.

Schmidt, V. (2008) 'Discursive institutionalism: Explanatory power of ideas and discourse', *Annual Review of Political Science*, 11: 303–326.

Seitz, R. (1993) 'Britain and America: towards strategic coincidence', *The World Today*, 49, 5: 85–88.

Stoddart, K. and Baylis, J. (2012) 'The British nuclear experience: The role of beliefs, culture and status', (Part 2), *Diplomacy and Statecraft*, 23, 3: 493–516.

Terriff, T. (2007) 'Of Romans and dragons: Preparing the US Marine Corps for future war', *Contemporary Security Policy*, 28, 1: 143–162.

Till, G. (2010) 'Great Britain gambles with the Royal Navy', *Naval War College Review*, 63, 1: 33–60.

Thelen, K. (1999) 'Historical institutionalism in comparative politics', *Annual Review of Political Science*, 2: 369–404.

Wallace, W. (2005) 'The collapse of British foreign policy', *International Affairs*, 82, 1: 53–68.

Wallace, W. and Phillips, C. (2009) 'Reassessing the special relationship', *International Affairs*, 85, 2: 263–284.

Walt, S. (1997) 'Why alliances endure or collapse', *Survival*, 39, 1: 156–179.

Wither, J. (2006) 'An endangered partnership: The Anglo-American defence relationship in the twenty-first century', *European Security*, 15, 1: 47–65.

Xu, R. (2016) 'Institutionalization, path dependence and the persistence of the Anglo-American special relationship', *International Affairs*, 92, 5: 1207–1228.

Young, O. (1980) 'International regimes: Problems of concept foundation', *World Politics*, 32: 331–356.

Book chapters and other publications

Alderson, A. (2013) 'Too busy to learn: Personal observations on British campaigns in Iraq and Afghanistan', in Bailey, J., Iron, R. and Strachan, H. (eds) *British Generals in Blair's Wars*, Ashgate, Farnham: 281–298.

Annis, F. (2020) 'Krulak revisited: The three-block war, strategic corporals and the future battlefield', Modern War Institute, West Point Military Academy, March, New York, https://mwi.usma.edu/krulak-revisited-three-block-war-strategic-corporals-future-battlefield/.

Aspin, L. (1993) *The Bottom-Up Review: Forces for a New Era*, Office of the Secretary of Defense, Washington DC, 1 September.

Bailey, J. (2013) 'The political context: Why we went to war and the mismatch of ends, ways and means', in Bailey, J., Iron, R. and Strachan, H. (eds) *British Generals in Blair's Wars*, Ashgate, Farnham: 5–25.

Baylis, J. (1998) 'The "Special Relationship". A diverting British myth?', in Buffet, C. and Heuser, B. (eds) *Haunted by History: Myths in International Relations*, Berghahn Books, Oxford: 117–134.

BBC News (2014) 'Military cuts mean "no partnership", Robert Gates warns', 16 January, www.bbc.co.uk/news/uk-2575487.

BBC News (2016) 'Trident lets UK punch above weight', 13 February.

BBC (2021) 'AUKUS: UK, US and Australia launch pact to counter China', 16 September, https://www.bbc.co.uk/news/world-58564837

Bellamy, C. (2003) 'Generals take note: peacekeeping requires more courage than war', The Independent online, 9 April, Christopher Bellamy: Generals, take note: peace-keeping requires more courage than war | The Independent |

Beloff, M. (1986) 'The end of the British Empire and the assumption of world-wide commitments by the United States', in Louis, W. and Bull, H. (eds) The 'Special Relationship': Anglo-American Relations since 1945, Clarendon Press, Oxford: 249–261.

Blair, T. (1999) 'The doctrine of the international community', Speech by Prime Minister Tony Blair, The Press Club, Chicago.

Blair, T. and Brown, G. (1999) Statement by the Prime Minister Tony Blair and Chancellor Gordon Brown, The Independent, 14 October.

Boyce, M. (2003) 'Challenges for the 21st Century', lecture at Gresham College, 27 October, available at https://www.gresham.ac.uk/lectures-and-events/challenges-for-the-21st-century.

British Army (1989) Design for Military Operations. The British Military Doctrine, The Stationery Office, London.

British Army (2010) 'Operation in Iraq, January 2005-May 2009, AC 71937 An Analysis from the Land Perspective', The Stationery Office, London.

Burt, A. (2016) 'Next steps in the United Kingdom's nuclear warhead programme. What future for the Atomic Weapons Establishment?' in Futter, A. (ed) The United Kingdom and the Future of Nuclear Weapons, Rowman and Littlefield, London: 107–120.

Callahan, T. and Jansson, M. (2008) 'UK independence or dependence?' in Mackby, J. and Cornish, P. (eds) US-UK Nuclear Cooperation after Fifty Years, CSIS and Chatham House, CSIS Press, Washington DC: 126–140.

Centre for Defence Studies (1998) The Strategic Defence Review: How Strategic? How Much of a Review? Brassey's for the Centre for Defence Studies, London.

Clarke, M. (2014) 'Brothers in Arms: The British-American Alignment', in A. Johnson (ed.) Wars in Peace: British Military Operations Since 1991, Royal United Services Institute, London: 237–255.

Codner, M. (2014) 'Fighting for peace, 1991–2001', in A. Johnson (ed.) Wars in Peace: British Military Operations Since 1991, Royal United Services Institute, London.

Cornish, P. (2010) 'Strategy in Austerity', Chatham House Paper, October, London.

Cowper-Coles, S. (2017) 'So what the hell were we doing in Afghanistan (and why did we stay)?' Saturday Review: Books, The Times, 19 August: 11.

Cox, S. and Ritchie, S. (2002) 'The Gulf War and UK air power doctrine in practice', in Cox, S. and Gray, P. (eds) Air Power History: Turning Points from Kitty Hawk to Kosovo, Routledge, Abingdon: Chapter 14.

Croft, S. (2001) 'Britain's nuclear weapons discourse', in Croft, S., Dorman, A., Rees, W. and Uttley, M., Britain and Defence 1945-2000: A Policy Re-evaluation, Longman, Harlow: 69–83.

Cross, T. (2013) 'Rebuilding Iraq 2003: Humanitarian assistance and reconstruction', in Bailey, J., Iron, R. and Strachan, H. (eds) British Generals in Blair's Wars, Ashgate, Farnham: 69–78.

Defence Select Committee (2004) 'Defence – Fourth Report', Minutes of Evidence by Air Chief Marshal Sir Jock Stirrup, House of Commons Session 2004–05, 20 October, The Stationery Office, London, paras 144–152.

Defence Select Committee (2010) 'The Strategic Defence and Security Review and the National Security Strategy', The Government's Response to the Committee's Sixth Report of Session 2010–12, 9th Special Report of Session 2010–12, House of Commons 1639, The Stationery Office, London.

Defence Select Committee (2011) 'Operations in Afghanistan', Fourth Report of Session 2010–12, House of Commons 554, 17 July, The Stationery Office, London.

Defence Select Committee (2012) 'Libya', Ninth Report of Session 2010–12, Volume 1, House of Commons, 25 January, The Stationery Office, London.

Defence Select Committee (2017) 'Lessons of Iraq', 3rd Report, Session 2003–04, House of Commons, The Stationery Office, London.

Defence Select Committee (2018) 'The indispensable ally? US, NATO and UK Defence relations'. Government response to the committee's eighth report, Ninth Special Report of Session 2017–19, House of Commons 1569, The Stationery Office, London.

Defence Select Committee (2018a) 'The indispensable ally? US, NATO and UK Defence relations', Oral evidence, House of Commons 387, 5 March, The Stationery Office, London, 5–34.

Defence Select Committee (2018b) 'The indispensable ally? US, NATO and UK Defence relations', HC 387, Evidence by Victoria Nuland, The Stationery Office, London, Q 90–140.

Defence Select Committee (2021) 'We are going to need a bigger navy', Third Report of Session 2021–22, HC 168, Evidence by Greg Kennedy, 7 December, The Stationery Office, London.

Dempsey, M. (2014) Statement by the Chairman of the US Joint Chiefs at the meeting of the US and UK Chiefs of Staff, London, 10 June.

Deni, J. (2012) 'The future of American land power: Does forward presence still matter? The case of the Army in Europe', Strategic Studies Institute, US Army War College, Carlisle, PA.

Department of the Navy (1992) 'From the Sea', US Department of Defense, Washington DC.

Department of the Navy (1994) 'Forward from the Sea', US Department of Defense, Washington DC.

Department of the US Air Force (1989) 'Air Force and US National Security: Global Reach – Global Power', US Department of Defense, Washington DC.

DCDC (Development, Concepts and Doctrine Centre) (2007) 'The Joint Medium Weight Capability Analytical Concept', 24 April, Shrivenham.

DCDC (Development, Concepts and Doctrine Centre) (2008) 'Security and stabilisation; The future land operational concept 2008', Shrivenham.

DCDC (Development, Concepts and Doctrine Centre) (2020) www.gov.uk/government/groups/development-concepts-and-doctrine-centre#doctrine), Shrivenham.

Dodd, T. and Oakes, M. (1998) 'The Strategic Defence Review White Paper', Research Paper 98/91, International Affairs and Defence Section, 15 October, House of Commons Library, London.

Downing Street (2021). 'Prime Minister and President Biden to agree new Atlantic Charter: 10 June 2021' [online]. Gov.uk. Available at: https://www.gov.uk/government/news/prime-minister-and-president-biden-to-agree-new-atlantic-charter-10-june-2021.

Dumbrell, J. (2013) 'Personal diplomacy. Relations between prime ministers and presidents', in Dobson, A. and Marsh, S. (eds) Anglo-American Relations: Contemporary Perspectives, Routledge, London: 82–104.

Eberle, J. (1986) 'The military relationship', in Louis, W. and Bull, H. (eds) The 'Special Relationship': Anglo-American Relations since 1945, Clarendon Press, Oxford: 151–159.

Echevarria, A. (2011) 'The Special Relationship and the British Army', in Codner, M. and Clarke, M., (eds) A Question of Security: The British Defence Review in an Age of Austerity, I. B Tauris, London: 187–195.

Edelman, E. (2009) 'The US-UK Special Relationship: The end of an affair?' The Bernstein Lecture, John Hopkins University, Washington DC, 10 November.

Fallon, M. (2017) 'Defence Secretary Speech at CSIS, Washington', 7 July, available at: https://www.gov.uk/government/speeches/defence-secretary-speech-at-csis-washington.

Farrell, T. and Bird, T. (2010) 'Innovating within cost and cultural constraints: The British approach to military transformation', in Terriff, T., Osinga and Farrell, T. (eds) *A Transformation Gap? American Innovations and European Military Change*, Stanford Security Studies, Stanford: 14–35.

Fiddes, J. (2017) 'Implementing post-Cold War Anglo-American military intervention: scrutinising the dynamics of legality and legitimacy', PhD Thesis, University of Aberdeen.

Fisher, L. (2020) 'RAF Typhoons knock out ISIS fighters in blitz on Iraqi caves', *The Times*, 6 May.

Foreign Affairs Select Committee (2009) 'Global Security: UK-US Relations', Written evidence of former US Ambassador to NATO, Robert Hunter, Special Report of Session 2009–10, House of Commons, 21 September, The Stationery Office, London.

Foreign Affairs Select Committee (2010) 'Global Security: UK-US Relations', Sixth Report of Session 2009–10, House of Commons, 18 March, The Stationery Office, London.

Foreign Affairs Select Committee (2010a) 'Global Security: UK-US Relations', Response of the Foreign Secretary, David Milliband, Third Special Report of Session 2009–10, House of Commons, 6 April, The Stationery Office, London.

Foreign Affairs Select Committee (2014) 'Government Foreign Policy Towards the US', House of Commons, 3 April, The Stationery Office, London.

Foreign and Commonwealth Office (2003) 'UK international priorities: a strategy for the FCO', December, www.fco.gov.uk/Files/kfile/FCOStrategyFullFinal.pdf.

Foster, J. (2008) 'Strategic perspectives through oral history', in Mackby, J. and Cornish, P. (eds) *US-UK Nuclear Cooperation after Fifty Years*, CSIS and Chatham House, CSIS Press, Washington DC: 276–278.

Fox, L. (2011) 'Strong economy, strong defence, strategic reach: Protecting national security in the 21st century', Speech of Secretary of Defence at Chatham House, 19 May, https://www.gov.uk/government/speeches/2011-05-19-strong_economy_strong_defence_strategic_reach

Freedman, L. (2004) 'Britain and the revolution in military affairs', in Dorman, A. Smith, M. & Uttley, M. (eds) *The Changing Face of Military Power: Joint Warfare in an Expeditionary Era*, Palgrave, Basingstoke: 111–128.

Friedman, B. (2009) 'The Navy after the Cold War. Progress without revolution', in Sapolsky, H., Friedman, B. and Green, B. (eds) *US Military Innovation since the Cold War. Creation without Destruction*, Routledge, London: 71–99.

Fry, R. (2014) 'Strategy and operations', in A. Johnson (ed) *Wars in Peace: British Military Operations Since 1991*, Royal United Services Institute, London: 215–237.

Garofano, J. (2004) 'The United States in Bosnia-Herzegovina: Points of tension and learning for the US military', in Callaghan, J. and Schönborn, M. (eds) *Warriors in Peacekeeping: Points of Tension in Complex Cultural Encounters*, George C Marshall European Center for Security Studies, Lit Verlag, Munster: 223–260.

Gomis, B. (2011) 'French-British Defence and Security Treaties', Chatham House Paper, March, London.

Gowing, M. (1986) 'Nuclear weapons and the "Special Relationship"', in Louis, W. and Bull, H. (eds) *The 'Special Relationship': Anglo-American Relations since 1945*, Clarendon Press, Oxford: 117–129.

Graham, A. (2013) 'Iraq 2004: The view from Baghdad', in Bailey, J., Iron, R. and Strachan, H. (eds) *British Generals in Blair's Wars*, Ashgate, Farnham: 97–108.

Haglund, D. (2013) 'Is there a strategic culture of the special relationship? Contingency, identity and the transformation of Anglo-American relations', in Dobson, A. and Marsh, S. (eds) *Anglo-American Relations: Contemporary Perspectives*, Routledge, London: 26–51.

Hague, W. (2010) 'Britain's foreign policy in a networked world', Speech by the UK Foreign Secretary, 1 July, Foreign and Commonwealth Office, London. https://www.gov.uk/government/speeches/britain-s-foreign-policy-in-a-networked-world--2

Hallion, R. (2011) 'US air power', in Olsen, J. (ed) *Global Air Power*, Potomac Books, Washington DC: 63–136.

Haynes, D. (2018) 'Cuts risk turning Britain into Belgium with nukes, says general', The Times, 12 January: 4.

Hendershot, R. (2013) 'Affection is the cement which binds us: Understanding the cultural sinews of the Anglo-American special relationship', in Dobson, A. and Marsh, S. (eds) *Anglo-American Relations: Contemporary Perspectives*, Routledge, London: 52–81.

Hennessy, P. (2007) 'Cabinets and the Bomb', British Academy Occasional Paper 11, Oxford University Press for the British Academy, Oxford.

Hermann, M. (2010) 'Understanding the UK-US intelligence partnership', in Tazuner, M. (ed) *Intelligence Cooperation Practices in the Twenty-First Century: Towards a Culture of Sharing*, IOS Press, Amsterdam: 17–19.

Hitchens, P. (2014) 'The special relationship uncovered', Broadcast on BBC Radio 4, 23 June.

Holmes, A. (2013) 'Transatlantic diplomacy and "global" states', in Dobson, A. and Marsh, S. (eds) *Anglo-American Relations: Contemporary Perspectives*, London, Routledge: 105–128.

Horne, A. (1986) 'The Macmillan years and afterwards', in Louis, W. and Bull, H. (eds) *The 'Special Relationship': Anglo-American Relations since 1945*, Clarendon Press, Oxford: 87–102.

Houghton, N. (2013) Chief of the Defence Staff General Sir Nicholas Houghton Annual Lecture, Royal United Services Institute, 18 December, London.

House of Commons (2010) 'The comprehensive approach', Session 2010–11, 28 July, London, https://publications.parliament.uk/pa/cm201011/cmselect/cmdfence/writev/comp/m01.htm

House of Commons (2016) The Report of the Iraq Inquiry: Executive Summary, Report of a Committee of Privy Counsellors, HC 264, 6 July, HMSO, London.https://assets.publishing.service.gov.uk/government/uploads/system/uploads/attachment_data/file/535407/The_Report_of_the_Iraq_Inquiry_-_Executive_Summary.pdf.

Iron, R. (2013) 'Basra 2008: Operation Charge of the Knights', in Bailey, J., Iron, R. and Strachan, H. (eds) *British Generals in Blair's Wars*, Ashgate, Farnham: 187–200.

Jackson, C. (2009) 'From conservatism to revolutionary intoxication. The US Army and the second interwar period', in Sapolsky, H., Friedman, B. and Green, B. (eds) *US Military Innovation since the Cold War. Creation without Destruction*, Routledge, London.

Joint Doctrine Publication JDP 3-40, (2009) *Security and Stabilisation: The Military Contribution*, 30 November, DCDC.

Joint Doctrine Publication 01 (2014) *UK Joint Operations Doctrine*, November, DCDC.

Joint Doctrine Publication 0-01 (2014) *UK Defence Doctrine*, 5th edition, November, DCDC.

Joint Doctrine Publication 0-10 (2017) *UK Maritime Power*, 5th edition, October, DCDC.

Joint Doctrine Publication 0-30 (2017) *UK Air and Space Power*, 2nd edition, December, DCDC.

Joint Warfare Publication 3-50 (2004) *Comprehensive Approach*, June, DCDC.

Jones, P. (2016) '*UK/US Naval Partnership*', *Speech of the Royal Navy First Sea Lord, Sir Philip Jones to the Cohen Group*, Washington DC, http://www.royalnavy.mod.uk/news-and-latest-activity/news/2016/may/17/160517-1sl-speech-to-the-cohen-group.

Kandiah, M. and Staerck, G. (2005) (ed.) *The British Response to SDI*, Centre for Contemporary British History, King's College London. https://www.kcl.ac.uk/sspp/departments/politicaleconomy/research/british-politics-and-government/witness-seminars/pdffiles/sdi.pdf

Kiszely, J. (2008) Coalition Command in Contemporary Operations, Whitehall Report 1–08, Royal United Services Institute, London.

Kiszely, J. (2013) 'The British Army and thinking about the operational level', in Bailey, J., Iron, R. and Strachan, H. (eds) *British Generals in Blair's Wars*, Ashgate, Farnham: 119–130.

Levi, M. (1997) 'A model, a method, and a map: rational choice in comparative and historical analysis', in Lichbach, M. and Zuckerman, A. (eds), *Comparative Politics: Rationality, Culture, and Structure*, Cambridge University Press, Cambridge: 19–41.

Lizza, R. (2011) 'Leading from behind', *The New Yorker*, 26 April, https://www.newyorker.com/news/news-desk/leading-from-behind.

Louis, W. (1986) 'American anti-colonialism and the dissolution of the British Empire', in Louis, W. and Bull, H. (eds) *The 'Special Relationship': Anglo-American Relations since 1945*, Clarendon Press, Oxford: 261–283.

Maciejewski, J. (2013) '"Best effort": Operation Sinbad and the Iraq campaign', in Bailey, J., Iron, R. and Strachan, H. (eds) *British Generals in Blair's Wars*, Ashgate, Farnham: 157–174.

Major, J. (1995) Statement by Prime Minister John Major on Bosnia, House of Commons, 31 May, https://johnmajorarchive.org.uk/1995/05/31/mr-majors-commons-statement-on-bosnia-31-may-1995/

March, J. and Olsen, J. (2009) 'The logic of appropriateness', Arena Working Papers, Centre for European Studies, University of Oslo, 4: 1–28.

Marsh, S. (2013) 'The Anglo-American defence relationship', in Dobson, A. and Marsh S. (eds) *Anglo-American Relations: Contemporary Perspectives*, Routledge, London: 179–207.

May, E. and Treverton, G. (1986) 'Defence relationships: American perspectives', in Louis, W. and Bull, H. (eds) *The 'Special Relationship': Anglo-American Relations since 1945*, Clarendon Press, Oxford: 161–184.

Mayer, P., Rittberger, V. and Zurn, M. (1997) 'Regime theory: state of the art and perspectives', in Rittberger, V. (ed) *Regime Theory and International Relations*, Clarendon Press, Oxford.

Mason, A. (2004) 'Kosovo: The air campaign', in Badsey, S. and Latawski, P. (eds) *Britain, NATO and the Lessons of the Balkan Conflicts 1991-1999*, Frank Cass, London: 39–66.

McCausland, J. (2009) 'When you come to a fork in the road, take it – Defence policy and the Special Relationship', in Bankcroft, J. (ed) *US-UK Relations at the Start of the 21st Century*, Nova Science Publishers, New York: 172–180.

McColl, J. (2013) 'Modern campaigning: From a practitioner's perspective', in Bailey, J., Iron, R. and Strachan, H. (eds) *British Generals in Blair's Wars*, Ashgate, Farnham: 109–118.

McInnes, C. (1991) 'Trident', in Byrd, P. (ed) *British Defence Policy: Thatcher and Beyond, Philip Allan*, London: 67–87.

McInnes, C. (2006) 'The Gulf War 1990-91', in Strachan, H. (ed) *Big Wars and Small Wars. The British Army and the Lessons of War in the Twentieth Century*, Abingdon, Routledge: 162–179.

Menon, A. (2010) *'Between faith and reason: UK policy towards the US and the EU'*, Chatham House Briefing Paper, July, London Paper: 1–18.

Michel, L. (2009) 'Observations on the Special Relationship in security and defense matters', in Bankcroft, J. (ed) *US-UK Relations at the Start of the 21st* Century, Nova Science Publishers, New York: 135–157.

Middup, L. (2011) The legacy of Vietnam and the Powell Doctrine: Four case studies, PhD Thesis, October, University of Nottingham.

Michta, A. (2019) 'The US-UK Special Relationship and the "Principled Realism" of the Trump Administration', in Johnson, R. and Haaland Matlary, J. (eds) *The United Kingdom's Defence after Brexit: Britain's Alliances, Coalitions and Partnerships*, Springer, Switzerland: 59–75.

Miliband, D. (2007) Speech of the Foreign Secretary David Miliband at Chatham House, 19 July.

Miller, F. (2008) 'Creating a bilateral nuclear policy framework', in Mackby, J. and Cornish, P. (eds) *US-UK Nuclear Cooperation after Fifty Years,* CSIS and Chatham House, CSIS Press, Washington DC: 172–178.

Ministry of Defence (1980) The Future United Kingdom Strategic Nuclear Deterrent Force, Defence, Open Government Document 80/23, July.

Ministry of Defence (1990) *'Options for Change'*, Command 1559, Her Majesty's Stationery Office, London.

Ministry of Defence (1998) *Strategic Defence Review, Command 3999*, Her Majesty's Stationery Office, London.

Ministry of Defence (2002) *Strategic Defence Review. A New Chapter*, Her Majesty's Stationery Office, London.

Ministry of Defence (2003) *'Delivering Security in a Changing World'*, Command 6041-1, Her Majesty's Stationery Office, London.

Ministry of Defence (2006) *The Future of the United Kingdom's Nuclear Deterrent,* Command 6994, Her Majesty's Stationery Office, London.

Ministry of Defence (2010) *'Adaptability and Partnership'*, Command 7794, Her Majesty's Stationery Office, London.

Ministry of Defence (2010a) *'A Strong Britain in an Age of Uncertainty'*: The Strategic Defence and Security Review, Command 7948, The Stationery Office, London.

Ministry of Defence and the US Department of Defense (2012) *Statement of Intent Regarding Enhanced Cooperation on Carrier Operations and Maritime Power Projection*, London and Washington DC.

Ministry of Defence (2015) *National Security Strategy and Strategic Security and Defence Review 2015: A Secure and Prosperous United Kingdom,* Command 9161, The Stationery Office, London.

Ministry of Defence (2021) *'Defence in a Competitive Age', The Integrated Review of Security, Defence, Development and Foreign Policy*, March, HMSO, London.

Moreland, S. and Mattox, J. (2009) 'Pressing contemporary issues', in Jasper, S. (ed) *Transforming Defense Capabilities: New Approaches for International Security*, Lynne Reinner, Boulder: 79–102.

Murray, P. (1995) 'An initial response to the Cold War: The build-up of the US Air Force in the United Kingdom 1948–156', in Miller, R. (ed) *Seeing off the Bear: Anglo-American Air power Cooperation during the Cold War*, Joint Meeting of the Royal Air Force Historical Society and the Air Force Historical Foundation, Air Force History and Museums Program, Washington DC: 15–24.

Navynews (2013) 'Aircraft handlers lay foundations for Queen Elizabeth by working on US flight decks' 25 February, https://navynews.co.uk/archive/news/item/7095

Newton, P. (2013) 'Adapt or fail: The challenge for the armed forces after Blair's wars', in Bailey, J., Iron, R. and Strachan, H. (eds.) *British Generals in Blair's Wars*, Ashgate, Farnham: 297–326.

Niblett, R. (2021) 'Global Britain, global broker. A blueprint for the UK's future international role', Chatham House Research Paper: 43, https://www.chathamhouse.org/sites/default/files/2021-02/2021-01-11-global-britain-global-broker-niblett_0.pdf. (Accessed 3 Nov 21)

Norton-Taylor, R. (2006) 'Britain's new top soldier: Can the military cope? I say – just', The Guardian Online 4 September.

Obama, B. (2011) *Speech of President Barack Obama to both houses of Parliament*, 25 May, London.

Office of Force Transformation (2005) '*US-UK Coalition Combat Operations during Operation Iraqi Freedom: A Network Centric Case Study*', March, US Department of Defense, Washington DC.

Office of Force Transformation (2005a) '*Force XXI Battle Command Brigade and Below*', US Department of Defense, Washington DC.

Olsen, J. (2007) 'Understanding institutions and logics of appropriateness: Introductory essay', Arena Working Papers, Centre for European Studies, University of Oslo, 13: 1–16.

O'Nions, K., Anderson, R. and Pitman, R. (2008) 'Reflections on the strength of the 1958 Agreement', in Mackby, J. and Cornish, P. (eds) *US-UK Nuclear Cooperation after Fifty Years*, CSIS and Chatham House, CSIS Press, Washington DC: 179–188.

Parker, N. (2013) 'Twenty-first-century operational leadership: Sierra Leone, Baghdad and Northern Ireland', in Bailey, J., Iron, R. and Strachan, H. (eds.) *British Generals in Blair's Wars*, Ashgate, Farnham: 131–138.

Peach, S. (2014) 'A contemporary perspective', in Finn, C. (ed) *Effects Based Warfare*, The Stationery Office, London: 79–101.

Peach, S. (2016) *Air Chief Marshall Sir Stuart Peach, RUSI Chief of the Defence Staff lecture*, 14 December, London.

Pounds, N. (2013) 'Southern Afghanistan 2006–2008: The challenge of a Comprehensive Approach to counter-insurgency', in Bailey, J., Iron, R. and Strachan, H. (eds.) *British Generals in Blair's Wars*, Ashgate, Farnham: 225–236.

Richards, D. (2009) *Chief of the Defence Staff General David Richards*, Chatham House lecture, 17 September, London.

Richardson, J. (2008) 'UK-US Air Force collaboration', in Mackby, J. and Cornish, P. (eds) *US-UK Nuclear Cooperation after Fifty Years*, CSIS and Chatham House, CSIS Press, Washington DC: 141–148.

Riley, J. (2013) 'NATO operations in Afghanistan 2008–2009: A theatre-level view', in Bailey, J., Iron, R. and Strachan, H. (eds) British Generals in Blair's Wars, Ashgate, Farnham: 237–248.

Rosamond, J. (2015) 'Britain's top Admiral: US, UK planning for "closer and stronger" naval alliance', USNI News, 16 July, https://news.usni.org/2015/07/16/britains-top-admiral-u-s-u-k-planning-for-closer-and-stronger-naval-alliance.

RAF (1991) 'Air Power Doctrine AP3000', First Edition, The Stationery Office, London.

RAF (1999) 'Air Power Doctrine AP3000', Third Edition, The Stationery Office, London.

RAF (2009) 'Air Power Doctrine AP3000', Fourth Edition, The Stationery Office, London.

Ruane, K. (2013) 'Britain, the United States and the issue of "Limited War" with China, 1950–54', in Young, J., Pedaliu, E. and Kandiah, M. (eds) *Britain in Global Politics, Volume 2: Security, Conflict and Cooperation in the Contemporary World*, Palgrave Macmillan, London: 62–81.

Russell, J. (2013) 'Into the Great Wadi: The United States and the war in Afghanistan', in Farrell, T., Osinga, F. and Russell, J. (eds) *Military Adaptation in Afghanistan*, Stanford University Press, Stanford: 51–82.

Rynning, S. (2010) 'From bottom-up to top down transformation: Military change in France', in Terriff, T., Osinga, F. and Farrell, T. (eds) *A Transformation Gap? American Innovations and European Military Change*, Stanford Security Studies, Stanford: 59–82.

Sanders, E. (2006) 'Historical Institutionalism', in R. Rhodes, S. Binder and B. Rockman (eds) *The Oxford Handbook of Political Institutions*, Oxford University Press, Oxford: 39–55.

Schmidt, V. (2010) 'Reconciling ideas and institutions through discursive institutionalism', in Bland, D. and Cox, R. (eds) *Ideas and Politics in Social Science Research*, Oxford University Press, Oxford: 47–64.

Sengupta, K. (2009) 'Army fury at refusal to bolster Afghan campaign', Independent, 31 May, http://www.independent.co.uk/news/uk/home-news/army-fury-at-refusal-to-bolster-Afghan-campaign.1693827.html.

Shapiro, J. and Witney, N. (2009) *'Towards a post-American Europe'* European Council on Foreign Relations, London.

Shaw, J. (2013) 'Basra 2007: The requirements of a modern Major-General', in Bailey, J., Iron, R. and Strachan, H. (eds) *British Generals in Blair's Wars*, Ashgate, Farnham: 175–180.

Simpson, J. (2013) 'The US-UK special relationship: The nuclear dimension', in Dobson, A. and Marsh, S. (eds) *Anglo-American Relations: Contemporary Perspectives*, Routledge, London: 240–262.

Stabilisation Unit (2014) *Analysis for Conflict and Stabilisation Interventions: What Works Series*, October, HMSO, London.

Stabilisation Unit (2017) *Joint Analysis of Conflict and Stability: Guidance Note*, June, HMSO, London.

Stabilisation Unit (2019) *The UK Government's Approach to Stabilisation*, HMSO, London.

Stewart, A. (2013) 'Southern Iraq 2003–2004: Multi-national command', in Bailey, J., Iron, R. and Strachan, H. (eds) *British Generals in Blair's Wars*, Ashgate, Farnham, 79–88.

Strachan, H. (2013a) 'British generals in Blair's wars', in Bailey, J., Iron, R. and Strachan, H. (eds) *British Generals in Blair's Wars,* Ashgate, Farnham, 327–346.

Swartz, P., Rosenau, W. and Kates, H. (2017) 'The origins and development of "A Cooperative Strategy for 21st Century Seapower"', CAN Analysis and Solutions, September, https://www.cna.org/cna_files/pdf/DRM-2015-U-012011-2Rev.pdf

Telegraph, The Daily (2013) 'Unreliable' British officers left out of US meetings in Syria', 2 September, http://www.Telegraph.co.uk/news/worldnews/middleeast/Syria/ 10282460, unreliable British officers left out of US meetings in Syria.html

Telegraph, The Daily (2015) 'UK defence spending "concerns" US Army Chief Raymond Odierno', 2 March, www.bbc.co.uk/news/uk-31688929

Terriff, T. and Osinga, F. (2010) 'Conclusion: The diffusion of military transformation to European militaries', in Terriff, T., Osinga, F. and Farrell, T., (eds) *A Transformation*

Gap? American Innovations and European Military Change, Stanford Security Studies, Stanford: 187–209.

Ullman, R. (1986) 'America, Britain and the Soviet threat in historical and present perspective', in Louis, W. and Bull, H. (eds) *The 'Special Relationship': Anglo-American Relations since 1945*, Clarendon Press, Oxford: 103–114.

US Air Force Doctrine Document 1, September 1997, Government Printing Office, Washington DC.

US Army Field Manual 100-5 (1982) '*Operations*', Government Printing Office, Washington DC.

US Army Field Manual 100-5 (1986) Government Printing Office, Washington DC.

US Army Field Manual 100-5 (1993) '*Operations*', Government Printing Office, Washington DC.

US Army Field Manual 3.0 (2001) '*Operations*', June, Government Printing Office, Washington DC

US Army Field Manual 3-24 (2006) '*Counterinsurgency*', Government Printing Office, Washington DC.

US Marine Corps Counterinsurgency Field Manual 3.24 (2007) Government Printing Office, Washington DC.

US National Security Strategy (1994) July, The White House, Washington DC.

Wampler, R. (1990) 'NATO Strategic Planning and Nuclear Weapons 1950–1957', Occasional Paper No. 6, Nuclear History Programme, Center for International Security Studies, University of Maryland.

Wampler, R. (1991) The Ambiguous Legacy: The United States, Great Britain and the Formulation of NATO Strategy, PhD Thesis, Harvard University, Cambridge.

Watt, D. (1986) 'Introduction: The Anglo-American relationship', in Louis, W. and Bull, H. (eds) *The 'Special Relationship': Anglo-American Relations since 1945*, Clarendon Press, Oxford: 1–16.

Washington Post Online (2001) Text: Rumsfeld's news conference, 18 October, https://www.washingtonpost.com/wp-srv/nation/specials/attacked/transcripts/rumsfeld_text101801.html

Watt, D. C. (1986) 'Demythologizing the Eisenhower era', in Louis, W. and Bull, H. (eds) *The 'Special Relationship': Anglo-American Relations since 1945*, Clarendon Press, Oxford: 65–86.

Weiner, S. (2009) 'Evolution in the post-Cold War Air Force. Technology, doctrine and bureaucratic politics', in Sapolsky, H., Friedman, B. and Green, B. (eds) *US Military Innovation since the Cold War. Creation without Destruction*, Routledge, London: 100–118.

Well, S. (1986) 'The United States, Britain and the Defence of Europe', in Louis, W. and Bull, H. (eds) *The 'Special Relationship': Anglo-American Relations since 1945*, Clarendon Press, Oxford: 129–149

Williams, H. (2016) 'Surviving a sea change. Trident and the Special Relationship', in Futter, A. (ed) *The United Kingdom and the Future of Nuclear Weapons*, Rowman and Littlefield, London: 107–120.

Xu, R. (2015) A Theory of Alliance Persistence within the Anglo-American Special Relationship in the Post-Cold War Era, PhD Thesis, University of Nottingham, April.

Documents from the National Archives

TNA, Air 8/2046, (1956) 'Chancellor of the Exchequer Letter to Minister of Defence', 24 November.

TNA, Air 8/2046, (1956a) 'Vice Chief of the Air Staff to Chief of the Air Staff', 29 November.

TNA, CAB 148/30, OPD (1967) '17th Meeting, Defence and Overseas Policy Committee', 21 April.

TNA, DEFE 5/60 (1955) 213 'Exchange of Military Information with the US', 30 August.

TNA, DEFE 6/33 JP (1955) Note 20 (Final) 'Anglo-American Strategic Policy', 11 October.

TNA, DEFE 6/32 JP (1955) 147, 'The Effectiveness of Nuclear Deterrence', 13 December.

TNA, DG 1/11/56 MD (1950) 12, 'Western Union Defence Organisation', 5 July.

TNA, FO 371-ZP5/02/G (1955), Ministry of Defence to Foreign Office, 'UK Defence', 31 March.

TNA, DEFE 7/964 (1955) Maudling letter to S. Lloyd, Minister of Defence, 30 August.

TNA, DEFE 4/82 JP (1956) 8 (Final) 'Military Problems in the Far East', 12 January.

TNA, DEFE 4/82 JP (1956a) 3 (Final) 'The Baghdad Pact – Interim Concept of Operations', 18 January.

TNA, DEFE 5/70 Annex to COS (1956) 276, 'The Size of the Deterrent', 15 September.

TNA, DEFE 5/72 COS (1956) 428, 'Relations between ANZAM and SEATO', 4 December.

TNA, FCO 371 (1957) 129306, 'Record of a Meeting Held at the Pentagon', 28 January.

TNA, DEFE 4/95 COS (1957) 11th meeting, 'NATO Overall Strategic Concept', 8 February.

TNA, DEFE 4/96 Annex to JP (1957) 28 (Final) 'CPX 7', 22 March.

TNA, DEFE 5/80, COS (1957) 280 Appendix, 'Minimum Essential Force Requirements for the Period up to 1963', 19 December.

TNA, DEFE 4/100 Annex to COS (1957) 77th Meeting, 'Earth Satellite', 8 October.

TNA, DEFE 4/101 COS (1957) '81st Meeting, Anglo-US Defence Policy', 21 October.

TNA, DEFE 4/101 JP (1957) 135, 'NATO Minimum Force Studies', 6 November.

TNA, DEFE 4/103 COS (1958) 6th Meeting 'The Effects on Soviet Policy of the Attainment by the USSR of Nuclear Sufficiency', 17 January.

TNA, DEFE 4/103, COS (1958a) '7th Meeting, Control of IRBMs', 21 January.

TNA, AIR 8/2400 (1958) 'Medium Bomber Force: Size and Composition'. Memorandum by the Secretary of State for Air. DB 10, 29 October.

TNA, DEFE 6/49 JP (1958) 32 (Final) 'Coordination of Defence Policy in South East Asia and Pacific', 9 April.

TNA, DEFE 5/84 COS (1958) 145, 'UK Reply to NATO Annual Review', 30 May.

TNA, CAB131/20 D (1958) 54, 'Germany and Nuclear Weapons', 3 November.

TNA, DEFE 6/60 JP (1959) Note 38, 'Assumptions for UK Force Requirements up to 1970', 14 December.

TNA, CAB 139/1929, FP (1960) 1, 'Future Policy Study', 24 February.

TNA, DEFE 6/61 JP (1960) 'Military Strategy for Circumstances Short of Global War 1960-70', 27 July.

TNA, DEFE 4/129, COS (1960) 55th meeting, 'NATO Strategy', 13 September.

TNA, PREM 13/124 (1965) 'Record of a conversation between the Prime Minister and Dean Rusk' May.

Interviews

Interview with former British Defence Attache to the USA (2012), London, 4 July.

Interview with former British Ambassador to Afghanistan (2012), London, 25 April.

Interview with former British Ambassador to Iraq (2012) London, 24 April.

Interview with former First Sea Lord (2012), London, 3 May.

Interview with Royal Navy submarine Captain rtd (2012) London, 4 July.

Interview with Royal Navy Admiral rtd (2012) London, 28 May.

Interview with Royal Navy Rear Admiral rtd (2012) London, 3 May.
Interview with Royal Navy Rear Admiral rtd (2012a) Liberal Club, London, 14 June.
Interview with Royal Navy Vice Admiral rtd (2012) London, 28 May.
Interview with British Army Lieutenant General rtd (2012) London, 14 May.
Interview with Royal Air Force Air Chief Marshal rtd (2012) London, 28 May.
Interview with British Army Major-General rtd (2012) London, 6 April.
Interview with British Army Major-General rtd (2012) London, 30 May.
Interview with British Army Major-General rtd (2012) London, 3 May.
Interview with former British Defence Attache to the USA (2013), Oakham, 29 December.
Interview with Royal Air Force Air Commodore rtd (2013) Nottingham, 26 May.
Interview with British Army Major-General rtd (2013) Nottingham, 28 October.
Interview with British Defence Attache (2014) British Embassy, Washington DC, 5 May.
Interview with British Army Colonel (2014) The Pentagon, Washington DC, 11 May.
Interview with former First Sea Lord rtd (2014) London, 5 June.
Interview with former Chief of the General Staff (2014) Millbank House, London, 11 June.
Interview with British Liaison Officer (2014) British Embassy, Washington DC, 5 May.
Interview with Royal Air Force Air Commodore (2014) British Embassy, Washington DC,
    5 May.
Interview with Royal Navy Captain (2014) British Embassy, Washington DC, 6 May.
Interview with British Army Brigadier (2014) British Embassy, Washington DC, 6 May.
Interview with Liaison Officer for the British Chief of the Defence Staff (2014) British
    Embassy, Washington DC, 7 May.
Interview with Counsellor for Defence Policy and Nuclear Issues (2014) British Embassy,
    Washington DC, 6 May.
Interview with Counsellor for Defence Acquisition and Technology (2014) British Embassy,
    Washington DC, 8 May.
Interview at Naval Ocean Processing Facility (2014) Norfolk, Virginia, 2 May.
Interview with Royal Navy Aircraft Carrier Liaison Officer (2014) Norfolk, Virginia, 2 May.
Interview with US Army Colonel rtd (2014) US Army War College, Carlisle Barracks, PA,
    7 May.
Interview with panel of US Army Colonels rtd (2014) US Army War College, Carlisle
    Barracks, PA, 7 May.
Interview with former First Sea Lord (2015) Palace of Westminster, London, 25 March.
Interview with Royal Navy Admiral rtd (2015) London, 30 April.
Interview with Royal Navy Admiral rtd (2015a) London, 28 April.
Interview with British Army Lieutenant General rtd (2015) London, 20 March.
Interview with British Army Lieutenant General rtd (2015a) Special Forces Club, London,
    30 April.
Interview with former Commander of British Land Forces (2015) Army and Navy Club,
    London, 9 March.
Interview with former Chief of the Defence Staff (2015) London, 12 April.
Interview by telephone with former British Army Liaison Officer to the US Training and
    Doctrine Centre (2019) 4 November.
Interview with Royal Air Force Air Marshal rtd (2020) Nottingham, 17 April.
Interview by telephone with Director of the Defence Concepts and Doctrine Centre (2020)
    3 March.
Interview with British Army Lieutenant General rtd (2021) Dorset, 12 July.

Index

For the benefit of digital users, indexed terms that span two pages (e.g., 52–53) may, on occasion, appear on only one of those pages.

Introductory Note

References such as '178–79' indicate (not necessarily continuous) discussion of a topic across a range of pages. Wherever possible in the case of topics with many references, these have either been divided into sub-topics or only the most significant discussions of the topic are listed. Because the entire work is about the 'Anglo-American military relationship', the use of this term (and certain others which occur constantly throughout the book) as an entry point has been restricted. Information will be found under the corresponding detailed topics. Cross-references in a form such as 'prime ministers *see also individual names*' direct the reader to headings in a particular class (e.g. in this case 'Blair, Tony') rather than a specific '*individual names*' entry.